*Virgin* Crossing Borders

TRANSFORMATIONS:
WOMANIST, FEMINIST,
AND INDIGENOUS STUDIES

Edited by AnaLouise Keating

*A list of books in the series appears
at the end of this book.*

# *Virgin*
# Crossing Borders

## Feminist Resistance and Solidarity in Translation

EMEK ERGUN

UNIVERSITY OF
ILLINOIS PRESS
Urbana, Chicago, and Springfield

Library of Congress Cataloging-in-Publication Data
Names: Ergun, Emek, author.
Title: Virgin crossing borders : feminist resistance and
     solidarity in translation / Emek Ergun.
Description: Urbana, Chicago and Springfield : University
     of Illinois Press, 2023 | Series: Transformations:
     womanist, feminist, and indigenous studies | Includes
     bibliographical references and index.
Identifiers: LCCN 2022032683 (print) | LCCN 2022032684
     (ebook) | ISBN 9780252044939 (cloth) | ISBN
     9780252087080 (paperback) | ISBN 9780252054099
     (ebook)
Subjects: LCSH: Feminist theory. | Translating and
     interpreting—Political aspects. | Women's studies—
     Political spects.
Classification: LCC HQ1190 .E74 2023 (print) | LCC
     HQ1190 (ebook) | DDC 305.4201—dc23/eng/20220712
LC record available at https://lccn.loc.gov/2022032683
LC ebook record available at https://lccn.loc.gov/2022032684

*To annem, babam, ablam, cici'm, and all my co-travelers*

# Contents

# Foreword

AnaLouise Keating

What does transformation look like? What's the relationship between language, reading, writing, and progressive social-justice work? How can we use words, ideas, theories, and stories to develop inclusive, life-affirming communities? How can we enact transformation in our daily practices, scholarship, and other areas of life? *Transformations: Womanist, Feminist, & Indigenous Studies* has its origins in these and related questions. Grounded in the belief that radical progressive change—on individual, collective, national, transnational, and planetary levels—is urgently needed and in fact possible (although typically not easy to achieve), this book series offers new opportunities for transdisciplinary scholarship informed by women-of-colors theories and post-oppositional thought. *Transformations* invites authors to take risks (thematically, theoretically, methodologically, and/or stylistically) in their work—to build on while simultaneously moving beyond disciplinary—or interdisciplinary-specific academic rules; and, through these risks, to invent new, transdisciplinary perspectives, methods, and knowledges.

Books in this series foreground women-of-colors theorizing because these theories offer innovative, though too often overlooked, perspectives on transformation. Women-of-colors theories give us the intellectual grounding and visionary-yet-pragmatic tools to understand, challenge, and alter the existing frameworks and paradigms that structure (and constrain) our lives. They are riskier, more innovative, and imaginative . . . rich with the potential to transform. Look, for instance, at post-oppositionality itself, which emerged from womanist thought and other woman-of-colors theories. As I define the term, "post-oppositional" represents deeply relational approaches to knowledge creation and praxis that transform dichotomous (us-against-them) worldviews into radically inclusive perspectives.

Post-oppositionality invites us to think differently, to step beyond conventional rules; to learn from, build on, and liberate ourselves from the dichotomous (us/them, mind/body, self/other, spirit/matter, winner/loser, etc.) worldview, theories, and practices we've been trained to employ. I describe these alternatives as "post-oppositional" to underscore both their inclusive relationships to binary-oppositional thought and their willingness to embrace yet move through oppositional perspectives. Post-oppositionality neither completely rejects nor entirely accepts oppositionality but rather works with and transforms it. Post-oppositionality's knowledge production, identity formation, and social change borrow from but do not become trapped within oppositional thought and action. Although post-oppositionality takes many forms, these forms typically share several traits: belief in our interconnectedness with all that exists; acceptance of paradox and contradiction; and the desire to be radically inclusive—to seek and create complex commonalities and broad-based alliances for social change.

Emek Ergun's Virgin *Crossing Borders: Feminist Resistance and Solidarity in Translation* beautifully illustrates and builds on these traits. Indeed, Ergun takes post-oppositionality in new directions: Centering translation studies and transnational feminist solidarities, she deepens our understanding of post-oppositionality itself while offering additional post-oppositional tools and tactics. She reminds us that post-oppositionality requires intellectual humility—a communal, open-minded attitude toward knowledge creation that allows space for additional perspectives and growth—seen, for example, in her frank self-reflection as she explores her translation work: She investigates her "mediating presence" in the translation process that brought Hanne Blank's book, *Virgin: The Untouched History*, to a Turkish-speaking audience; and Ergun's book to western/US readers. She acknowledges the "geopolitical anxieties" that this recursive translation evokes, and yet she proceeds, despite the risks.

By enacting this risky translation work, Ergun offers new post-oppositional strategies and tools. Here, I'm especially drawn to "differential universalization" as a post-oppositional reading practice. Post-oppositionality builds community by enacting a twofold gesture: it replaces the desire for sameness with a quest for commonalities; it reframes difference as relationship (rather than opposition). By definition, "sameness" implies the eradication of difference: When we posit sameness between ourselves and others, we must ignore the very real differences that also exist. However, when we shift our language from sameness to commonalities, we make room for differences to coexist with (and within) the commonalities. This shift, in turn, enables us to reframe differences relationally, in less oppositional terms. By positing commonalities (rather than sameness), we allow points of connection to emerge while also simultaneously acknowledging the very real differences among us. Differential universalization enacts this subtle negotiation, thus enabling us to more fully discern relational differences that coexist with (and within) commonalities. This complex reading process avoids "replicat[ing] the hegemonic gesture of ethnocentric western feminisms."

As her theory of differential universalization suggests, Ergun demonstrates profound faith in her readers and in the act of reading itself. She demonstrates that reading can be transformational. She boldly invites us (all of us, but especially those of us colonized by oppositional thought) to release our preconceptions, to intentionally "read . . . against the colonial grain." She encourages nonhierarchical, post-oppositional reading practices, and she demonstrates some of the ways these practices can unfold. And, she reminds her western, US-based readers of how others read us: as too hierarchical in our conventional reading practices, too trapped within the hegemonic binaries that we ostensibly deplore. This recognition is crucial because it fosters the intellectual humility that can energize and transform us, enabling us to create new "connectionist frameworks" of feminist solidarity.

# Preface

## Traveling (with) Books

> How do we learn about each other? How do we do it
> without harming each other but with the courage to
> take up a weaving of the everyday that may reveal deep
> betrayals? How do we cross without taking over?"
> —Lugones, "Decolonial Feminism," 755

Virgin *Crossing Borders* is a book that tells the story of a traveling book—
Hanne Blank's *Virgin*, a western feminist history book about virginity that
crossed the Atlantic via my translation to be transplanted in Turkey and is
now coming back to the United States as yet another book expanding the
transnational web of relations that *Virgin*'s translation initiated over a decade ago. Undertaken as an epistemic project of transnational feminism, the
story of *Virgin*'s border crossing is deeply interwoven with my own story as a
transnational feminist subject who has been shuttling back and forth between
Turkey and the United States, between Turkish and English, in a constant
cycle of mobility—of displacement, translation, resettlement, transformation, and growth. Although I came across *Virgin* on this precarious path
of entanglement and decided to build a bridge of translation with it while
walking that path, the journey that brought us together had in fact started
long before I came to the United States.

I was born and raised in Turkey with parents whose unabated encouragement and unyielding dedication made it possible for me to pursue higher
education so I could become an independent, self-reliant, and self-defined
person. I grew up with an inspiring older sister whose fearlessly rebellious
stance of justice for all both introduced me to intersectional feminist politics
and enabled me to see firsthand how one could fight for social justice on
multiple fronts of resistance. My family equipped me with epistemic hunger,
intellectual humility, political curiosity, ethical sensitivity, and subversive energy that have over the years been sustained by many people, most of whom

I have never met face to face but benefited immensely from through their books. In fact, I was very young when I started learning about the subversive power of books—particularly books that exposed injustices, condemned inequalities, and ingrained in me the wisdom of resistance and solidarity early on. After all, I grew up surrounded with banned books. Books, I came to understand, were consequential. Words mattered. Stories mattered even more. They carried dreams that could be mine. That could become ours. Books moved us as they moved among us. So, wherever I went, I carried a book with me. My passion of traveling with books, literally and figuratively, began with that early faithful bond.

Growing up in Turkey in a working-class, leftist, profoundly secular, and Alevi[1] family, navigating, surviving, and resisting simultaneously functioning systems of oppression was a skill I had to learn early on, and reading books was a central component of that coping process. Books were where I took refuge when the oppressive and fear-ridden realities of gender, class, religion, and political affiliation were too much to bear on my own. As I traveled to the worlds of stories hidden in books, I learned that books had their own stories as well. And those stories could be just as powerful as the books themselves. For instance, the stories my parents told me numerous times about their heartbreaking book-burning incidents in the repressive aftermath of the 1980 military coup showed me that reading books could be a form of resistance to hegemonic power structures as well as a threat to fascist regimes. At the time, like many people in Turkey, my parents had to burn almost all of their "politically suspect" books so that in case their house was raided by the military police, they would not be imprisoned for working for an underground communist party. In fact, my father named me, born one year before the coup, *emek* (literally "labor" in English) in honor of that communist party, perhaps without foreseeing that it would bring on some not-so-amusing encounters with police years later. Over time, the story of my "burning" name and the story of the burning books melted into each other, solidifying my belief in the power of words and books. It was no wonder that when I heard my parents tell me those painful stories of destroying their books in the face of possible government retaliation, it felt as if they were mourning after fallen comrades. It was then that I found out that one could indeed mourn after lost books; books that leave long-lasting traces on one's self and let them see the world from different places and lead them to different paths of life. And years later, when I helped my sister hide her "politically suspect" books so neither our parents nor the police would find them in case of a search, the thrill I felt was because I now knew how important that "game" of saving books was. We had to make sure those books lived on so that their theories of liberation, stories of resistance, and dreams of justice continued inspiring. So, we hid them well. I had not yet learned that books also "lived on" in translation, as Walter Benjamin famously said (*Illuminations*).

There were other incidents that helped crystalize my political vision of books. I was in seventh grade, when one day our Turkish literature teacher asked us to bring poems to class. I went home and chose a poetry book I found on the bookshelf. It had many beautiful poems, and I was certain any one of them would impress my teacher. As I was trying to decide which poem, my sister asked me why I was reading "that" book. Upon hearing that it was for a class assignment, she told me to leave it and instead find one that praised Atatürk, Turkey's "founding father." When I asked her why, she said that my teacher, who used to be her teacher as well, was a fascist and would fail me if I took that book to class. Again, my child self asked, but why? It turned out the book was by Ahmed Arif, a Kurdish communist poet who had been imprisoned for years on political grounds in Turkey. I had picked one book that my parents could not bring themselves to burn a decade ago. I never took that book to school, but I devoured every poem in it and never forgot one—a short one called "İçerde" [Inside/Locked Up] that spoke of hope despite the ruling presence of captivity.

Through these and other similarly transformative encounters with books (and stories about books), I discovered early on that some books were so powerful that their words could spill out of the pages and pour onto the streets and spark protests of social change—also send you to prison or the principal's office, for that matter. When I eventually encountered feminist books, my conviction about the political power of books to make dreams and actions of resistance solidified even more. I became aware of, in Sara Ahmed's words, "how feminist community is shaped by passing books around; the sociality of their lives is part of the sociality of ours. There are so many ways that feminist books change hands; in passing between us, they change each of us" (*Feminist Life*, 17). And some of those books I could read, and be changed by, only because translators had labored hard to rewrite them in my mother tongue. Thanks to that cross-border act of retelling and sharing called translation, I could encounter stories rooted in different lands and landscapes and expand the boundaries of myself beyond the familiar limits of my immediate world. Thanks to translation, I could develop an early appreciation for the distant, the unknown, the foreign, the other. My passion of translating feminist books, telling the transatlantic journey of *Virgin*, and researching the political potential of translation is rooted in this personal history marked, both epistemically and affectively, by those indelible book memories. Virgin *Crossing Borders* is a product of this passion of traveling with books and the ethico-political responsibility that comes with it, which Audre Lorde beautifully explains in *Sister Outsider* (43):

> And where the words of women are crying to be heard, we must each of us recognize our responsibility to seek those words out, to read them and share them and examine them in their pertinence to our lives. That we do not hide behind the mockeries of separations that have been imposed upon us and which so often we accept as our own.

How did my path cross with *Virgin*'s, then? After I received my bachelor's degree in translation studies in Turkey, where I learned to conceive translation as a political and ethical question of intersubjectivity and cross-border interconnectivity, I came to the United States to get my master's degree in women's studies, which congealed my already primed interest in feminist politics. It was in this time and space of displacement that my fascination with feminist translation emerged, an interest that was kindled by the very act of my traveling into the United States, where, much to my dismay, I was feeling disconnected from the feminist movement in Turkey. My sister, who was the editor of the renowned monthly feminist periodical, *Pazartesi*, suggested that I translated news articles on global women's issues for the periodical. While volunteering for *Pazartesi*, I realized that translation enabled me to stay connected to as well as serve the feminist movement in Turkey—no matter how small-scale—despite thousands of miles of distance. Moreover, it facilitated the cross-border flows of feminist stories and lessons from around the world into Turkish, increasing a sense of global affinity and solidarity among feminists. This is when I started asking questions about "feminist translation." And soon I discovered that I was not alone. There were many scholars and translators, particularly in Quebec, Canada, who had already done it and written about it. Once again, I was reading books that deeply touched me.

It was also in this period that I met Hanne Blank and her book, *Virgin: The Untouched History*. At the time, I was working on my master's thesis on the medical and legal construction of virginity in Turkey and struggling to find a comprehensive feminist source that demedicalized virginity and substantiated that with historical data. My thesis both aimed to condemn medical virginity tests and virginity violence in Turkey, which was already done by local feminists, and, more importantly, sought to reveal that virginity was a fabricated idea—that it could not be "tested" or dis/proven even by medical doctors trained to believe so. Besides, without such a comprehensive source, my thesis, written in English for an Anglo/American audience with its focus on Turkey, ran the risk of orientalizing virginity and presenting it as if it were an exclusively Middle Eastern problem or "tradition"—Lata Mani's ("Multiple Mediations") and Lila Abu-Lughod's ("Orientalism") questions about "multiple mediations" and "multinational reception" were fresh on my mind. Then, one day, I saw a flyer on campus that was announcing an upcoming talk on the history of virginity by a visiting scholar, Hanne Blank. I was awestruck. After I met Blank following her thought-provoking talk, which summarized the key findings of her archival research, I realized that I had finally found a feminist book on virginity that would not only help me demedicalize virginity, but also alleviate my geopolitical anxieties about writing a thesis on Turkey's virginity politics for an Anglo/American feminist audience. *Virgin* appeared at that very moment when I needed a credible source that would help me conceptualize virginity as a cross-cultural problem. And it did help prevent the topic from becoming a "Turkish problem" in my thesis, even though I exclusively focused on the "Turkish face" of the issue.

After our initial encounter, Hanne Blank was generous enough to share with me an unpublished version of *Virgin*. The manuscript dismantled longstanding heteropatriarchal virginity myths, including the most long-lasting ones fabricated by western medicine, so compellingly that I decided to translate it into Turkish as soon as it was published in English. I did not want this book to continue missing from Turkey's feminist repertoires. In the meantime, Blank became a member of my thesis committee and the vigorous archival research that produced *Virgin* shaped my own virginity research and thesis—the thesis that would eventually become an introduction to the Turkish translation of *Virgin* and travel back to Turkey. By the time *Virgin* was finally published in 2007, I had already started my doctoral studies researching the political potential of translation as an apparatus of transnational feminist knowledge production and solidarity making. Could the translation of *Virgin* become a transnational bridge between feminists in Turkey and those in the United States? Would feminists in Turkey walk across that bridge despite the well-archived oppositional gulf—the west versus the east—that the traveling book attempted to cross? Virgin *Crossing Borders* explores these questions. And it further asks, could Virgin *Crossing Borders* itself become such a transnational bridge? Given that "to bridge is to attempt community, and for that we must risk being open to personal, political, and spiritual intimacy, to risk being wounded," will you, dear reader, walk across that bridge with me and the feminist readers of Turkish *Virgin*, whose stories in/of generosity, hospitality, vulnerability, and solidarity are not only uplifting, but also eye-opening and inspiring (Anzaldúa, "Preface," 3)? I/we hope you accept this invitation because, in Anzaldúa's ("Now Let Us Shift," 576) words,

We are ready for change.
Let us link hands and hearts
together find a path through the dark woods
step through the doorways between worlds
leaving huellas for others to follow,
build bridges, cross them with grace, and claim these puentes our
    "home"
si se puede, que asi sea, so be it, estamos listas, vámonos.
Now let us shift.

## Traveling (with) Virgin *Crossing Borders*

Virgin *Crossing Borders* not only tells the story of the cross-border journey
of *Virgin* from the United States to Turkey but is itself a traveling book bringing back stories from Turkey. Borrowing from Richa Nagar's inspiring book
on "hungry translations," where she asks, "what possibilities for justice can
be created by rethinking translation as an enterprise of ethical and ever open
mediation across space, time, and struggle," (*Hungry Translations*, 26–27)
I invite you to consider the translational processes that make this book as
"a series of 'retellings' being passed along from one person to the next" and
position yourself as a responsible agent of "telling in turn" (Merrill, *Riddles
of Belonging*, 5, 43). You are a crucial part of this journey, and how you read
and retell the stories here will matter for what kinds of networks of meanings it establishes in and beyond its immediate reception context. You are, in
Christi Merrill's words, "part of this ocean of streams of story, contributing
to it and redirecting its flow" (5).

In a world that is violently divided into two supposedly irreconcilable
opposites, which I cautiously continue to call "the west versus the east," zigzagging those borders back and forth is risky business, to say the least. My
mediating presence, which has been in every part of this transatlantic journey
as the reader, translator, researcher, and writer, is particularly bold in this
phase of the journey because the orientalist meaning-making regime of the
border economy within which Virgin *Crossing Borders* is to be read and interpreted increases my geopolitical anxieties immensely. As a transnational
subject whose liminal positionality poses distinct challenges and opportunities for retelling stories across borders, I find myself caught between the
desire to retell my feminist co-travelers' inspiring stories and the fear of this
polyphonic text being appropriated into the simplistic interpretive schemes
of existing oppositional regimes. I do not want this book to re-activate the
persistent colonial imagery of "the Oriental Woman," fantasized by both
patriarchal and feminist agents of knowledge-making as an abject object of

western pity and rescue. The geopolitical conditions of possibility that govern the reception context of the book, and thus the political fate of its stories, do not yield immediate trust in the meaning-making mechanisms, conventions, and practices awaiting this traveling book.

Therefore, as I worked on the book, I frequently found myself asking the same question: will the readers of Virgin *Crossing Borders* be ethically and politically responsible co-travelers in this cross-border journey (do I dare, sister?)?[2] Or in María Lugones's moving words, "do I trust myself to you" (*Pilgrimages*, 45)? This is a crucial question because "without such accountability, Euro-American feminist critical practices will not sufficiently examine the material conditions of 'information retrieval,' ignoring the politics of reception in the interpretation of texts, information, and points of view from the so-called peripheries" (Kaplan, *Questions of Travel*, 169). However, my desire (duty?) to (re)tell is bigger than my fear of being unheard or misheard, no matter how precarious the hope (of mutual trust, vulnerability, and generosity) that sustains the stories in the rest of the book is. All these intermingled affective states—of desire, fear, doubt, as well as hope—are justified because "When we speak of violence directed to us, we know how quickly that violence can be racialized; how racism will explain that violence as an expression of culture. . . . We must still tell these stories of violence because of how quickly that violence is concealed and reproduced. . . . But it is risky: when they are taken out of hands, they can become another form of beating" (Ahmed, *Feminist Life*, 72). Taking that risk is about continuing the cross-border dialogue, no matter how difficult, tentative, and unpredictable it is, while "reminding ourselves and one another of the violent histories and geographies that we inherit and embody despite our desires to disown them" (Nagar, *Hungry Translations*, 43). And who articulates this simultaneous presence of hope and doubt, fear and commitment, frustration and faith in our political narratives better than Audre Lorde's following manifesto-like words (*Sister Outsider*, 40–41):

> I have come to believe over and over again that what is most important to me must be spoken, made verbal and shared, even at the risk of having it bruised or misunderstood. . . . My silences had not protected me. Your silence will not protect you. But for every real word spoken, for every attempt I had ever made to speak those truths for which I am still seeking, I had made contact with other women while we examined the words to fit a world in which we all believed, bridging our differences.

I believe in the transformative potential of translational journeys enough to invite you into the stories retold in this book. You will have to constantly shift geopolitical gears to read them against the colonial grain, but it will be worth the effort because the stories you read will then summon your own (perhaps untold, perhaps mistold, or perhaps overtold) stories, which may or may not stick to you with the same affection after the cross-border encounter. However, regardless of the outcome, the stories you read and the stories you re/tell will have faced each other against a colonial backdrop that threatens but does not preclude ethical encounters. It is that possibility of clogging, corroding, disrupting, and decelerating, if not demolishing yet, the age-old colonial machinery of cross-border meaning making and story re/telling that makes the translational encounter between the self and the other worthy of risk. We can, indeed, radically touch and budge one another beyond the relational dictates of domination, but we must be ready to break the mold, share our intimate stories regardless of what might become of them, and become vulnerable in each other's presence. This is why,

> I invite each one of you, the reader and the co-learner, to also retell your own locations, journeys, encounters, and struggles and to bring them into conversation with texts, moments, and movements that have inspired you. Then, we can together learn how to meet, cross, counter, and re-spect the borders between self and other as an essential part of grappling with politics that are simultaneously intimate and global (Nagar, *Hungry Translations*, 208).

The reward of being such a geo/politically grounded and ethically attentive reader is not only self-transformation, but also intervention into existing relations of domination, which in the case of translation is both local and global. The traveling stories you read in this book attest to the simultaneity of such an inward-looking and outward-turning movement in translation, so I hope you let them tempt you with their connectionist lessons. If you read these stories with responsibility, hospitality, generosity, and vulnerability, they will show you how to encounter the other ethically in translation and how to become anew and expand with them and their traveling stories. And that means getting one step closer to that dream of a just, peaceful world of coexistence in difference that fuels feminist movements across the world. This polyphonic dream-world that is yet to come is possible only if "you" and "I" let translation bring "us" to each other and together across languages, differences, and borders, because, as Judith Butler beautifully says, "I am nowhere without you" (*Precarious Life*, 49):

> What was once thought of as a border, that which delimits and bounds, is a highly populated site, if not the very definition of the nation, confound-ing identity in what may well become a very auspicious direction. For if

I am confounded by you, then you are already of me, and I am nowhere without you. I cannot muster the "we" except by finding the way in which I am tied to "you," by trying to translate but finding that my own language must break up and yield if I am to know you. You are what I gain through this disorientation and loss.

Virgin *Crossing Borders* is a product of that dream of/in translation that will bring "me" to "you" and "you" to "me." So that together we can muster the transnational "we/s" necessary for justice and liberation for all—and, until we get there, for survival because "we need each other to survive; we need to be part of each other's survival" and we can only survive together in translation (Ahmed, *Feminist Life*, 235).

# Acknowledgments

This book, which I started writing at the University of Maryland, Baltimore County (UMBC), is a product of a collective journey during which I had the company of a large group of remarkable co-travelers. Without their gentle and generous presence in my life, navigating the intimidating, if not utterly disheartening and alienating, terrains of academia, which as Sadiah Qureshi says, is terribly "pale, male, and stale," would not give me the nurturing and inspiring experiences that enabled this book ("Manifesto for Survival"). Walking side by side with them has taught me so many precious lessons about feminist collaboration and solidarity that I am not sure if I can do justice to all of them in this limited space, but I will do my best. Needless to say, all errors in this book are my own.

My first big thanks goes to my outstanding research participants: Ayşe, Ayşegül, Bilge Su, Çise, Defne, Deniz, Dicle, Dîlan, Ece, Ekin, Gülümser, Kırmızı, Leylak, Lorin, Milena, Müjgan, Nil, Pembe, Selma, Sezen, Şeyma, and Yasemin. I can only thank them with their pseudonyms, but my gratefulness to each of them is immeasurably, indescribably real. Dear readers of *Virgin* in Turkish, who dedicated enormous time and energy to this project, I will forever be in your debt. I hope I have done justice to your stories. And thank you Amargi Women's Academy, for hosting the focus group sessions, and thank you Esen Özdemir, for facilitating the focus groups and being such a big-hearted friend.

My dear mentor and friend, Carole McCann, how do I thank you? Since the day we first met in 2006, I have been thanking the universe for crossing our paths because you have always believed in me, challenged me, inspired me, and fostered my intellectual curiosity—in so many ways that I cannot begin to describe here. It has been a true pleasure to continue to work with you and I am looking forward to future collaborations. I also owe heartfelt thanks to Jessica Berman, Christine Mallinson, Bev Bickel, and Pat McDermott, for showing me firsthand how rewarding, energizing, and enriching interdisciplinary collaborative work can be.

I am also grateful to those who made it possible for me to cross borders with *Virgin: The Untouched History* and do so with a feminist agenda. First of all, dear Hanne Blank, thank you for sharing your wonderful book with me. And thank you my dear editor, Aksu Bora; editor-in-chief (late), Nihat Tuna; cover designer, Suat Aysu, and Tanıl Bora from İletişim Press for your trust and collaboration.

At UMBC, I would like to thank Devin Hagerty from Global Studies for being a great friend and colleague; Jodi Crandall, Denis Provencher, Craig Saper, and Liz Steenrod of the treasured LLC community; and Elle Trusz, Kate Drabinski, and Amy Bhatt from GWST for their feminist friendship. At UMBC, I also found a wonderful community of friends who always offered inspiring conversations and comforting hugs when needed: Ruken, Doaa, Satarupa, Rachel, Aynur, İbrahim, Sema, Emerald, Felix, Violeta, Heidi, Uzma, Autumn, Amy, Landry, and Kevin, thank you all for your friendship.

At UNC Charlotte, I am grateful for the immense support I have received from the Women's and Gender Studies and Global Studies communities and beyond. In particular, I owe many thanks to Janaka Lewis, Dale Smith, Sonya Ramsey, Katie Hogan, John Cox, Elisabeth Paquette, Kelly Finley, Jennifer Byrd, Amal Khoury, Charles Houck, Garth Green, Carmen Soliz, Oscar de la Torres, Andrea Pitts, Lara Vetter, Kirk Melnikoff, Min Jiang, Amanda Binder, Paula Martinac, Chris Mellinger, and Jeffrey Killman. And thank you, the one and only Vicky Harris.

I am very grateful to my undergraduate professors at Boğaziçi University's Translation Studies Department who planted in me an immense political and intellectual curiosity and passion for translation: Dilek Dizdar, Şehnaz Tahir-Gürçağlar, İsmail Kaplan, and Şebnem Bahadır. I am also grateful to my professors at Towson University's Women's Studies Department, where I started combining that curiosity and passion for translation with my feminist curiosity and passion: Karen Dugger, Toni Marzotto, Cindy Gissendanner, Cecilia Rio, and Esther Wangari.

I thank my colleagues and friends at Keene State College for such a warm, welcoming first year fresh out of PhD and giving me precious feedback on my work: Patricia Pedroza Gonzaléz, Jennifer Musial, Lisa DiGiovanni, Amber Davisson, Emily McGill, Armağan Gezici, and Darrell Hucks. Also, thank you, Cindy and John Cole Brewster, for giving me that fabulous tree house in

New Hampshire, where a lot of the revisions of this work got done peacefully while surrounded by your flower fields.

Over the years, I have received considerable institutional support that made this work possible. The Dresher Center for the Humanities at UMBC honored me with a Residential Fellowship Award in 2013 and two Scholarly Development Fund awards in 2012 and 2014, all of which gave me the necessary space to focus on my writing and share my research at various academic venues. National Women's Studies Association (NWSA) not only supported my research by giving me the 2013 Graduate Student Award, but also gave me precious feedback and further encouragement for my work when I was elected a finalist for the NWSA and Illinois University Press First Book Prize in 2015. Finally, UNC Charlotte awarded me a Faculty Research Grant in 2017 that enabled me to do a follow-up interview study with the participants of my earlier reception study in Turkey.

I also received terrific feedback on portions of this work at keynote addresses and lectures I gave at Boğaziçi University (Istanbul, 2020 & 2021), Warwick University (UK, 2021), UNCC English Graduate Student Association Conference (Charlotte, 2019); 6th Conference of the International Association for Translation and Intercultural Studies (IATIS) (Hong Kong, 2018), Smith College (Massachusetts, 2018), and Middlebury College (Vermont, 2018). Thank you to those who organized these events to have critical conversations about the politics and ethics of translation: Carolyn Shread, Karin Hanta, María Laura Spoturno, Robert John Neather, Mona Baker, Mila Milani, Ceyda Elgül, Şule Demirkol, and Sara Eudy. And thank you to all the audience members, especially students, whose questions and comments not only kept my research going but also helped me refine it.

There are a lot of scholars, teachers, activists, and artists that have become co-travelers in my feminist journey. Many of these amazing human beings I do not know personally, such as Audre Lorde and Gloria Anzaldúa. But some I have been lucky enough to meet, even work with. I am grateful to Patricia Hill Collins, Richa Nagar, AnaLouise Keating, Claudia De Lima Costa, Kathy Davis, Sonia Alvarez, and Luise von Flotow for their trailblazing works and feminist camaraderie.

I owe many thanks to my students at UMBC, Keene State College, and now at UNC Charlotte who have constantly reminded me why all this matters. Regularly engaging with students in and out of the classroom and exploring feminist questions of justice and equality with them sustains my hope for a planetary future for all. I am also thankful to the graduate students of the "Feminist Theory and Its Applications" class of Fall 2021 for reading a draft of this work and giving me invaluable feedback.

I cannot express the deep gratitude I feel for my series editor AnaLouise Keating, acquisitions editor Dominique Moore, and assistant acquisitions editor Ellie Hinton at the University of Illinois Press. You have been a delight to work with. Dear AnaLouise, thank you for creating the Transformations series and giving this book the best home possible. I am also immensely thankful to the anonymous reviewers who read my book and offered me amazing feedback to make my arguments sharper and stronger.

My dear İlkim, *iyi ki varsın,* thank you for sending me that first email and never stopping since then. And thank you for helping me conduct the focus group discussions. My dear Olga, *grácies* for being a wonderful friend and a fantastic collaborator. My dears Ritika, Ella, and Penny, thanks for being my family in Charlotte. Your goofy and loving presence on this planet makes everything better.

*Canım annem, canım babam, canım ablam, canım Cici'm,* and *canım Zeynep'im,* thank you for being the best family I could have asked for. This book is for you. I love you all so very much.

And finally, my dear sweetheart Tim, Charlotte is home thanks to you. I love you.

*Virgin* Crossing Borders

# Translation in Feminism/ Feminism in Translation

Each of us is here now because in one way or another
we share a commitment to language and to the power
of language, and to the reclaiming of that language
which has been made to work against us. In the
transformation of silence into language and action, it
is vitally necessary for each one of us to establish or
examine her function in that transformation and to
recognize her role as vital within that transformation.
—Lorde, *Sister Outsider*, 43

Ten years after activist and survivor Tarana Burke coined the phrase "MeToo" in 2006 and started a movement to raise awareness on sexual violence and empower other survivors of sexual abuse (particularly women and girls of color), it turned into a massive global awareness campaign in 2017 when the hashtag #MeToo went viral on social media in response to US actor Alyssa Milano's Twitter call (following allegations of sexual harassment and assault against movie mogul Harvey Weinstein). Despite critiques for turning into an exclusionary feminist platform, the online movement quickly became a transnational phenomenon[1]: "Direct translations of #MeToo have been shared by Arabic speakers in Africa and the Middle East and by Spanish speakers in South America and Europe, while activists in France and Italy have developed distinct hashtags to express the sentiments of the movement. In less than a month, some form of #MeToo had reached 85 countries" (Dennis, "#MeToo Movement," 1). In fact, a recent UN Women's brief analyzing the global presence of #MeToo found that "There were over 24 million impressions using the #MeToo hashtag on Twitter between October 2017 and December 2019" (Sen, *#MeToo*, 2). The multifarious and multidirectional travels of #MeToo have not only turned a US-based movement into a transnational platform, but also revealed the vital work of translation in enabling such border crossings and feminist remakes. The case, however, also raised an important question: Can we speak of global reciprocity in the translational flows and exchanges of feminist discourses? After all, similar cases of online feminist protests against violence against women had emerged,[2] for example, in several African countries before #MeToo, but "did not receive the same international support or attention" (Ajayi, "#MeToo, Africa").

Then, in July 2020, Instagram was flooded with black-and-white selfies of women accompanied by #ChallengeAccepted, #womenempowerment, and #womensupportingwomen, in what seemed like a liberal feminist plot to celebrate "sisterhood"—perhaps best encapsulated by Ivanka Trump's post: "Gratitude for the sisterhood . . . Let's be kind to each other. Let's choose to love, support and strengthen one another."[3] As millions of glamour shots filled up Instagram from across the globe, some started asking where this challenge came from and what it meant. For instance, Rae Alexandra reported on the public media outlet KQED's website, "On initially encountering these images yesterday—especially with zero context—it was hard for me to fathom what the 'challenge' was exactly" ("Empowerment"). Then, she added, "What is now a light-hearted expression of female solidarity in America was originally, in Turkey, a campaign inspired by both the soaring rates of violence against women and the brutal murder of a 27-year-old student named Pinar Gültekin." The selfies were meant to refer to a funeral tradition in Turkey, where mourners pin on their clothes black-and-white mugshots of the deceased, femicide victims in this case (and to the routine circulation of those mugshots in Turkish news). Those Instagram posts implied that each of us could be a victim of male terror in Turkey, which has one of the highest femicide rates in the world. And despite such prevalence of violence against women, a few days before the Instagram challenge, the Turkish government had announced their intention of withdrawing from the Istanbul Convention, the first international binding agreement created in 2011 by the Council of Europe to prevent and combat gender-based violence. This is why the central hashtag of the Turkish #ChallengeAccepted campaign was #istanbulsözleşmesiyaşatır (Istanbul Convention Saves Lives), which, however, quickly got lost as the challenge traveled to the United States. The Turkish hashtag was not reposted, translated, or adapted, but rather simply dropped from the vocabulary of the campaign while the English hashtags were allowed to cross borders only to be resignified as watered-down liberal claims of female empowerment.[4]

How come #MeToo transformed into a polyversal transnational feminist movement, while #ChallengeAccepted simply got flattened into a glamourous showcase of "global sisterhood"?[5] What was it that facilitated the smooth travels of #MeToo across countless borders without causing any major losses in the "original" movement's political and affective load, while #ChallengeAccepted's global expansion came at the expense of its radical critiques and demands of gender justice? These questions bring us back to the other question I posed in the previous paragraph: Can we really speak of global reciprocity in the translational flows and exchanges of feminist discourses? Virgin *Crossing Borders* explores this question of transnational feminism by not only tracing the translational journey of a feminist book on virginity from the United States to Turkey, but also itself bringing back stories of gender violence and lessons of feminist resistance and solidarity from Turkey to the United States. While revealing at-times-hopeful and at-times-woeful pictures of feminist border crossings, the book invites its readers to reconsider transnational feminism as a platform in/of translation and reposition themselves as ethically and politically responsible agents of meaning-making across borders.

Recognizing the intricate relationship between "transnational" and "translation," Virgin *Crossing Borders* aims to bring translation from the margins to the center of contemporary thinking on transnational feminism revealing the ways in which translation contributes to the political project of feminisms by enabling retellings and exchanges of feminist theories, stories, knowledges, and affects across borders. In this context, translation is considered simultaneously an interlingual, intercultural, and intersubjective art of recreation; a form of intellectual activism grounded in and in-between different political histories and social justice movements; a productive mode of negotiating difficult points of encounter across geohistorically contentious borders; and a means of transnational traveling and networking of political discourses and actors across asymmetrically positioned localities. In short, by reconceptualizing translation as a formative, transformative, and performative force of transnational feminist politics, Virgin *Crossing Borders* explores the crucial, yet largely ignored, role that translation plays in the operations of discursive border crossing, cross-cultural dialogue, and coalition building across differences.[6] As Patricia Hill Collins writes in her preface to *Feminist Translation Studies*, "There is no way to know our world without crossing linguistic, cultural and epistemological borders" (xvi).Virgin *Crossing Borders* provides crucial lessons on how to do that cross-border knowing and epistemic sharing in ethically responsible, affectively moving, and politically connectionist ways.

In particular, Virgin *Crossing Borders* reveals the trans/formative role of translation by unpacking the ways in which the subversive virginity knowledges of Hanne Blank's *Virgin: The Untouched History*, a US-American popular history book on the western configurations of virginity, traveled to Turkey through my politically engaged translation, which I call *Bekâret* in the rest of the book.[7] Comparing the United States and Turkey, two unevenly positioned cultures with different configurations of virginity, different feminist legacies of resistance, and different geohistorical conditions of possibility, the book examines how a western feminist book was cross-culturally mobilized to unsettle Turkey's heteropatriarchal virginity codes and what kinds of political impact it created among a group of feminists. Thus, within a comparative framework, Virgin *Crossing Borders* reveals the political potential of translation to facilitate cross-border flows of feminist theories, enable feminist interventions into local heteropatriarchal regimes of truth, connect feminist activists across differences and divides, and thus help forge transnational feminist solidarities. This interventionist practice of cross-border knowledge production is called "feminist translation"—a form of intellectual activism, where the political figure of the translator uses language to disrupt hegemonic gender regimes.

Virgin *Crossing Borders* investigates the interventionist power of feminist translation by focusing on two key aspects of *Virgin*'s cross-border journey: the textual and material production of the Turkish translation, *Bekâret*, assigned with the feminist mission of disrupting Turkey's severely medicalized virginity regime and the reception of the traveling western book in Turkey among a group of feminist activists. The analyses of *Virgin*'s Turkish translation and its reception—framed respectively as subjective, local, and transnational processes of resignification—reveal crucial insights on how to build feminist solidarities in a world organized around mutually sustaining oppositionalities. Starting with the subjective (and the intimate) and zooming out the analytical scale to the local (Turkey's feminist movement) and then to the global (transnational feminism) enables me to reveal how cross-border flows are individually and collectively experienced across geopolitical divides and cultural differences.

When we consider the fact that *Virgin* is framed as a *western* history of virginity, which in the context of the book includes the ancient Greek, early Christianity, Europe, and the contemporary US, the book's travel from the US to Turkey (and its "back" travels to the US via my research activities and this very book) appear as a thorny case of global flows. Indeed, in a world divided into two supposedly irreconcilable opposites, which I cautiously refer to as "the west versus the east," crossing (and coalescing) across those borders is risky, to say the least. For instance, the exclusive geohistorical focus of *Bekâret* could easily lend itself to immediate nationalist rejection in Turkey on the grounds of being a culturally irrelevant text or being an imperialist product of the US disseminating—potentially "degenerate"—western values. Hence, the geopolitical directionality of *Virgin*'s flow, which seems to replicate the colonial trend of "from the west to the rest," could bring to mind concerns of "feminism as cultural imperialism" (Davis, *How Feminism Travels*, 11). Analyzing *Virgin*'s travel from the US to Turkey is important precisely because only a detailed account of the book's reception in Turkey can unpack and complicate such a totalizing verdict of western cultural imperialism. That is, Virgin *Crossing Borders* recognizes "translational relationalities" and the fact that "a passport does not stamp a determinate national character on a person, a text, or a discourse. Nor culture and knowledge production conform to tidy political boundaries or obey the mandates even of the most authoritarian regimes" (Stam and Shohat, *Race in Translation*, 298). Then, is *Virgin*'s travel from the US to Turkey a case of discursive colonialism? How did the traveling book's feminist readers respond to that charge? My analyses reveal that rather than meekly absorbing *Bekâret* as the authoritative voice of the western feminist expert, the readers actively negotiated with the text and its (geohistorically partial) truth claims based on their own affectively and corporeally experienced epistemic repertoires and locally grounded political expertise. They neither rejected the text for its "foreign" identity and scope, nor passively agreed with everything it said about virginity.

By reasserting the interpretive agency of the translation's readers (including that of the translator) and situating them as cross/cultural brokers, Virgin *Crossing Borders* contributes to the larger postcolonial efforts to intervene into hegemonic globalization narratives that configure women of the global south as docile consumers of cultural products of the global north. Moreover, Virgin *Crossing Borders* is itself conceived as part of the transatlantic journey initiated by the Turkish translation of *Virgin*. Indeed, as I noted in the preface, the feminist knowledges produced by *Bekâret*'s readers have already traveled back to the US through my research, which I have shared in several academic settings, i.e., conferences. Hence, by addressing questions of reception in regard to potentially orientalist readings, my work further adds to postcolonial critiques of assimilation of Third World women's narratives of resistance and resilience into colonial discourses about "Third World women's misery." By stressing the geopolitics of reception, Virgin *Crossing Borders* reminds us that transnational solidarity requires different translation and reading strategies depending on meaning-making agents' locations.

In short, the textual flows that are analyzed in this book are not as unidirectional as they might seem at first glance. Hence, I agree with Clare Hemmings' warning that "conceptualizing of Anglo-American feminist theory's travels as direct *dissemination* fails to capture the transitions and translations that mark its movements back and forth and that highlight the nature of international engagement with its various forms" (*Why Stories Matter*, 15, emphasis original). Cross-border discursive travels are messy, and Virgin *Crossing Borders* testifies to those complexities by providing a unique case study of translational feminist knowledge production across various geopolitical directionalities.

## Theorizing Textual Travels

Feminisms travel with their discourses and practices circulating, transforming, and generating on their multidirectional routes across geopolitical and historical borders within contentious terrains of encounter marked by unequal power structures at local and global scales.[8] In fact, the theoretical body of politics that we call "transnational feminism" itself is a direct product of feminisms/feminists traveling in translation across and beyond borders. Yet, despite countless contributions of rejuvenation, expansion, and growth that are brought about by translational migrations of feminisms, the geohistorical specificities of such global mobilities have not received the scholarly attention they deserve in feminist scholarship. By renovating Edward Said's traveling theory, Virgin *Crossing Borders* offers a complex theoretical model to study such translational flows of feminist discourses.

"Traveling theory," or more accurately the theory of traveling theory, was first formulated by Said in his 1983 book, *The World, the Text, and the Critic*, and later revised in his 1994 article, "Traveling Theory Reconsidered." The theory addresses the question, "what happens to a theory when it moves from one place to another" (*The World*, 230)? Despite its lack of a complex formulation of the notion of travel, the explanatory power of Said's theory derives from his conceptualization of theory as a situated, dynamic, and mobile form of discourse and his recognition of the inherently transformative and intellectually generative nature of such cross-border mobilities. As he puts it (226),

> Like people and schools of criticism, ideas and theories travel—from person to person, from situation to situation, from one period to another. Cultural and intellectual life are usually nourished and often sustained by this circulation of ideas, and whether it takes the form of acknowledged or unconscious influence, creative borrowing, or wholesale appropriation, the movement of ideas and theories from one place to another is both a fact of life and a usefully enabling condition of intellectual activity.

Said explains his traveling theory through a case study on the borrowings (or citations in the largest sense of the term) and appropriations of Hungarian Georg Lukács's Marxist theory of reification first by Lucien Goldman in Paris and then by Raymond Williams in Cambridge. He argues that theories "originate" at specific locations and times as a response to certain historical and political conditions.[9] Since they often acquire their power from the circumstances in which they are made, when theories move to different geohistorical contexts they get domesticated, or "tamed" in Said's words, and lose their "original" subversive, even revolutionary power (238). Said argues that this is what happens to Lukács's theory as a result of its domestications in different sociopolitical settings (236).

Although, in his 1983 essay, Said only emphasizes the loss that Lukács's theory suffers from in the travel process, the model is actually open ended as it does not specify the nature and effect of the transformation caused by traveling. However, despite the apparent flexibility of his model, Said has been criticized for ignoring the possibility of positive transformation of traveling theories (Clifford, "Notes on Travel"). It is important to recognize, as Said does, that theories might indeed lose their power of resistance and "rebelliousness" in different sociocultural settings and even be turned into reactionary discourses ("Traveling Theory," 436). Gayatri Spivak, for instance, in her article on the postcolonial feminist politics of translation, similarly notes the possibility of traveling texts generating different political effects in different contexts, which, she argues, requires translators to be cautious while choosing texts to translate (Teaching Machine, 211). However, it is equally important to recognize that even when they become profoundly appropriated, mobile theories can produce counter-hegemonic effects within their new environments. Said's theory has been justly criticized for overlooking this possibility.[10] As a response, he revisited his theory in 1994 to consider the possibility of traveling ideas being rearticulated and revitalized to achieve anti-hegemonic effects in their new surroundings. He called this "an alternative mode of traveling theory" or a "transgressive theory" ("Traveling Theory," 438–40). However, some other major critiques remained unaddressed.

One major problem in Said's model is his lack of focus on the geohistorical contingencies of traveling and lack of acknowledgment of actors, particularly translators, involved in those processes of cross-border mediation.[11] Interestingly, Said, whose landmark Orientalism has been translated to at least thirty-six languages, completely sidesteps the translation issue and discusses traveling theories as if they circulate by themselves without any human actors involved. Although in his analysis of Lukács's traveling theory, Said discusses individuals, such as Goldman, he does not ascribe a particular role to them. In fact, his 4-stage model does not mention any agents. Rather, the exclusive focus of his theory remains on the antagonistic makeovers that mysteriously befall traveling theories. Hence, Lydia Liu rightly asks, "Indeed, who does the traveling? Does theory travel? If so, how? Granting theory such subjectivity leads to a further question: What is the means of transportation" (*Translingual Practice*, 21)? Underlining the importance of translation as a vehicle of traveling theories, she further adds, "With the suppression of that vehicle, travel becomes such an abstract idea that it makes no difference in which direction theory travels (from West to East or vice versa) and for what purpose (cultural exchange, imperialism, or colonialism?), or in which language and for what audience" (21).

To compensate for the shortcomings of Said's theory and enhance its explanatory potential for studies on translational travels and encounters of feminist texts and discourses, I borrow analytical tools from a number of inter/disciplines, including transnational (and women of color) feminisms, translation studies, indigenous feminisms, reception studies, comparative literature. These additions enable me to intervene in Said's theory on four fronts: feminist politics of translation, geopolitics of translation, post-oppositional ethics of interconnectivity, and politics of reception.

## Feminist Politics of Translation

One essential theoretical framework that I add to Said's traveling theory comes from feminist translation studies, which inform the textual reproduction of *Bekâret* and help bring the political agency of the translator into the center of analysis, rather than disguising their mediation of the text, which is often dictated by the conventional ethics of "fidelity" in translation. The praxis of feminist translation originated in Quebec, Canada in the 1970s and 1980s—a period marked by the "second wave" feminist movement and the Quebec sovereignty movement, both of which highlighted the centrality of language in securing hegemony and organizing resistance.[12] The praxis emerged and evolved in line with the growth of feminist experimental works, where language was critiqued for silencing women and reclaimed through innovative linguistic usages to make women's gendered experiences and protests visible. In the course of translation, these experimental writings required correspondingly subversive and creative rewriting strategies to unsettle and transform language. Feminist translation was officially born from those experimental translations.[13]

Feminist translation studies conceive translation not as a straightforward and transparent cross-linguistic transfer of prefixed meanings, but rather as an ideological practice of interpretive transformation, which is precisely why the feminist translator's political disclosure (on their interventions in the text) is celebrated both as a claim of their creative labor and as a principle of ethics. Moreover, feminist translation studies recognize that "translation [is] politically and theoretically indispensable to forging feminist, prosocial justice and antiracist, postcolonial, and anti-imperial political alliances and epistemologies" (Costa and Alvarez, "Dislocating the Sign," 558). Similarly, by expanding the definition of translation beyond textual recreation and reformulating it as a means of facilitating global conversations and collaborations, Virgin *Crossing Borders* explores the possibilities and drawbacks of translational/transnational feminism, seeking to increase the epistemological and political visibility of translation as a catalyst for social justice movements.

## Geopolitics of Translation

Transnational feminism's direct focus on the intersections of geopolitics and gender politics makes it a particularly useful theory to explore global circulations and translational crosspollinations of feminisms.[14] Indeed, the conceptualization of "transnational" as a contentious space of translational mediations and contestations where both new political possibilities and challenges emerge helps frame a translation as a case study of transnational feminist formations. In other words, the theory's emphasis on border crossings as well as the possibility and desirability of transnational alliances among differently situated constituencies of feminists helps me configure the making of *Virgin* into *Bekâret* not only as a case of traveling feminist discourses, but also as a political project of transnational collaboration and solidarity building. Geopolitics—simply defined as politics of space and spatiality—constitutes one of the key analytical categories of this book because it "acknowledges the travels and travails of feminism as it migrates across multiple borders, adapting itself to new conditions" (Friedman, *Mappings*, 5).[15] Moreover, paying attention to geopolitics, or what Jessica Berman calls "transnational optics," helps us disrupt the binary of "the local versus the global" by highlighting the interdependency between those two forms of spatiality (*Modernist Commitments*, 9–11, 28–32). As Susan Friedman explains, the local and the global are always implicated in one another and constantly inform and transform each other by continuous, creative contact (*Mappings*, 5). Anna Tsing calls those unequal, messy, and unpredictable interactions between the local and the global "frictions" (*Friction*, 4). And translation is a perfect example of how the local and the global are always implicated in one another, as it is not only an act of localization shaped by global power dynamics, but also an act of globalization enabling transnational movement of ideas and ideologies, if not more. In this regard, translation could be conceived as "friction" that "makes global connection powerful and effective" while also getting "in the way of the smooth operation of global power" (6). That is precisely why, "attention to friction [and translation] opens the possibility of an ethnographic account of global interconnection," which is what Virgin *Crossing Borders* seeks to reveal (6).

In short, transnational feminism is a productive theory because it frames cross-border movements of feminisms as both historicized and spatialized acts of transplantation. Unfortunately, these translational frictions have largely been neglected in feminist literature, where in-depth studies of discursive flows and local rearticulations are rare. Also, transnational feminism helps us recognize the directionality of cross-border mobilities as a central factor in shaping the course and fate of such flows. In reformulating traveling theory, it is necessary to incorporate directionality as an analytical question because discourses are not assessed on equal terms when they travel from the west to the east and vice versa.[16] Indeed, when Turkey's precarious relation to the west and *Bekâret*'s trajectory are considered, the book's journey appears much more complex than the linear travel process suggested by Said's model. In light of these theoretical insights, Virgin *Crossing Borders* can be envisioned as a case study of transnational feminism, which "acknowledges the historically and geographically specific forms in which feminism emerges, takes root, changes, travels, translates, and transplants in different spacio/temporal contexts" (Friedman, "Locational Feminism," 15). Translation cannot be fully understood without considering the geopolitical context within which it is performed and signified. Enabling such contextualization, the theory of transnational feminism allows me to engage in an in-depth analysis of "the geopolitics of translation," to use Rebecca Comay's term, in the process of which neither destination nor source remains untouched ("Geopolitics of Translation," 79).

## Post-oppositional Ethics of Interconnectivity

The third intervention into Said's traveling theory is an extension of the previous one, which highlighted translational border crossings as a function of a contentious world divided along various power lines, particularly ones demarcated by orientalism. I add an ethics of post-oppositionality to the geopolitics of transnational feminism to not only criticize the orientalist relationalities that oversee and ensue during *Virgin*'s journey from the US to Turkey, but also reveal interpretive strategies to go beyond the separatist economy of that geopolitical binary and connect across the assumed gulf between the east and the west. By proposing a relational worldview, post-oppositionality, AnaLouise Keating ("Citizen of the Universe," 60) explains, invites us "to move beyond the binary-oppositional frameworks that we generally use in identity formation and social change." This connectionist ethical stance rejects the oppositional binary logic that "reduces our interactional possibilities to two mutually exclusive options: Either we are entirely the same or we are entirely different" (61). This is precisely why post-oppositionality is very relevant to the study of translational flows and encounters because it not only helps us reveal the connectionist power of translation but also, very much like translation, reminds us that we are neither entirely the same nor entirely different. That is, post-oppositionality, like translation, highlights commonality and solidarity as the desired and sustainable ground of relationality and political action, rather than sameness or oppositionally coded difference. In a similar vein, committed to highlighting the interconnectivity between the self and the other, Virgin *Crossing Borders* simultaneously recognizes and challenges the antagonistic operations of orientalism that pit the western stories of *Virgin* and its readers in Turkey against each other. I do that by drawing particularly on Gloria Anzaldúa's metaphysics of "nepantlera" ("Now Let Us Shift"), AnaLouise Keating's theory of "radical interrelatedness" (*Transformation Now*), Maria Lugones's philosophy of world traveling (*Pilgrimages*), and Richa Nagar's theory of "radical vulnerability" and "hungry translations" (*Hungry Translations*), all of which recognize the interdependent and mutually transformative relationship between the self and the other (or between the traveling textual other and its new situated reader) outside the oppositional parameters of identity politics. In this framework, commonalities and solidarities across borders are not automatically denied as impossible fallacies of western humanism and universalism but perceived as products and processes of difficult, relational work that acknowledges the presence of differences and the possibility of forging political alliances (Anzaldúa, "Foreword" and *Interviews*; Keating, "Citizen of the Universe" and *Transformation Now*; Tsing, *Friction* and "Transitions;" Boer, *Uncertain Territories* and "Remastering"). By engaging this body of works, I emphasize the transculturally relational—bridge building—potential of translation, which is missing from Said's theory.[17] Adding post-oppositional theories to Said's traveling theory helps me reclaim the possibility of translational feminist solidarities from the oppositional grips of orientalism and engage in a more relational analysis of textual border crossings.

Here, I should add a cautionary note on my use of "west/east" as the organizing scheme of my geopolitical analyses. While I do recognize that "the west" and "the east" are problematic binary markers that reinscribe the authoritative, homogenizing, oppositional voice of colonialism, I continue to use them here for several reasons. First, *Virgin* itself is framed as a western history of virginity so the book has activated the binary logic from the beginning, whether I like it or not. This does not mean that I do not recognize the heterogeneous, unstable, and interdependent nature of these categories. On the contrary, I argue that even *Virgin*, which claims exclusively to tell the *western* history of virginity, in fact admits, almost accidentally it seems, the translational/transnational formation of "western virginity" (and the west by extension). For instance, speaking of Persian physician Avicenna, Blank writes, "Translated into Latin by Gerard of Cremona sometime around the mid-twelfth century, Avicenna's description became the second influential model of the physical aspects of female virginity" (*Virgin*, 49). So, "west" and "east" are not pure oppositional categories but should rather be conceived as hybrid (and symbiotic) geohistorical nodes (Shohat and Stam, *Unthinking Eurocentrism*, 13–15). I am indeed using these terms to reveal their concealed interdependency, hybridity, and illusive nature. That is, I employ the terms to destabilize the geopolitical hierarchies they claim and undermine their antagonistic energies, rather than repeat their essentialist, oppositional load of meanings.[18] Second, the binary has been historically deployed to delineate Turkey's geopolitical positionality in the global order, as well as its self-adopted identity as a nation-state aspiring to the west.[19] That is, the oppositionality between the west and the east is deeply infused into Turkey's (trans)national composition and collective consciousness. Third, I use the markers because they heavily shape the Turkish and US-American cultural imaginaries and their (oppositional) relations.[20]

Finally, I deploy the orientalist terminology of "west/east" because as much as this binary claims fictional categories, invented identities, and imaginary cartographies, it also describes (and dictates) actual relations of ruling with very material consequences for the subjects and subjectivities it summons locally and globally—particularly in regard to the cross-border encounters, relationalities, and political formations those subjects and subjectivities participate in. In Nanda Shrestha and Dennis Conway's words, "the past is still very much with us and Occident/Orient cultural distinctiveness is still with us, so Said's (1978) original argument that the West's subordination of 'things Eastern' is a colonialist, or post-colonialist, denigration of the cultural faces of the 'Others' continues to have merit as an insightful depiction of the continuity of social power relationships at the global scale" (Shrestha and Conway, "Globalization's Challenges," 209). In short, I use the language of "west/east" to explore a particular set of translational encounters and exchanges between the US and Turkey and to expand our understandings (and improve our practices) of cross-border feminist connectivities and collectivities, rather than to further exaggerate or broaden the assumed gulf between them. As Zillah Eisenstein beautifully puts it, "West and non-West are both real and made-up as coherent geographical/cultural locations. The flows between empires and their colonies, between colonizer and colonized, between slave and slave-master, between colors of the skin, are misread as separateness and opposition. Feminisms have palpably suffered from this overdrawn divide" (*Against Empire*, 183). Virgin *Crossing Borders* explores whether that "overdrawn divide" has prevented the emergence of transnational feminist affinities and engagements in *Virgin*'s cross-border travels.

## Geo/Politics of Reception

Another important gap in Said's traveling theory is that it bypasses questions of reception. Hence, it neglects the systematic tracing of the text's movements through the translation's receptions in its new, differently populated reception context. The failure to attend to translation's reception is also seen in feminist studies and feminist translation studies. One exception has been the vast attention given to the reception of "French feminism" in the US.[21] Although these studies are invaluable for illustrating the processes of feminist discourses' crossing the Atlantic through translation, their focus is limited to feminist encounters taking place between western contexts.[22] What happens when feminist discourses travel outside the west and become subjected to asymmetrical geopolitical forces? What happens to readers' subjectivities when they encounter feminist texts traveling "from above"? These questions have somewhat been addressed by postcolonial feminist scholars who revealed the ways in which third world women's texts are often otherized in the face of orientalist discourses and imperialist motives (Abdo, "Textual Migration"; Amireh and Majaj, *Going Global*; Burwell, "Reading Lolita"). Yet, these reception studies largely neglect the translation question.

I draw on two theoretical bodies to explore the processes of reception: (a) Dorothy Smith's sociological textual analysis to study texts as active participants in the formation of subject positions and relations of ruling and, (b) reception theory to analyze the active involvement of readers in meaning making. These two theories, both of which conceptualize reading as an active, embodied, and geohistorically contingent practice, complement both Said's traveling theory and each other as they emphasize two different, yet interacting, aspects of the reading process. Smith's textual analysis model (*Texts and Conceptual Practices*), which Kathy Davis describes as, "an analysis that explores the active and constitutive relationship between texts and readers, as well as the role texts play in organizing and regulating power relations," rejects the idea of readers passively consuming texts (*How Feminism Travels*, 143). Smith acknowledges both the active engagement with the text by the reader, who arrives at the practice as an already constituted (yet not fixed) social subject, and the interpretive schemata that the text brings into the meaning-making process to shape the reader's perceptions of social reality. Smith sees the text as a "form of participation in social relations," which is crucial for a study that conceives translation as a form of intervention in gender regimes (*Texts*, 4). Smith's notion of "disjuncture" is also useful for my study (*Conceptual Practices*, 92, 96, 142). The concept refers to a discrepancy between the reader's subjective experiences and the way these experiences are represented ideologically (exclusively hegemonically in Smith's analyses) in the text.[23] Although Smith pessimistically conceives the result of disjuncture as the reader succumbing to the text's ideology, Kathy Davis expands that notion as "taking up a resistant position" to the text's ideological standpoint (*How Feminism Travels*, 149). The key point here is that if the reader experiences a disjuncture, they can reject the subject position offered by the text. When the text is trying to produce resistant subjects participating in a transnational epistemological project of feminism, this failure to recruit the reader might suggest the failure of the project (at least for that particular reader). This notion has considerable explanatory power for analyzing *Virgin*'s travels to Turkey, where the reader might experience serious geopolitically produced disjunctures between their epistemological and experiential configurations of virginity and the western narratives of the text that challenge those locally grounded configurations. Hence, the notion of disjuncture raises important questions such as: Do *Bekâret*'s readers reject the knowledge claims of the book for being products of the west and carrying the authoritative voice of the west? How do they overcome the geopolitical boundaries and estrangements installed by the east/west binary? Finally, what role does the textual construction and organization of the book (by the author and the translator) play in generating or forestalling such disjunctures?

While Smith's theory highlights how texts create subject positions for readers to adopt and situate them in relation to a context of power relations, it does not highlight the reader's active engagement with the text as much as reception theory does.[24] Since a text's subjective and social impact cannot be known without accounts of actual readers, reception theory adds a crucial analytical layer to my study.[25] As David Morley puts it, "meaning produced by the encounter of text and subject cannot be read off straight from its 'textual characteristics' or its discursive strategies" ("Texts, Readers," 170). According to reception theory, readers bring their own experiences, knowledges, and "horizons of expectations" (Jauss, *Aesthetic of Reception*) to the meaning-making process, which takes place within the discursive boundaries of certain "interpretive communities" (Fish, *Is There a Text*). Similarly, my study argues both that readers with preformed experiences and knowledges produce contingent meanings in their engagement with the text, and that this engagement happens in a specific historical setting where the circulating ideologies with their available subject positions influence the ways in which the reader signifies the text. While supplementing Said's largely agentless traveling theory, reception theory also increases my work's potential contribution to translation studies, which has not devoted much attention to readers and "their habits of reading translation" (Tahir-Gürçağlar, *Kapılar*, 166).[26] Also, it is particularly important to study readers' interpretations of ideologically marked and performed translations, such as feminist translations, so that we can assess the political impact of their specific translation strategies and make more informed choices in future translations.

In this section, I have described four areas of intervention into Said's traveling theory, which is now theoretically capable of answering the question, what happens to feminisms when they travel across localities characterized by dissimilar discursive and political heritages and situated unevenly in the global economy. That is, with its renewed attention to translational procedures and agents of travel, geopolitical directionality of global flows of feminist texts, politics of reading translation, and ethical formations of post-oppositional connectivities across borders, the enhanced theoretical model of Said's traveling theory can now examine the displacements and appropriations that translated gender discourses go through as they cross contentious geopolitical borders in translation and engage in discursive and material encounters with a different set of historical conditions of possibility. In the next section, I discuss the methodological framework that I developed from that interdisciplinary conversation to analyze the particularities of *Virgin*'s political journey from the US to Turkey.

## Researching Textual Travels

Award-winning feminist poet from Turkey, Gonca Özmen once said, "Translation is a kind of metamorphosis. It is a journey to the Other—a journey to another mind, a journey to another language and tradition, a journey to another culture, a journey to another realm. It is a re-creation, re-voicing, re-vision, re-evaluation and re-writing. Translation can resurrect the dead. Translation can change the flow of the river."[27] Virgin *Crossing Borders* explores whether *Virgin*'s feminist translation changed the flow of the "virginity" river in Turkey—or did it at least cause some slowdowns, commotions, or disruptions in the river's flow?—and what kinds of journeys the traveling text facilitated to the Other in its encounters with a differently situated set of readers—between two unevenly positioned cultures with different configurations of gender, sexuality, and virginity and distinctive histories of feminist resistance. By answering this question, Virgin *Crossing Borders* seeks to contribute to the formation of a feminist politics and ethics of translation that can help us develop better—more just and justice-oriented, more responsible, more generous, more humble, more compassionate—strategies of retelling to transform the antagonistic energies of borders into post-oppositional, connectionist energies that are indispensable to the formation of cross-border feminist solidarities and resistances.

As I noted before, much of recent scholarship on translational flows and border crossings acknowledge global circulation of ideas and texts as key transcultural processes, but rarely studies the particularities of how subversive (or normative) discourses travel across the globe and become localized. One crucial exception is Kathy Davis's innovative book on the translational travels and receptions of Boston Women's Health Book Collective's *Our Bodies, Ourselves (OBOS)*, "a distinctively U.S. book," very much like *Virgin (How Feminism Travels*, 6). Similar to my work, Davis also describes her study as a "test case" undertaken "to assess the pitfalls of global feminism or, alternately, . . . the unexpected possibilities of transnational alliances for the circulation of feminist knowledge" (81). However, because my study focuses on a single translation, as opposed to Davis's focus on numerous translations, it allows for a more exhaustive analysis of the textual production and reception of a transnational knowledge project. Davis's book is also invaluable because the ideological standpoints and the geopolitical directionality of the translations we analyze are similar. So, the research questions she asks are worth quoting at length as they closely relate to the questions I explore here (6):

> What happened to the book when it traveled? How did it change in order to address the concerns of women in such different contexts? And finally, what can the travels of *OBOS* tell us about how feminist knowledge and politics circulate transnationally? In what ways have these border crossings been shaped by, but also subverted, globally structured relations of power between what has critically been referred to as the "West and the rest"? (Hall 1992)

To address these questions regarding *Virgin*'s cross-border journey, I analyze the complex phenomenon of translation/travel in three steps, each with a distinct methodological approach. The first methodological step of my study investigates how, as *Virgin*'s feminist translator, my political subjectivity and intersubjective dialogues with the text and my "implied readers" affected my translation decisions, including the initial decision to translate the book (Iser, *Implied Reader*). I look at how I consciously (and unconsciously) structured the text to facilitate transgressive readings and to position the readers as feminist subjects. More specifically, I analyze my text choice (why I translated *Virgin* in the first place), my lexical choices (e.g., the translation of the term "hymen"), my syntactical decisions (e.g., translations of English gender pronouns into Turkish, a language that has no gender pronouns), and the paratextual commentaries I added to the book (e.g., the composition of my preface) (Genette, *Paratexts*). So, this step reveals the textual manifestation of the translator's feminist agency.

It is important to note here that it is not the most common practice among translation scholars to study their own translations,[28] which could be regarded as a conceited behavior flouting the expected norms of the translator's humility and invisibility. As Lawrence Venuti notes, in doing so, a translator-scholar risks "the cynical charge of self-promotion that tends to be leveled at any translator who attempts to describe the choices and effects of his or her work" ("Translating Derrida," 257). Moreover, analyzing one's own translation within the acclaimed scientific discourse of translation studies might give rise to a charge of "subjective bias." However, my study does not share an empiricist understanding of objectivity as the condition under which an unsituated researcher is presumed to observe and articulate an immediately present, transparent reality unmediated by discourse. Rather, reflecting the feminist critiques of empiricism and celebrations of self-reflexivity, my study emphasizes that the researcher's geohistorical, experiential, and affective positionality, as well as that of the translator and the research participants, shapes the ways in which they collaboratively build situated and partial knowledges. As I am multiply positioned in Virgin *Crossing Borders* as a reader, researcher, researched, and translator, it is even more important to continually describe and analyze my involvement in the making of this re/writing project, rather than pretend I was not there.

The second methodological step of my study explores the publisher's promotions (e.g., the repackaging of the book) and media receptions of the traveling book (e.g., reviews and interviews with the translator and the author) and how those media representations responded to the textual strategies used by the translator to activate subversive readings within Turkey's discursive fields. Such a synchronic analysis of the reviews of a single work is of great importance because they influence the reception context of the text and might affect the reading experiences of individual readers.

The third methodological step, which is the most complex part of the research study, looks at readers' interpretations of *Bekâret* to understand to what extent the political claims of the feminist translator are materialized in reading practices. The analysis also examines what kinds of readings exceeded that intent and reveals the ways in which the readers activated the text to their own (unanticipated) ends. I used three methods to gather data on readers' receptions: semi-structured reading diaries, focus group studies, and semi-structured interviews conducted with twenty-two cisgendered women in Istanbul in the summer of 2010.[29] The participants were all self-selected—they responded to my "call for participants" circulated in feminist listservs in Turkey. They were between the ages of 18 and 38. While one participant was a high school graduate (and equipped with a wealth of knowledge on feminist and critical scholarship), eight were college graduates, six were college students, five were graduate students, and two were doctoral students. Except for the college students, all were employed (as a lawyer, teacher, school counselor, civil servant, accountant, graphic designer, journalist, etc.). Eighteen participants identified as heterosexual (plus one as "so far heterosexual"), two as bisexual, and one declined to say (possibly asexual). At the time of the study, four participants were married and the remaining eighteen were single. All the participants lived in major cities, with the majority being in Istanbul. While I did not ask the participants' ethnicity, at least two identified as Kurdish.

The participants were self-identified feminists, yet the extent to which they were engaged in feminist politics differed significantly in terms of types of activism, organizational commitment, and personal history of involvement in feminist politics. While some of the participants were longtime active members of relatively larger feminist and/or LGBT+ organizations (such as Amargi, Socialist Women's Collective, Mor Çatı Women's Shelter, Eğitim-Sen Union Women's Commission, Lambda Istanbul, Kaos GL), others were "newcomers" in the movement or only engaged in smaller-scale women's initiatives (for instance, feminist and LGBT+ college student organizations like "Cins Klüp" at Sabancı University). I actively sought feminist-identified participants, rather than a more diverse group of readers regarding political standing and background, because I wanted to see whether and how the translation fostered transnational feminist connectivities among feminists situated differently and whether the traveling text could be viewed as a transnational feminist solidarity-building project. In 2018, I also completed a follow-up interview study with seventeen of the same participants to bring my earlier findings up to date.[30] Considering Turkey's increasingly repressive political environment where feminist dissidence has become both more vital and risky, this follow-up study has been critical for uncovering the book's continuing transgressive impact and honing my critical arguments.

The analyses of the reading narratives that I collected from *Bekâret*'s feminist readers in 2010 and 2018 reveal crucial insights on the multiple roles of feminist translation in enabling the trans/formation of feminist subjectivities, expanding local repertoires of feminist knowledge and action, and facilitating transnational feminist connectivities in a world organized around mutually sustaining oppositionalities. The organization of the book, which I explain in the next section, reflects the analysis of those distinct roles by respectively bringing into spotlight the subjective, local, and global politics of feminist encounters and engagements taking place in and through translation.

## Chapter Summaries

Virgin *Crossing Borders* is composed of six analysis chapters. Chapter 1 recounts the virginity politics of Turkey and the US in a comparative framework to help readers geohistorically contextualize *Virgin* and *Bekâret* as well as the text's travels. Without such contextualization, the study runs the risk of romanticizing the notion of global circulation by depicting a picture of agentless and fixed discourses floating freely across unideological terrains and routes of a "global village" untainted by power hierarchies. Texts do not transcendentally flow in a neverland but are performed by ideological agents within specific conditions of possibility. To understand the contingencies of *Virgin*'s travels, first, the local and global geohistoricity of Turkey needs to be described. The chapter reveals the similarities and differences between the reception contexts of *Virgin* and *Bekâret*. By describing the ways in which the heteropatriarchal virginity codes as well as the feminist resistances of the US and Turkey depart from each other, Chapter 1 reveals the differently interventionist agendas pursued by the two books. The next chapter discusses how that agenda materialized in the translation of the Turkish text.

Chapter 2 first describes *Virgin* as a popular feminist history book dedicated to dismantling virginity myths by revealing its constantly changing configurations throughout the western history. The rest of the chapter analyzes the book's remaking in Turkish and introduces "feminist translation" as a political project that seeks to intervene into local heteropatriarchal truth regimes and enable cross-border flows of subversive epistemologies and transnational feminist connectivities. The chapter examines the manifestation of that feminist agenda by particularly focusing on the politics of text choice, lexical choices, the translator's preface as an interventionist discursive space, and finally, the material remaking of the book (especially its new cover).

Drawing on the reception study, the following four chapters, each with a distinctive analytical scale—subjective, local, and transnational—examines the political impact of those feminist translation strategies among a group of feminists in Turkey.

Chapter 3 explores how feminist subjectivity is transformed in and through contact with traveling texts. The first part of the chapter explores translation as a dialogic expansion in the process of which the reader's situated subjectivity engages with the "alien" discourses of the traveling text and becomes transformed by that encounter. The next section, conceiving reading as an embodied encounter, asks how *Bekâret*'s readers responded to a border-crossing text within which they were bodily implicated while also being implicated outside its geohistorical scope. Chapter 4 takes off from the fact that *Bekâret* to this day remains the only feminist book in Turkish that is exclusively dedicated to challenging virginity codes and conventions, which explains why the book has a steady sales record, and asks how *Virgin*'s Turkish translation could settle in Turkey despite its exclusively western scope and identity and unsettle Turkey's cultural economy of virginity. The chapter investigates the local political impact of this exceptional book by drawing on the reception study and reveals that the book has significantly contributed to the feminist politics in Turkey by (1) providing counter knowledges on virginity and, (2) raising critical awareness and acting as a call for feminist action.

By shifting the analytical scale to the transnational, Chapter 5 explores translation's role in building cross-border feminist solidarities and asks pressing questions about the promises and risks of transnational feminism by using *Bekâret* as a case study. Given the precarious positionality of Turkey regarding the "west vs east" binary as opposed to the US' hegemonic status as the current face of western imperialism, *Virgin*'s translation and reception in Turkey provide a great opportunity to analyze the potentials and pitfalls of transnational feminism. The chapter reveals two primary connectionist reading strategies used by *Bekâret*'s readers, "comparative accretion" and "differential universalization," during which the readers populate the text's foreign virginity narratives while inhabiting the discursive and material locality of their "home." During those connectionist engagements with the traveling text that flout the oppositional schemes of orientalism, the readers question the virginity politics of both "home" and "abroad" in a relational manner and come up with a universal narrative of resistance that recognizes both similarities and differences across localities.

Continuing with the transnational focus, Chapter 6 shows that a crucial outcome of *Bekâret*'s readers' post-oppositional reading strategies was the formation of imagined translational feminist communities bonded by a common vision of a world free from virginity oppression. The first section argues that when ethically practiced and read, translation fosters a sense of cross-border political affinity and interconnectivity. The second section, drawing on the follow-up reception study, discusses the readers' responses to a hypothetical question: how do you think western feminists would react to a similar feminist book that dismantled virginity by examining the geohistorical realities of the east? This question, which I also revisit in the conclusion, reveals crucial insights on the issue of cross-border trust in the other's reciprocity, hospitality, and vulnerability. Hence, by exploring the issue of the geopolitics of trust from two different angles of cross-border intersubjectivity—one yielding a hopeful picture of post-oppositional transnationality, while the other remaining doubtful of it—the two sections of this chapter provide us with mutually complementary lessons about imagining (and building) transnational feminist connectivities and communities in and through translation.

In the final chapter, I conclude the manuscript by highlighting translation's political potential to facilitate empowering interactions between resistant texts and feminist readers and to mobilize feminist connectivities across borders. The first section brings up cautionary tales about transnational feminist politics as implicated by *Virgin*'s transatlantic travels. I ask, what would happen if the geopolitical composition, position, and direction of the traveling text were reversed? Then, I discuss two scenarios illustrating some of the disturbing reactions that Virgin *Crossing Borders* received at western academic settings. Those oppositional responses are worth noting because they highlight the urgency of assuming ethical responsibility when it comes to hearing one another across borders. In the third section, I underline the importance of cultivating a new cultural ethos of cross-border translation and reception that simultaneously celebrates the indeterminate alienness of the other, the fluidity and vulnerability of the self, and the fine possibility of hybridization. I end the manuscript by inviting further research on translational travels of feminisms. Translation, I contend, deserves more attention from feminist scholars because in a world that is inhabited by/in numerous languages, the only way to achieve justice across borders and differences is to ethically translate and hear each other's stories so that our partial truths can join forces in our common pursuit of global resistance and change.

## CHAPTER 1

# Comparative Geohistories
# of Virginity

November 2019: Rapper TI's disclosure on the *Ladies
Like Us* podcast about taking his daughter to an annual
gynecological exam to confirm her virginity makes the
headlines in (and beyond) the United States.

December 2019: The first episode of the popular
TV drama *Sefirin Kızı* [*The Ambassador's Daughter*]
is aired in Turkey and becomes one of the most
controversial topics on social media.

In November 2019, US rapper and producer TI went on the *Ladies Like Us* podcast and shared that he took his daughter to a gynecological exam every year before her birthday to confirm that she was still a virgin. As the internet exploded in response to his confession, the hosts apologized and pulled down the episode. In the following days and weeks, several columns, particularly those written from feminist perspectives, appeared throughout the media revealing that virginity tests were not as uncommon in the United States as people thought, condemning virginity tests as a violation of women's bodies and rights, and dispelling supposedly scientific myths about the hymen.[1] Clearly, America's obsession with virginity had not come to an end despite claims of a sexual revolution. Interestingly, within hours after the TI scandal hit the news in the United States, every major and minor news outlet in Turkey was reporting it on their online venues, typically using "shock" or "shocking" in their titles. What was so shocking about this event for Turkey's audience—so much so that it only took a few hours for the news to travel to Turkey in translation? Was it because such a locally familiar practice was being performed by Americans too? That such a patriarchal practice was being embraced by Americans too? Or that such a conservative ideology of sexuality was being pursued by Americans too?[2] What was it that the

Turkish audience expected from Americans that this event contradicted in a "shocking" way?

A few weeks after America's TI scandal shocked the Turkish-speaking audience, another sensational virginity story, this time a locally procured one, left them open-mouthed. On the night of December 11, 2019, a popular TV drama called *Sefirin Kızı* [The Ambassador's Daughter] made its debut in Turkey and caused a huge controversy on social media[3] because of its "first night of marriage" scene where the main woman character is kicked out by her newly wedded husband for not being a virgin (that is, for not bleeding after intercourse). She admits to being raped by an acquaintance, but the husband does not believe her and insists she cheated on him. The drama tells the rest of this "legendary" love story as she comes back to the town years later with a daughter conceived that very first night. As soon as the show aired on TV, numerous tweets critiqued the drama for upholding patriarchal norms like virginity and honor and contributing to a misogynist ethos that bolstered violence against women in the country. Such a flood of criticism carried heavy feminist undertones, although none pointed out the fact that the show perpetuated myths about the hymen and vaginal bleeding, except for gynecologist Irmak Saraç's newspaper column titled "Erkeklik Zarı" (The Membrane of Manhood), which appeared on *BirGün*. This article begins with a reference to the TV drama, asking, "How do we feel when we see in a new TV series a man who raises hell because the woman he has married does not bleed on the night of their marriage and a woman who has to hide the fact that she was raped?"[4] Saraç, then, continues to discuss a series of myths and facts about virginity and the hymen, which separates her critique from others' since hers seeks to break the false association between virginity and the hymen, not just condemn the virginity norm. Interestingly, most of the details in the article, including Saraç's use of the term *himen*, are directly borrowed from *Virgin*'s Turkish translation, *Bekâret* and the translator's preface. So, the article, which ends with, "Women will keep writing, talking, and struggling against *himen* until they control their own bodies," reveals the continuing relevance of *Bekâret* more than ten years after it was first published in Turkish.

I started this chapter with these two "virginity scandals" not only because they reveal the enduring heteropatriarchal prominence of women's virginity in the United States and in Turkey but also because they have been protested and challenged most effectively by feminists who are well informed about the myths of the hymen and virginity.[5] I should also note that both of those locally grounded virginity events have later become translational border crossings, and it is through such transnational circulation that the geopolitical reach of their biologically essentialist virginity lessons has expanded.[6] That is, both of those traveling narratives uphold virginity as an empirical fact that can be medically tested and proven by "hymenal bleeding," reinforcing virginity's presumed universality.[7] It is that phallocentric universality that highlights the urgency of producing and circulating feminist virginity knowledges across borders because it is only through such a concerted transnational effort of counter-epistemology that we can disrupt that violent universality claim.[8] I situate the publications of *Virgin* and *Bekâret* as part of this concerted effort to create a transnational front of resistance against virginity violence. In the rest of this chapter, I first discuss the configuration of virginity in Turkey's national context and then briefly introduce the United States' virginity politics in a comparative framework.

## Policing Virginity as a Nationalist Assignment

The Republic of Turkey was officially founded in 1923 by a group of nationalist "revolutionaries" led by Mustafa Kemal Atatürk (the last name literally meaning "the fore/father Turk") as a successor state of the 600-year-old Ottoman Empire, which had been economically and politically deteriorating and territorially dissolving, particularly after the First World War.[9] The new nation-state came into being after defeating and driving out the invading European forces and overthrowing the Ottoman state, whose sovereignty was already questionable as the country was under occupation. For the next ten years, the new state undertook many reforms[10] in pursuit of its ideology of secular modernization and westernization blended with a carefully crafted form of Turkish nationalism.[11] These reforms included secularization and unification of education, replacement of religious courts by a secular legal system,[12] language reforms including the adoption of Turkish as the (only) national language,[13] creation of the Translation Bureau in 1940,[14] adoption of the Roman alphabet,[15] and new dress codes.[16]

Until the late 1940s, the state was governed by a single-party system that solidified the status of Atatürk as the nation's "father." After the multi-party system was launched in 1945, the country experienced three military coups (1960, 1971, and 1980), all of which resulted in temporary periods of direct military rule.[17] The country went through a difficult path of political instability until 2002, when the neoliberal conservative Justice and Development Party (AKP)[18] came to power under Recep Tayyip Erdoğan's leadership (the current president) and formed a single-party government (repeated in the later national elections). Even though AKP might appear to have brought some stability to Turkish politics, particularly due to its domination of the parliament and continuing power as a single-party government, the country has, in fact, been experiencing major economic troubles and tremendous political turmoil and repression, especially on issues regarding Kurdish liberation, secularism, women's rights, LGBT+ rights, freedom of speech, environmental justice, and neoliberal capitalist expansion in guise of "urban renewal" and "development," which have resulted in substantial decline in national economy, severe ideological polarization, and awfully violent, authoritarian state policies.

This short national history provides some useful background information to situate the history of Turkey's women's movements. Aside from the Ottoman women's movement (1868–1922), the history of the republic witnessed two "waves" of women's collective activism.[19] The first one is the short-lived (1923–1935) first wave that continued from the Ottoman women's movement and was repressed by the Turkish state. The second wave has been going on since the 1980s.[20] Tekeli calls the period between the two waves as "barren years" (Tekeli, "Birinci ve İkinci," 337)—or, as others have (problematically) called it, the era of "state feminism," which refers to "the state-led promotion of women's equality in the public sphere [that] monopolized women's activism" (White, "State Feminism," 155). The emergence of the feminist movement in the 1980s is often regarded as paradoxical since this is the highly restrictive aftermath of the 1980 coup during which the military-state suppressed all political action, especially that of political parties and labor unions and sought to depoliticize all aspects of life in Turkey. Paker notes this paradox, saying, "the coup cleared the way for a women's movement to begin to assert its independence" (Paker, "Unmuffled Voices," 273).

It was in this period that a feminist language, discourse, and consciousness started to develop among women, many of whom had been involved, yet largely in secondary positions, in leftist (and male-dominated) political organizations prior to the coup. These women activists began forming consciousness-raising groups to discuss their experiences of discontent with the existing regime of male domination and express their opposition to its multiple configurations of oppression. At the time, they did not seem to pose a serious threat to the military-state and were ignored until an organized independent feminist movement grew out of these small groups, which is deemed to be "the first democratic movement to emerge after the coup" (Kardam and Ertürk, "Gender Accountability," 187).[21] One key development of this period was the Women's Circle (*Kadın Çevresi*), a feminist translation collective. Founded in 1983 by a group of feminist scholars and activists, the Women's Circle is described as "the first feminist group" in the history of Turkey's contemporary feminist movement. It played a central role in the

1980s' feminist movement by translating primary feminist works into Turkish and facilitating the growth of a local theoretical and conceptual repertoire of feminism.[22] In Timisi and Gevrek's words, who attribute the emergence of academic feminism in 1990's Turkey to the translation of feminist literature in the 1980s, "With the support of the translations carried out in the 1980s, a substantive feminist literature began to develop in the academia" ("Feminist Hareket," 38). The Women's Circle also contributed greatly to the formation of a feminist language in Turkish that would enable women to articulate their experiences from a gender-political perspective. Şule Aytaç, one of the members of the Women's Circle and translators of Juliet Mitchell's *Woman's Estate*, explains this as follows (Kum et al., *Özgürlüğü Ararken*, 39–40):

> We noted that there was no "language of feminism" in Turkish to begin with. So, if we translated some of the terms used by Mitchell or Millett into Turkish literally, feminism could not be understood in Turkey, and a feminist movement could not develop. Thus, we decided to use Mitchell's work to create the [feminist] concepts. . . . So, we decided not to hurry to translate the text right away because we would create a feminist language from it.

Following this comment, the translation of "male domination" as *erkek egemenliği* is mentioned as a case of translational making of a local feminist language. Ayşe Gül Altınay discusses another case of such translational production of local language: the Turkish appropriation of "sexual harassment" as *cinsel taciz* in the 1990s (Altınay, "Bedenimiz ve Biz," 324–25)—in fact, the English term itself was relatively new coined in the 1970's United States (Mansbridge and Flaster, "*Male Chauvinist*," 268–69).[23] Her words clearly illustrate the contested process of importing foreign terminology:

> After the name of the campaign [against sexual harassment] was debated at length and "*cinsel taciz*" was decided on, it was criticized a lot for being an incomprehensible, unfamiliar translation of a foreign phrase. . . . I don't know how many women today would say that *cinsel taciz* is a translation from another language. Obviously, we have already made it "ours."[24]

Today, these terms are so firmly established in both feminist *and* mainstream language that it is hard to see them as products of translation and grasp their roots in creative acts of cross-border borrowing, especially when no historical accounts of their importation are told in feminist historiography.[25]

The introduction of such concepts into Turkish should not be underrated since these naming practices paved the way for the creation and legitimization of new critical discourses and practices and helped carve alternative political spaces. As Şirin Tekeli says about the Women's Circle, "When we got together in our translation group, the breaking point was this: we all in fact had experienced sexism but had not given it a name" (*İsyan-ı Nisvan*). It was because of such translational operations of naming that a feminist language and consciousness began to develop in Turkey. I see *Virgin*'s feminist translation into Turkish as an extension of that legacy passed on by the Women's Circle.

Another key development of the post-1980 era was the emergence of feminist historiography, which peaked in the 1990s and 2000s when numerous works recovering the erased/forgotten histories of women's activism were published.[26] These pioneer studies uncovered both the Ottoman women's movement (1868–1922) and the movement of the early republican era (1923–1935) and advanced "the formation of a feminist consciousness and memory" in Turkey (Çakır, "Feminism," 61). They revealed the political voices and struggles of Ottoman and republican women activists, which were suppressed by Atatürk's totalitarian regime. This erasure of the early women's movement from the official historiography was partly secured by the language reforms, especially the Turkification of language and the adoption of the Roman alphabet in 1928,[27] which created a major gap between pre-1928 documents written in the Persian-Arabic script and vocabulary and the post-1928 generations who were taught in state schools only to read and write in the Roman alphabet equipped with the "purified Turkish" vocabulary. Therefore, those works of women's history should also be considered as works of translation since they transplanted in history a part of women's past that was condemned by the masculinist official historiography to dusty archives and rewrote it for a new generation of feminists whose collective memory now includes both Ottoman and early republican women's struggles.

One of the most significant outcomes of those historical studies has been the problematization of the national discourse on women's rights, which claims that women in Turkey did not fight and did not need to fight for their sociopolitical rights as those were generously bestowed upon them by the "modern and progressive" Turkish state and Atatürk (hence the notion of "state feminism" often used to describe Turkey's early gender politics) (Zihnioğlu, *Kadınsız İnkılap*, 23).[28] As Çakır notes, "this androcentric discourse designated Atatürk as the sole emancipator of Turkish women" ("Feminism," 62). Hence, Turkey's so-called "state feminism" was established on its suppression and erasure of "civil feminism" from the official history (Altınay, "Giriş," 24). This official discourse has been constantly repeated in Turkey not only to ensure women citizens' ideological and embodied loyalty and commitment to the new republic, but also more importantly to portray the image of a "progressive, democratic, secular, modern, and western" nation-state in the international arena (as opposed to the Ottoman Empire, which became Turkey's Other in the nation-building process). In this regard, women were cast as the "iconic embodiments" of the new nation and deployed to symbolize the newly designed national identity.[29] As Lewis notes, "policies advocating female emancipation were of huge symbolic importance for the new regime as a way of signalling their distance from an antiquated and morally impoverished empire" (*Rethinking Orientalism*, 115). That is, in the making of the nation-state, women became the chief mark of the Turkish modernization and westernization project with their gender and sexual identities, embodiments, and roles configured and constrained by the state under the general rubric of "the New Modern Turkish Woman."[30]

In fact, "how should the New Turkish Woman be?" was a major question of debate in the republic's early years (Zihnioğlu, *Kadınsız İnkılap*, 225–30). The question reflects the state's investment in constructing a specific model of woman citizen whose social, political, and moral roles were to be defined within the gendered parameters of the new nation-state. As part of the "collective identity architecture" of the Kemalist project, the New Turkish Woman was imagined as a "Child Woman" whose connections to the Ottoman past were severed and whose new national identity was created on the basis of the annihilation and historical denial of local civil feminism (228). In this patriarchal formulation, Atatürk was positioned as her "father" and the state as her paternalistic source of guidance and protection. The New Turkish Woman was supposed not to remember the Ottoman past so that her complete integration into and internalization of the republican paradigm could be ensured. She was expected to be docile, loyal, thankful, and content with the rights "given" to her by the state.

Yaprak Zihnioğlu argues that this is one reason why women affiliated with the first wave (e.g., Nezihe Muhiddin) were suppressed by the state since they did not fit in the image of the submissive and quiet "Turkish Child/Woman" (*Kadınsız İnkılap*, 227–30, 262–64). On the contrary, these women were bold and loud in their demands. They posed a threat to Atatürk's plans to use women's rights as leverage for Turkey's inter/national performance of a western/modern identity. Plus, these women's activism began in the Ottoman times and was carried over into the republican era. They did not deny their Ottoman pasts but symbolized the continuity between the empire and the republic, which was in opposition to the ideological project of the new state that depended for its new identity on collective amnesia. In fact, the ongoing activism of those women demonstrated that even though the new state and its gendered citizens were redefined against their Ottoman Other through historical detachments, all of these ruptures were "surrounded by mental and structural continuities shaped fundamentally by patriarchy" (Berktay, *Tarihin Cinsiyeti*, 100). That is, the patriarchal gender regime continued from the Ottoman context into that of the republic, so did women's resistance, both of which were strategically elided while writing the official history. The translational work undertaken by feminist historiographers, who retold pre-republican texts in Turkish, played a central role in uncovering these historical continuities. This importantly shows that translation is not just a matter of spatial reworking of texts, but also a temporal resignification of history, both can be crucial feminist projects.

As the New Woman of the Turkish nationalist imaginary was defined as modern, her appearance and social roles were redesigned to resemble that of "the Western Woman" with veiling being discouraged in public and women being encouraged to enter the public spheres of education and workplace. In fact, the admonishing of the veil, which was the emblem of the Ottoman Empire in orientalist western discourses, was a key geopolitical gesture to establish the contours of the new ideal nationalist femininity and outline the gendered boundaries of the nation in accordance with the west. Since "the veil (in all its versions) is the ultimate sign by which the west distinguishes the Oriental woman from the Occidental," it was strategically deployed by nationalists to anchor the identity of Turkishness within the imagined boundaries of the modern west (Lewis, *Rethinking Orientalism*, 231).

Because the New Turkish Woman's identity was modeled after the (imaginary) unveiled (read: promiscuous and immoral) Western Woman, the national anxiety over her "dangerous" sexuality and assumed potential to cause "moral degeneration" was resolved with the addition of "modest" to the equation. Hence, "the nationalist project both initiated women's access to modernity and set the limits of desirable modernity for them" (Sinha, "Gender and Nation," 254). Or as Perin Gürel puts it, "Chastity and modesty, along with nationalist commitment, constituted the line between selective and excessive westernization" (*Limits of Westernization*, 70). The new nationalist gender formulation sought to highlight the ideal Turkish Woman's similarity to, yet at the same time difference from, the imagined Western Woman: "Unveiled and yet pure, the new woman was to be 'modern' in appearance and intellect but was still required to preserve the 'traditional' virtue of chastity and to affirm it constantly" (Parla, "Honor of the State," 75). With the "Modern But Modest Woman" ideal came the strict state control over women's bodies as well as a renewed emphasis on virginity, marriage, family, and motherhood, which once again points at the patriarchal continuities from the Ottoman context into the republican one. This re/formulation required women to be either "unmarried virgins" or "married nonvirgins." In the making of this identity, women were assigned the role of asexual "comrades," "whose honour and chastity remains intact in spite of her active participation in the struggle to liberate and improve her nation" (Sirman, "Feminism in Turkey," 12). And as that identity got further endorsed, premarital virginity crystallized both as a heteropatriarchal gender code and as a nationalist trope that legitimized the state's authority to regulate and police women's sexualities.

The making of the Modern Turkish Woman, however, should not exclusively be assessed in local terms, but also situated in a global arena, where the "Modern Girl/Woman" has had many appearances across national contexts, which should be analyzed as cases of "multidirectional citation" or translations (Modern Girl Around the World Research Group, *Modern Girl*, 4–5).[31] While the Modern Girl has been variously deployed as a key constituent of capitalist, anticolonialist, racist, imperialist, and modernist projects across nations, in the Turkish case, the symbolic and pragmatic construction of the Modern Girl repertoire has been most prominent in relation to the nation-building project.

The Turkish Modern Girl, who emerged as a state-sanctioned nationalist project, was an object of *both* celebration and control. Her new image was bounded by marriage and motherhood, especially to prevent her transgression of patriarchal sexuality codes of (e.g., virginity) adopted surreptitiously from the officially rejected Ottoman Empire. That is, she was used to cement nationalist ideals, yet, in ways that put her under the patronage of her father and Atatürk, the symbolic father of the nation (Ergun, *Erkeğin Yittiği Yerde*, xi). Then, the Turkish Modern Girl differs from other nations' Modern Girls for the concurrent disciplining she was subjected to by the state and the state endorsement she received, particularly regarding education and employment. Hence, Deniz Kandiyoti's diagnosis of the condition of "the new republican woman" as "emancipated but unliberated" ("Emancipated"). The Turkish Modern Girl's both restricted and promoted appearance in the nationalist discourse highlights her distinction from other cases where the Modern Girl was either condemned (e.g., China) or fostered by the state as a racialized "signifier of 'healthy' and 'civilized' national femininity" (e.g., Nazi Germany) (Modern Girl Around the World Research Group, *Modern Girl*, 16).

An example that illustrates this paradoxical bond is the case of Sabiha Gökçen, who was one of Atatürk's adopted daughters and known to be the world's first woman combat pilot. Gökçen was deployed in the constitutive rhetoric of the republic to promote a modern image of the nation through her depiction as a "modern but modest" (unmarried and virgin) woman soldier. According to Gökçen's memoirs, when she asks for Atatürk's permission to join the military operations undertaken to suppress the ethnically defined Dersim uprising (of the Kurdish Alevi population)[32] in 1937, his first question is what she would do if she had to surrender to a "gang of bandits" (Altınay, "Ordu-Millet-Kadınlar," 268–69). Gökçen answers that she would not surrender alive. Upon this satisfactory response, Atatürk gives her his own gun and tells her not to hesitate to kill others or herself in case her "honor" (read: virginity) comes under threat. Gökçen reports this encounter under the title, "The Gun That Will Protect My Honor!" (268). So, her performance of the "Modern Turkish Woman" identity is celebrated only under the condition of her embodiment of the sexual modesty norm whose key constituent is virginity. The norm is deemed even more important than her (or others') life. The story attests to the centrality of premarital virginity in the construction of the New Turkish Woman.

Since those early years of the republic, women's bodies and sexualities have consistently been kept under state scrutiny in Turkey, particularly through the institutions of family, law, medicine, education, and military. The practice of virginity tests has played a key role in this disciplining and it was one of the first issues problematized by the women's movement in the 1980s. Up to the 1980s, there is a gap in feminist and mainstream literatures on Turkey's virginity regime. Its sociolinguistic conceptualizations (cultural conventions), institutional operationalizations (medical, legal, and other normative definitions and practices), and experiential manifestations (subjective dis/embodiments) are not questioned publicly. This epistemic silence does not necessarily mean that the nation's virginity regime was never contested or disrupted. Rather, the silence indicates the lack of a public debate on the issue, which is not surprising given that virginity constitutes a taboo in Turkey and without the critical force and voice of an organized feminist movement, which did not fully emerge until the 1980s, it would be difficult, if not impossible, to frame virginity and virginity tests as public issues.

The controversy over virginity tests first received some public interest in 1988 when the General Command of Mapping, a branch of the Turkish Armed Forces, required virginity reports from its prospective women staff as a condition of their employment. Due to the feminist movement's protests, the issue drew some attention in the media, but it was not until 1992 that virginity tests became a major topic in the mainstream media. In 1992, two female high school students committed suicide after the principals of their schools ordered them to undergo virginity tests. Despite the public outcry generated by national and international women's organizations, the Ministry of Education issued a regulation in 1995 that enabled school authorities to require virginity tests from "suspicious" female students. In 1999, the Ministry of Justice issued another regulation limiting the right to request virginity tests to judges or prosecutors in sexual assault or "prostitution" cases. The issue erupted again in 2000 when the Minister of Health imposed virginity tests on female students at Vocational High Schools of Health. For decades from the 1980s till the 2000s, the state continued to police women's virginity and refused to take legislative action to end virginity tests.

In the course of the Turkish Penal Code (TPC) amendments in 2004, the government's reluctance to outlaw virginity tests had to subside to some extent in the face of growing pressure from the women's movement and the European Union. The TPC is the most important legal document pertaining to virginity, and unfortunately, the amendments were not satisfactory with regard to the issue. The term "virginity examination" is not even used (hence, not explicitly criminalized) in the TPC but legitimized under Article 287 titled "Genital Examination."[33] The article limits the authorization of the practice to prosecutors and judges; yet, it is still problematic because if deemed "necessary" by these authorities, women can still be *legally* forced to undergo virginity tests.[34] So, the Turkish state provides its judicial agents with continuing power to control women's sexualities.[35]

Moreover, the legal code assumes that the hymen is a physical proof of virginity, which is inaccurate because, as Blank argues, the hymen is "just another of the various ridges and folds of the female genitals" (*Virgin*, 43).[36] In fact, it came into being as a discrete membrane only after being named as such and signified as proof of virginity by Flemish anatomist Andreas Vesalius in 1544 (50). The hymen was found precisely because it was looked for by patriarchal western medicine (94). What we call the hymen is so diverse in shape, size, appearance, and structure that "saying that someone has a hymen is, all by itself, a bit like saying someone has skin" (41). Moreover, the hymen is so unstable for many reasons other than sexual intercourse that Blank rightly asks, "if the hymen can change all by itself, can we ever accurately call it 'intact' or 'unaltered'?" (38, 94). The medical configuration of the hymen as a distinct, palpable, and diagnostic vaginal entity is a case of normative standardization where one type of a membrane becomes naturalized as intact and resistive in the masculinist imaginary. This is why I claim that the hymen is as invented as virginity itself is, yet "objectively" anchored in women's "biological" bodies and designated within the authoritative field of anatomy as *the* marker of virginity. Throughout history, there have, in fact, been many (imaginary) tests of virginity, which, however, "can only tell us whether or not she conforms to what people of her time and place believe to be true of virgins" (77). In short, by perpetuating the flawed belief that virginity can be definitively bodily verified, the TPC reinforces the scientific myth of hymenal virginity. Therefore, Turkey's "Modern But Modest Woman" ideal resides not only in the patriarchal virginity ideology (that women should not engage in premarital sex), but also in the scientifically fabricated imaginary of the hymen.

## "Turkish Virginity" vis-à-vis "American Virginity"

The local picture of virginity that I just described gets more complicated when we consider the global context within which it appeared. As noted, Turkey was built on the remnants of the Ottoman Empire, *the* orient in the European imaginary.[37] Since its conception in the late 19th century, Turkey has endeavored to build an identity defined not only in opposition to the oriental Ottoman, but also in alignment with the west. However, very much like "the bridge between the east and the west" metaphor often used to describe Turkey's transcontinental positionality, the country has been stuck between an inherited, yet rejected, identity informed by orientalism and an aspired to, yet never fully attained, identity informed by occidentalism.[38] As Meltem Ahıska writes, "Turkey has been trying to cross the bridge between the East and the West for more than a hundred years now, with a self-conscious anxiety that it is arrested in time and space by the bridge itself" (*Occidentalism*, 353). According to Fatmagül Berktay, the mode of being stuck in the east/west binary and oscillating between the two poles without ever becoming one has caused a trauma in Turkey's collective psyche (*Tarihin Cinsiyeti*, 150–56).[39] As a result, the New Turkish Man has developed a deep state of paranoia toward his internal Other, the New Turkish Woman, whom he ceaselessly attempts to control by constraining her new modern identity and actions so that his already unstable identity would not come under further threat.

In fact, the new nation's anxiety, whether experienced consciously or not, over the New Turkish Woman's threatening sexuality has been caused by Turkey's deeply entrenched anxiety over its boundary position between the east and the west. The sexual modesty ideal with its central component of premarital virginity has been imposed to resolve those two conflating geopolitical anxieties. This should be considered while analyzing *Virgin*'s travels to Turkey because the text's western "origin" (implied in the very name of its author and explicitly claimed and performed by the text) does have an impact on the readers' meaning-making patterns. That is, since the reception of the text takes place in a national context that has neither successfully left behind the oriental identity nor acquired the western identity, it is crucial to ask how this perpetual state of in-betweenness has affected the readings and translation of a text carrying the authoritative voice of the US-centered west that could potentially unsettle everything the local readers knew and experienced about virginity.

The orientalist and occidentalist discourses circulating in Turkey also have important implications for the perceptions of the United States, the "originating" location of *Bekâret*, in the Turkish imaginary. One of the dominant images of the west (particularly the United States) in Turkey is that of the "Western Woman," who allegedly loses her underappreciated virginity at a young age outside marriage and lives her sexuality "freely" (read: immorally) without being constrained by her family, culture, or state. As discussed before, this image of "the sexually liberated Western Woman," which Gürel argues was best symbolized by the image of "the flapper," was the main reason why the New Modern Woman ideal was a source of moral panic and conceived consequently as "modern but modest" in Turkey (*Limits of Westernization*, 71). This anxiety seems to have persisted, perhaps even escalated as the nation's connections with the United States have intensified over time. In other words, "the Western Woman" appears as an object of both aspiration and aversion in the Turkish imaginary and it is this contradictory mold that positions *Bekâret*, a sexuality book written primarily by, about, and for western women, in a precarious relationship with Turkey's audience, who has been persistently warned against potential "westoxification" particularly at the hands of overwesternized, treacherously immoral women.

The image of the "sexually liberated" Western Woman, further promoted by the popular notion of "the sexual revolution," is partly dismantled by *Virgin*,[40] which shows how virginity plays a disciplining function in the west, especially in the United States, which "of all the countries of the developed world . . . is the only one that has to date created a federal agenda having specifically to do with the virginity of its citizens" (238).[41] The history of abstinence policies as told in *Virgin* presents a picture of "western virginity" that is different from the one domineering the Turkish imaginary. Indeed, this is one reason why the media coverage of the US abstinence policies in Turkey usually contains an element of surprise. For instance, several news reports on the results of a 2011 survey done by the US Department of Health and Human Services used an exclamation point in their titles expressing the "surprising" finding that virginity was on the rise among people aged 15–29—e.g., "Yeni Trend Bekaret!"[42] [The New Trend Is Virginity!] and "ABD'de Yeni Kadın Modası: Bekâret!"[43] [The New Women's Fashion in the US: Virginity!]. Or remember the media stories that reported the TI virginity scandal, most of which similarly used the word "shock/ing" in their headlines—e.g., "Ünlü Şarkıcıdan Şok İtiraf" [Famous Singer's Shocking Disclosure].[44] The fact that these events were deemed newsworthy enough to be extensively covered in

Turkish mainstream media is itself quite telling in regard to the country's perception of US women's (hyper)sexuality, coded as perverse, out-of-control, and immoral. Also, these events are often presented in the news in a way that both reinforces the image of the "sexually liberated Western Woman" and justifies policing women's virginities by implying that too much sexual freedom is dangerous for the well-being of society ("teen pregnancy" is the key citation here) and needs to be kept under control. For instance, in a news article on the "back-to-virginity movement," the United States' sexual revolution is portrayed as a social event that "has gone to extremes" and is therefore being countered with the conservative, corrective abstinence movement ("Batı'da Bekarete Dönüş"). In this regard, such representations of "Western Woman" serve to solidify Turkey's "Modern But Modest Woman" ideal by pitting the public image of "the honorable Turkish Woman" against the imagined subject of "the dishonorable Western Woman."

Indeed, abstinence-based sex education programs and the federal policies that endorse and fund these seem to constitute the biggest concern with regard to virginity in the contemporary United States. Having been "well entrenched in American public policy since its (re)emergence in the 1980s" and implemented most rigorously during the George W. Bush administration, abstinence-based sex education has caused quite a stir in the cultural landscape of the United States within the last decade (Carpenter, *Virginity Lost*, 199). Under the apparent goal of precluding teenagers from engaging in premarital sex (again, "teen pregnancy" is the key citation), abstinence programs have been shown to define for the US population an ideal "public morality" inspired by a conservative Christian ideology while reasserting traditional gender roles conceived within the contours of heteropatriarchal marriage and family (Greslé-Favier, "Sexual Abstinence"). As a result of these programs, the virginity norm, which was assumed to have lost its allure as an ideal for most Americans since the "sexual revolution," resurfaced in the national agenda as a topic of intense discussion. *Virgin* was written in this context marked by a public debate that the resurrected abstinence/virginity ideology generated.[45] So, like its Turkish translation, Blank's *Virgin* itself has been a discursive intervention into the officially reclaimed virginity regime of the United States, seeking to unsettle its "troubling" reactionary rhetorics and gender practices (243).

Then, in both the United States and Turkey, the state is actively involved in conservative virginity politics—through abstinence policies in the United States and virginity testing policies in Turkey. Moreover, in both contexts, virginity is heavily medicalized with the hymen occupying the center in the symbolic and practical repertoires of virginity. Yet, virginity tests do not constitute a state-sanctioned practice in the United States (although they are widely practiced across the country).[46] The second crucial difference is the strong association of (male/family) "honor" with virginity in Turkey, which does not seem to have a ruling cultural presence in the United States. These two contextual divergences point to a larger difference between the two settings: Turkey's virginity politics seem to generate more systematic, prevalent, and deadly forms of violence against women—particularly virginity tests and "honor killings."[47]

Given this comparison of virginity politics in Turkey and the United States, it becomes clear that the reception contexts of *Virgin* and *Bekâret* differ considerably, a difference that is also manifest in the motivations to produce the texts. Blank explains her interest in virginity as "spurred by the questions of some adolescents with whom I was working as a sex educator" (*Virgin*, ix). Her initial virginity research sought to find a definitive sketch of the concept so that she could help adolescents struggling with reconciling their diverse sexual experiences with the inconsistent and obscure virginity definitions they encountered. Upon realizing the immense historical data on virginity, yet the absence of a fixed definition, she wanted to "solve the puzzle," which turned into the project of writing *Virgin* (Ergun and Akgökçe, "Neyle Ölçerseniz," 60). In the process, Blank also disrupted the myth of the "singular body" with supposedly singular virginity experiences in particular and sexuality in general (*Virgin*, 95):

> There is no single virginal body, no single virginity experience, no single virginal vagina, not even a single virginal hymen. There is only the question, how do we know whether this woman is a virgin? The answer has been written innumerable times, with alum and doves' blood and urine and decoctions of mint and lady's mantle, with charts and graphs and clinical photography. But no matter how many times someone attempts to inscribe it, no matter how firmly they press the pen to the paper, we are left forever with the same blank page.

In short, *Virgin* reinscribed the western history of virginity with such an open-ended universal (a "blank page" where only the nonexistence of virginity is a constant) that it simultaneously dismantled oppressive virginity discourses, recognized geopolitical and experiential differences, and left little, if any, room for other seemingly absolute gender-oppressive codes to be dictated.

In comparison, my incentive to translate *Virgin* might appear more explicitly interventionist than that of Blank's. While we both wanted to destabilize local virginity codes by disclosing the misogynist politics behind their fabrication, I assigned to the book the much more urgent mission of disrupting a medical ideology that induced multiple forms of violence against women in Turkey. As the massive power of medicalization[48] is combined with the brutal force of the masculinist codes of "honor/shame" in Turkey, the disciplining function of virginity becomes further endorsed. The US book does not appear to be motivated by such a pressing problem of systematic (and deadly) violence against women but is framed more as addressing an issue of adolescent sexuality—an issue that has received a lot of public attention in the United States with the rise of the abstinence-based sex education debate.

In conclusion, this chapter revealed not only that there are substantial commonalities and differences between the virginity regimes of the United States and Turkey, but also that the "Sexually Liberated Modern Western Woman" and the "Modern But Modest Turkish Woman" have been defined in the Turkish imaginary in terms of both similarities and irreconcilable differences. What happens, then, when a book that (supposedly) speaks to and about western women comes to Turkey and engages with a different constituency of women whose sexual history and subjectivity carry the traces of different political, social, and cultural traditions and legacies? How does the Turkish-speaking audience respond to the similarities and differences surrounding the traveling book? Can they forge transnational feminist connectivities across geopolitical divides? In light of such questions raised by this (partial) comparative reading of Turkey's and the United States' virginity politics, it becomes obvious that *Virgin*'s translational travel to Turkey cannot be viewed as a straightforward transfer of meanings. In the next chapters, I first discuss how I translated the book into Turkish with a new interventionist agenda and then explore whether that discursive potential has materialized into subjective and collective forms of feminist consciousness—or defused and rejected under the reception setting's nationalist discourses.

## CHAPTER 2

# Re-visioning Virginity in the Rewriting of *Virgin*

Re-vision—the act of looking back, of seeing with fresh eyes, of entering an old text from a new critical direction— is for women more than a chapter in cultural history: it is an act of survival. Until we can understand the assumptions in which we are drenched we cannot know ourselves. And this drive to self-knowledge, for women, is more than a search for identity: it is part of our refusal of the self-destructiveness of male-dominated society. A radical critique of literature, feminist in its impulse, would take the work first of all as a clue to how we live, how we have been living, how we have been led to imagine ourselves, how our language has trapped as well as liberated us, how the very act of naming has been till now a male prerogative, and how we can begin to see and name—and therefore live—afresh. . . . We need to know the writing of the past, and know it differently than we have ever known it; not to pass on a tradition but to break its hold over us.

—Rich, *Lies, Secrets, and Silence*, 35

*Virgin*'s Turkish translation, *Bekâret*, from the moment of its inception, has been conceived as a project of feminist "re-vision," in Adrienne Rich's terms.[1] By rewriting the history of virginity from a feminist perspective, *Virgin* invites readers to interrogate their own place within that historical discourse. In doing so, it enables them to see the heteropatriarchal ideology of virginity afresh and reimagine their embodied gendered selves. In fact, by providing the readers with critical conceptual, epistemological, and political tools, the book helps readers rearticulate their experiences and live afresh, and thus, helps break the ideological and material hold of virginity over women. The book's potential of generating such interruption—of the apparent naturality, uniformity, and continuity of the hegemonic virginity regime—was the main rationale of my translation, which I discussed in the preface, and this chapter discusses the ways in which I reworked political potentiality in Turkish. Focusing on the discursive and material specifics of the book's production, promotion, and packaging, I explore how *Virgin*'s feminist re-vision was carried out by various actors situated in and in between the United States and Turkey.

The chapter's focus is on the embodied translating subject, the feminist translator, and my political agency as articulated in the reworking of the text. The analysis of the feminist translator's involvement in the project emphasizes not only my mediating role in the production of meanings, but also my negotiations with limited discursive resources and limiting institutional practices as well as my sense of ethical responsibilities. In fact, the very act of writing this chapter enacts my understanding of the translation ethics to which I subscribe. This ethical stance is informed by the feminist translation theory's simultaneous emphasis on the translator's visibility as a co-creator of the text and on self-reflexive disclosure of their politically imbued resignification of the text. That is, instead of pretending that the translator is unsituated/uninvested—objective, in the conventional sense—and concealing my ideological stance creating an illusion of an "unmediated" transfer of meanings, I pursued in *Bekâret* an ethics of political openness and accountability. This chapter is a testament to this ethical standpoint, yet a necessarily partial and incomplete one, as no act of self-reflexivity can account for all the choices and decisions made consciously and unconsciously in the translation process. The chapter is informed both by my decision-making practices as recorded in my translator's journal and observations from comparative textual analyses. Some of these analyses were induced by insightful comments made by readers who drew my attention to certain stylistic aspects, linguistic elements, and thematic features that I was not fully cognizant of during translation and might not have noticed in my analyses.

Drawing mainly on the theoretical and methodological insights of feminist translation studies, the chapter diachronically traces *Bekâret*'s production by first introducing *Virgin*—its core contents and stylistic features. An overview of the book's reception in the United States is also included here based on a partial analysis of its reviews. The chapter, then, moves on to the remaking of *Virgin* for a new setting and audience, and with a new set of political goals. Here, after describing the conversations that took place between the translator, the publishers, and the main editor, which emphasizes the multi-agentic nature of translation, I self-reflexively analyze the specifics of the translation process. I focus on some of my key significatory decisions and major translation dilemmas and discuss the ways in which I, as a situated political agent, dealt with them in pursuit of the feminist re-vision project that I had imagined and intended. In the final section of the chapter, I examine the material production of *Bekâret* by focusing on the ways in which the book was distinctively appropriated, packaged, and promoted in its new reception setting for a new audience. In short, the analytical mapping of the chapter responds to the question, "How, why, when, where, and by whom was *Virgin* transformed into *Bekâret*?"

## Reading *Virgin*

Before *Bekâret*'s publication, virginity's reification as "a medical fact" was not challenged by feminists in Turkey, who condemned virginity tests as a state-endorsed violation of women's bodily integrity but mostly left the concept itself alone. It was not common practice to ask where the concept came from, what it meant, and whether it always meant the same thing. *Virgin* could answer those critical questions and defy the epistemic basis of virginity tests. The book was finally published in the United States in 2007 after an extensive editing process, during which almost one-third of Blank's original submission was cut.[2] *Virgin*, which can be described as popular history in terms of genre, is a feminist account of the various configurations of virginity "within the vast and complicated framework of what we loosely call the West" (8). The book was promoted as the first comprehensive western history of virginity.

Readers first meet *Virgin* via the bold and humorous opening sentence of the prologue titled, "Extra Virgin": "As I worked on this book, I joked with friends that I was going to give it the subtitle Everything You Think You Know About Virginity Is Wrong" (ix). The sentence sets the book as a counter-discourse although it does not read as an arrogant statement because Blank situates herself as part of the constituency wronged by the hegemonic virginity discourse (ix). The next sentence situating Blank's work in "women's and gender studies" also hints that the counter-position taken is a feminist one. The prologue invites the readers to discard their preformed notions of virginity and engage in the text with an open mind, simultaneously giving the book an adventurous tone. It ends by asserting the legitimacy of studying virginity, which even Blank herself initially considered "to be a trivial topic" (ix). The prologue, then, justifies the book, saying "virginity has been, and continues to be, a matter of life and death around the world, very much including within the first world" (ix, xi). This statement is also crucial for its foresighted emphasis on "the first world" as a place of virginity violence, which seems to be highlighted to prevent Anglo/American readers from interpreting the claim as an orientalist affirmation of virginity oppression being an irrelevant phenomenon for the west, but rather exclusively a problem of the "third world." *Virgin*'s first chapter starts with a striking statement (3):

> By any material reckoning, virginity does not exist. . . . We invented it. We developed it. We disseminated the idea throughout our cultures, religions, legal systems, bodies of art, and works of scientific knowledge. We have fixed it as an integral part of how we experience our own bodies and selves. And we have done all this without actually being able to define it consistently, identify it accurately, or explain how or why it works.

Taking off from this thought-provoking statement the book continues to unsettle and dismantle every apparently factual, taken-for-granted notion about virginity by revealing the misogynist story of its continuous fabrication throughout the western history. In this sense, *Virgin* is a feminist mythbuster.

*Virgin* is comprised of two sections. The first part, "Virginology," starts by highlighting the indefinable, yet momentous phenomenon called virginity and explains why it has been such an important organizing, regulatory, and normative concept throughout the western history. Here, Blank also argues that virginity is fundamentally female, heterosexual, and white in the hegemonic western imaginary. Then, she delves into history that shows how the construction of this concept has evolved as western societies have gone through major transformations. This is where the book reveals the diversity in the formulations of virginity across time and space. The examples drawn from different geohistories are upsetting as they are fraught with stories of social, psychological, and physical violence against women. Yet, they confirm that there is no single, universal way of defining and testing female virginity and never has been. This review of virginity's cultural heterogeneity convincingly articulates the concept's ideological fabricatedness and defies any claims that insist on its universal standardized materiality. It is also this part of the book that traces the scientific constructions of virginity and problematizes its flawed association with the hymen, revealing the key role that the medical institution has played in fixing virginity as a scientific fact. Due to this central deconstructive emphasis on the medicalization of virginity, Part One constitutes perhaps the most interventionist section of the book.

The second part, "Virgin Culture," investigates the history of the cultural formations and transformations of virginity from early Christianity, through the Middle Ages and the Renaissance, until the present-day United States. Multiple configurations of virginity such as Queen Elizabeth and her public image as the Virgin Queen, colonization and its exploitative construction of the "New Lands" as virgin women, the fetishizing and manufacturing of virginity in pornography, and the US federal policies on abstinence-based education constitute some of the major discussions of the second part. The section also analyzes modern-day virginity tropes as they appear in various movies and television series.

*Virgin* received considerable media attention in the United States—for instance, in book reviews published in mainstream venues such as *New York Times* and *Washington Post* and feminist venues such as *Bitch* magazine.[3] The reviews mostly offer positive appraisals for the book's research, contents, writing style, and contributions to popular studies of cultural history, gender, and sexuality. Like my own reading, they evaluate *Virgin* as a mythbuster. In fact, Blank's reconceptualization of virginity as nonexistent is emphasized as the book's most crucial contribution since it elevates an ambiguous, critical discourse on virginity. Iris Blasi, in her *Bitch* magazine review, concurs: "As comprehensive as her history of virginity is, Blank hasn't submitted a con- clusive answer for all present and future questions. Instead, she has started a discourse where before there was none" ("Virgin Territory," 72). In a similar vein, Anna Jane Grossman asks in her review: "What would our world be like if for us, too, the idea simply did not exist?" ("2000-Year-Old Virgin"). One of the main reasons why I was drawn to *Virgin* is that by activating that "what if" question, it invites the reader to imagine otherwise—a question that has immense potential to generate an ontologically, epistemologically, affectively, and politically transformative reading experience that could en- able imagining new ways of embodied knowing, being, doing, and relating. Thus, *Virgin* both interferes with the normative virginity regime and offers the means to replace it with a non-normative truth regime.[4] This is why it is a useful political tool for feminists working against virginity violence. As feminist novelist and cultural historian Marina Warner's review in *Washing- ton Post* notes, "This entertaining history is a passionate polemic, brimming with a genuine spirit of emancipatory activism" ("Virgin Territory").

*Virgin* also received some noteworthy critiques. One issue raised by Ma- rina Warner and Kelly Mayhew and some readers on online blogs is that the book falls short of scholarly expectations and standards, which is understand- able given that *Virgin* is not an academic work in the strict sense of the word (Mayhew, "Pure"). For instance, Mayhew notes, "in trying to keep 'Virgin' breezy and accessible, she drops in bits of information that are often either not supported in the bibliography . . . or difficult to pull out of the biblio- graphic entries."[5] Although Mayhew admits that *Virgin* is a popular history, a genre that does not welcome heavy footnoting, she adds that "a bit more explication, a few footnotes and a more substantive bibliography . . . would have been a nice addition to this otherwise wonderful book." In fact, such a reference-making strategy could not only increase the legitimacy of *Virgin*'s truth claims, and in turn, expand its political reach, but also reveal Blank's intertextual engagements and conversations with other feminist scholars. The fact that *Virgin*, while pursuing an interventionist agenda of feminist re-visioning, cites very few feminist authors does a disservice to the arduous accumulation of feminist critique and knowledge, particularly in the field of feminist body politics.

Indeed, *Virgin* is a remarkably intertextual text, but also because it rewrites women's history by excavating, rearranging, and reinterpreting historical narratives of virginity.[6] The book incorporates numerous references to religious texts, medical studies, scientific reports, legal documents, literary works, pop culture sources, print and online media materials, institutional practices, and so forth, which immensely increases the visibility of its intertext. Beyond all that, *Virgin* is also intertextual because it is a project of re-vision built on decades of epistemological and theoretical accumulation of feminist politics, particularly regarding body politics, violence against women, women's sexuality, and women's health. Yet, *Virgin* does not make its feminist intertext visible, at least not in the main body of the text. That is, *Virgin*'s feminist citationality is not explicitly stated through specific referential, lexical, or discursive markers. Even the terms "feminism" and "feminist" are mentioned only five times in the main text, mostly in the last chapter, titled "The Day Virginity Died?" It is also this chapter that mentions almost all the feminist scholars noted in the book—Barbara Ehrenreich, Deirdre English, Gloria Steinem, and Marilyn Frye—although only Frye is introduced as a feminist. Such avoidance of feminist "jargon" could be a strategic (capitalist) move not to alienate mainstream or non-feminist readers and delimit the book's audience. The motive could also be to avoid widespread stereotypes about feminists, which could easily be used to undermine the book's epistemological merit. Or maybe the author simply did not want to situate her book in feminist history. Whatever the reason, due to its lack of direct referencing or alluding to key feminist intertexts and non-deployment of feminist terminologies and discourses, *Virgin* misses an opportunity to create a distinct feminist intertextual memory on virginity, and thus, its indebtedness to previous feminist work on gendered bodies and sexualities remains hidden in its subtext (de Lotbinière-Harwood, *Re-belle*, 129).

Despite its shortcomings as a scholarly work, *Virgin* still cogently demonstrates that virginity is an imaginary concept (though with embodied and often detrimental consequences for real subjects) that has taken multiple forms and meanings across time and place. Among these, virginity's function of keeping women's bodies and sexualities under the control and in the service of male-dominant, heteronormative institutions seems to be the most consistent and persistent one. This does not mean that this pervasive concept is always passively complied with. In fact, *Virgin* discusses several cases of women's negotiations with and exploitations of virginity regimes for personal empowerment.[7] Moreover, it gives readers several plausible reasons and epistemic tools to resist and dismantle hegemonic virginity ideologies. This is exactly why I translated *Virgin* into Turkish, so that it would offer women an alternative virginity discourse—non-prescriptive, non-dichotomous, non-phallocentric, non-gendered, non-heteronormative, and non-medicalized—that can help destabilize Turkey's institutionalized virginity regime. Although *Virgin* is not an academic book, I saw a potential of sociocultural intervention in it that did merit cross-border investment. In the next section, I discuss the details of translating *Virgin* to mobilize this disruptive potential in Turkish.

## Rewriting *Virgin*

Feminist translation conceives translation as a political and creative act of cross-border meaning making with transformative power. Contrary to the conventional view of translation bounded by the principles of fidelity (to a supposedly fixed "original" text) and equivalence (between purportedly fixed meanings), feminist translation revisits the notion of fidelity by highlighting the politics and ethics of translational endeavors and encounters. Fidelity in this new formulation implies concurrently exercised political commitments to the translator's own interpretation of the text, to the author and the "original" text, to the audience for whom the translation is produced, and to the political mission ascribed to the text. So, very much like Haraway's "feminist objectivity" ("Situated Knowledges," 581), feminist fidelity recognizes textual, sociocultural, and political interventionism as an inevitable and justified aspect of translation: "Far from being blind to the political and interpretative dimensions of their own project, feminist translators quite willingly acknowledge their interventionism" (Simon, *Gender in Translation*, 29). In translating *Virgin*, I also performed an ethical stance of feminist fidelity.

Before I begin analyzing the translation of *Virgin*, I should note that feminist translation is a form of praxis where theory, practice, and politics are often so intertwined that they may not be analytically separable and easily traceable. As José Santaemilia writes, "Although there is a clear, explicit activist agenda on the part of the translator, it is always difficult to point to the materialisation of this intention" ("Feminists Translating," 75). This is particularly so given that feminist translation promotes social justice not only through textually overt and more easily detectable linguistic and paratextual actions (e.g., lexical interventions and the use of prefaces), but also at the more covert and less visible ideological levels (e.g., introducing new concepts and political practices, opening counter-hegemonic discursive spaces, and activating critical consciousness).[8] That these contributions are not always readily identifiable within the instantaneity or the immediate textuality of the translation does not mean that the feminist translation project has failed (Shread, "On Becoming," 286–87). This is important to note since this chapter analyzes both the visible textual decisions of my translation praxis and the less immediately visible ideological implications of them. That being said, the following analysis is a partial testament to my claim of the inseparability of theory and action in the making of feminist translation praxis, which may or may not manifest itself easily to the naked eye. The fact that not every politico-discursive element of feminist translation can easily be seen makes comparative analyses like this one even more valuable for they reveal both the visible and invisible aspects of translations and illustrate that every textually detectable translation choice has an ideological facet to it. It is indeed this junction between the textual and the ideological that generates the activist force of feminist translation.

## Feminist Politics of Text Choice

When feminist translators choose a text to rework, their choice signifies not only a commitment to a political and ethical engagement with the text, but also a material investment of time, embodied energy, and intellectual and affective labor. Given these limitations, one can only translate so many texts in a lifetime. Then, every translation decision comes at the expense of other texts that do not get translated. This highlights the importance of text choice and the question "which text and why?" becomes critical in explaining the political and ethical reasoning behind the decision to translate. In this section, I first answer this question regarding *Virgin*'s Turkish translation and then examine the initiation procedures and the agents that played a key role in that process.

As noted, I decided to translate *Virgin* because I believed unless the imaginary, yet successfully naturalized, making of virginity was exposed, feminist critiques of virginity practices, like virginity tests, would not go far enough to end the oppressive effects of the concept. The issue, as I saw it, was not only that virginity tests should not be done, but also that they cannot be done because, as Blank convincingly demonstrates, virginity has no embodied existence that can be "dis/proven."[9] I wanted to add this missing piece to Turkey's feminist canon. So, after *Virgin* came out in 2007, I contacted

Aksu Bora, a prominent feminist activist and scholar in Turkey, who also was a translator and editor at İletişim Press, Turkey's leading press in social sciences and humanities.[10] My translational mission seemed to fit well with İletişim's mission emphasizing sociocultural and political transformation through publishing critical books and facilitating public conversations on key political issues.[11]

İletişim immediately accepted my proposal and invited me to write an additional chapter on Turkey's virginity history, which fit well with their mission to encourage local knowledge production. İletişim, indeed, sees publishing both translations and local works as "complementary" for they stimulate and sustain each other and open new intellectual and political fields of discourse and inquiry (Eker, "Building Translations," 86).[12] In full support of the feminist agenda ascribed to *Virgin*'s translation, İletişim also assigned Aksu Bora as my editor facilitating a mutually enriching collaboration between the two of us that lasted beyond the translation project. Such a feminist collaboration also took place between me and Hanne Blank during and beyond *Virgin*'s translation. In fact, close collaborations between the translator and the author have been a celebrated practice among feminist translators (Levine, *Subversive Scribe*, xiii). In much of the feminist translation literature, such collaborations are told in a spirit of feminist solidarity, which also applies to my case. Although I did not directly cooperate with Blank in the textual rewriting process, her constant support of the project played a crucial role in the remaking and promotion of the book. For instance, she enthusiastically endorsed the preface I wrote for *Bekâret* by giving the publisher (copyright) permission for it. The same spirit of solidarity continued after *Bekâret* was published in 2008 when Blank and I gave joint interviews to *Agos*, the Armenian-Turkish newspaper (Tosun, "Kanla Yazılan") and *Psikeart*, a Turkish magazine on psychiatry and art (Ergun and Akgökçe, "Neyle Ölçerseniz").

Blank has always publicly expressed her gratitude for my initiation of *Virgin*'s translation. For instance, in the *Agos* interview, she answered how she felt about *Virgin*'s Turkish translation, saying,

> I am delighted to see my book translated into Turkish for many reasons, one of which is that I have had the very unusual pleasure of having a wonderful translator whom I already knew, liked, and knew I could trust. With any book there are concerns about the accuracy of translation, but with a topic that can be as controversial and emotional as virginity, those concerns are magnified enormously . . . Knowing that I could trust Emek not just to be accurate but also politically and culturally savvy was an enormous gift (Tosun, "Kanla Yazılan," 13).

This statement reflects Blank's awareness (and justified concern) about translation politics, as feminist texts can ideologically be turned less effective or even ineffective or reactionary by patriarchal translation practices.[13] The response also illustrates her collaborative stance as she emphasizes the weight of political affinity and mutual trust between the author and the translator. As she elaborates later in the same interview, such rapport was key in *Virgin*'s translation since the book was intended to facilitate critical dialogues on virginity in Turkey and our voices, when joined together, could further expand the book's interventionist potential. In this regard, our cooperation was an act of transnational feminist solidarity or in de Lotbinière-Harwood's words, "The two women's signatures on the translated text identify it as a joint project realized in the spirit of solidarity" (*Re-belle*, 155).

In addition to the collaboration with Blank, *Bekâret* was also a product of other collaborations. For instance, without the enabling conditions of possibility that were provided to me by the agents of İletişim, particularly my editor Aksu Bora, my initial correspondent Tanıl Bora, and the editor-in-chief Nihat Tuna, *Bekâret* would probably not have the same politically dissident voice. Such collaboration with the publisher highlights the importance of the feminist translator having institutional support. In this context, my cooperation with my editor Aksu Bora was the most decisive. During production, Bora always gave me constructive feedback and never authoritatively intervened in my textual or paratextual choices. Her suggestions only sharpened *Bekâret*'s feminist discourse and tone.[14]

Another crucial platform of collaboration materialized between the translator and local feminist activists who enthusiastically promoted the book, and its re-visionist agenda, in a variety of settings. Several book reviews were written by feminist journalists in both mainstream and marginal news venues.[15] These publicity endeavors were also crucial for initiating public conversations on virginity. Although I have never met most of these reviewers face-to-face—neither has Blank—their contributions to the making of *Bekâret* indicate the formation of an imagined community of feminists who have not met in person but come together through their encounters with the book and worked toward building a shared subversive discourse against hegemonic virginity regimes.[16] In short, feminist collaboration in translation is crucial not only for making the traveling text more overtly polyphonic and dialogic, but also for inspiring broader, cross-border feminist collectivities.

## What Is in a Word?

Since language as a meaning-making system too often reproduces and naturalizes the male norm, feminist translators must find innovative ways to refrain from perpetuating phallocentrisms and infuse language with feminist intentions and claims. They achieve this by integrating *discourse* (microanalysis of textual particularities) and *Discourse* (macroanalysis in a Foucauldian sense) in their praxes and attending closely to the interplay between subjective language use and regulatory "relations of ruling," in Dorothy Smith's terms (*Conceptual Practices*, 14). Extending this perspective of language and translation as an ideological exercise of mediation with political implications, in this section, I explain the reasoning behind some of my linguistic strategies in *Bekâret*. Rather than focusing on whether the choice I made is a "correct" equivalent or loyal to the "original," I attend to the micro and macro-politics of choice in the situated language use of translation.

My predominant translation strategy in *Bekâret* was "familiarization" as I sought to produce a book that would be readily available, amply meaningful, and politically useful to a diverse group of readers across various educational levels.[17] I wanted the book's transgressive contents to be as accessible as possible, so I refrained from convoluted sentences and obscure words that could overstrain readers who did not possess the necessary symbolic capital (e.g., intellectual affinity with feminist discourses) to read dense texts.[18] By employing a relatively unalienating, user friendly language, I believed, *Virgin*'s counter-discourses could reach a wider segment of society, not just an elite group of readers. Familiarization, in this context, meant helping expand the geopolitical borders of virginity resistance and transgression, rather than assimilation of the foreign.

The textual performance of my resistance-driven familiarization strategy can be traced in *Bekâret* from the beginning onward. For instance, *Virgin* begins with the assertion, "By any material reckoning, virginity does not exist" (3). I translated this sentence as, *"Neyle ölçerseniz ölçün bekâret aslında yoktur"* (*Bekâret*, 45). (Backtranslation: "No matter what you measure it with, virginity does not in fact exist.") The sentence is drastically domesticated in terms of not only syntax and lexis, but also the discursive force with which its truth claim is articulated. Part of my intervention in the sentence (e.g., the deletion of "material") was caused by the resulting awkwardness of a more literal translation in Turkish. If I used the phrase "material reckoning" in Turkish (e.g., as *"maddesel ölçüm"*), the book's first sentence would not only sound inept and perhaps even incomprehensible, but also lose all the political starkness and striking force it had in English. Since this was the very first sentence of the first chapter, it was of great importance that the reader entered the text through an intriguing and compelling statement. Given that reading requires a good deal of investment, it is essential to greet the reader with a vehement enough interpretive incentive to keep going, especially in politically defined projects like *Bekâret*. If the reader stops reading, the project fails. Also, since I read this sentence (and the first two paragraphs that follow it) as one of the most critical claims of the book, I wanted to articulate it in Turkish in a way that would be comprehensible and stimulating. Hence, my addition of the phrase "in fact," which increases both the fluency of the sentence and the assertiveness of its truth claim. This turned out to be one of the most frequent citations from the book in the Turkish reviews and interviews. For instance, the *Psikeart* interview had it as its title, and Kurnaz incorporated it in the headline of her review (Ergun and Akgökçe, "Neyle Ölçerseniz;" Kurnaz, "Bedenden Öte").

Another example of familiarization came up in the fifth chapter, "The Virgin and the Doctor," where Blank cites "an anonymous Elizabethan doggerel" while discussing greensickness—"the disease of virgins"—whose cure was believed to be penile-vaginal intercourse (69).[19] My familiarizing translation strategy once again prioritized creating a semantically accessible but subversive discourse, rather than a stylistically or lexically estranging one. This verse was challenging because it was not only in Elizabethan English, but also rhymed and acrostic. I wanted to rewrite the verse in such a way that its content, rhyming, acrostic structure and designation, and humorous and archaic tone would also be expressed in Turkish. After days of experimenting, I ended up emphasizing the first four features of the doggerel at the expense of its archaism.[20] The Turkish verse that I created told the humorous story, replicated the rhyming rhythm, and reproduced the acrostic naming of the English version. Yet, the antiquated language of the verse, which generated a strong alienating effect even in English, was forfeited to achieve a gesture of "emasculation." That is, in the translation process, "a prick" designation of the verse (which becomes visible when the verse is read acrostically as dictated by the last line) became "*bir çük,*" which in Turkish slang refers to a little boy's penis. Instead of using other terms that could signify a "potent" adult penis, I preferred the belittling *çük* to undermine the phallocentrism of the virginity discourse of the time in which "greensickness" was embedded.[21]

Another set of feminist familiarization cases emerged because of the grammatical differences between English and Turkish. For instance, "virgin" grammatically refers to both women and men in English, although, as Blank notes, virginity is female unless stated otherwise (10–11).[22] However, in Turkish, *bakire* refers to a virgin woman and *bakir* refers to a virgin man. The term "virginity," on the other hand, translates as *bekâret* for all genders. In the translation, I used *bakire* unless "virgin" clearly implicated a man or a mixed group, in which case I preferred *bakir/e*. Using feminine *bakire* as generic accentuated the Turkish book's feminist critiques of hetero/sexist constructions of *women's* virginity. There was one key exception to my feminine reworking of virgin as *bakire*, which appeared in the book's title, *Virgin: The Untouched History*. I decided to translate the title's "virgin" as *bekâret* (virginity): *Bekâretin "El Değmemiş" Tarihi* [Virginity's "No Hands Touched" History].[23] This choice highlighted the systemic, ideational constructedness of *virginity* much more than the subjective reference of *bakire* as it named the phenomenon itself, rather than the person affected by the phenomenon. Hence, the reworked Turkish title did not deflect attention away from the emphasis on virginity—a taboo subject that is supposed to be kept out of conversations, particularly critical ones hinted by the title.[24]

My concern with achieving textual visibility for women and not erasing feminist critiques of gender practices—a common concern in the feminist translation literature—also informed my familiarization decisions regarding gender pronouns. Unlike English, Turkish does not have gender pronouns, which at times causes problems for translators who want to emphasize the gendered configuration of certain characters, concepts, or objects, to either positively represent women as historical agents or criticize heteropatriarchal codes. As the next example shows, I compensated for feminine pronouns (personal, possessive, or reflexive) by sometimes adding "woman" to the text. In this subheading, *her* refers to both Queen Elizabeth and the unexploited lands and hypersexualized women in the "New World," all of whom share the adjective "virgin" in the colonial imaginary:

> Source text: "Her treasures having never been opened" (*Virgin*, 187)
> Translation: "Hazineleri hiçbir zaman açılmamış kadın" (*Bekâret*, 279)
> Backtranslation: "The woman whose treasures have never been opened"

Since this subheading emphasizes the configuration of the lands and women of the "New World" as female virgin embodiments, whose "treasures" have not been "opened" by (white western male) colonialists, I did not want to erase the postcolonial gender critique underlining it by using a genderless pronoun. Although this translational gesture could be interpreted as (re)imposing the gender binary onto the text, the intervention only sought to highlight the intersectional nature of the issue at hand (colonialism and heteropatriarchy sustaining each other). In fact, the concept of virginity itself perpetuates the gender binary (and heteronormativity), so regardless of the pronouns used in the translation, gender binary would still be at the very center of the discussion, more or less saliently.[25]

Translating *Virgin* brought on another pronoun dilemma, this time about geopolitics, rather than gender. Throughout the book, Blank uses an all-embracing style of addressing the reader through her use of "we" and its associative forms. She incorporates the reader in the text through inclusive statements such as "we invented it" and "we know very little about the hymen" (3, 34). Given that *Virgin* is almost exclusively about the west and has been primarily marketed to an Anglo-American audience, such use of inclusive language may be reasonable. However, when the book travels to Turkey, that inclusive language becomes tricky since its readership changes although the book's western scope remains.[26] I did not intervene in any of these pronouns in the translation process. In fact, I thought a familiarizing strategy would bring about a transgressive opportunity. So, *Bekâret* ended up having the same inclusive language *Virgin* had. Yet, the translated "we" was now semantically a much bigger, transnational, and more contentious category. Indeed, *Bekâret*'s "we" blurred the seemingly fixed borders between the east and the west that supposedly positioned the book against Turkey's cultural landscape. This gesture, I hoped, would increase the text's connectionist capacity.[27]

Familiarization, however, was not the only translation strategy I used to unsettle Turkey's virginity regime. Occasionally, I used defamiliarization to serve the same political end, and one of these cases became the feminist translator's signature in *Bekâret*: the seemingly straightforward translation of "hymen." "Hymen" proved to be one of the most challenging and consequential decisions I made while translating *Virgin* as the stakes were high regarding the potential repercussions of such a politically charged and frequently used term. So, how was I to translate this term into a phallocentric language, Turkish, that stipulated womanhood on the basis of penile penetration of the vagina?

In Turkish, *kızlık zarı* literally translates as "the membrane of girlhood" and is the most widely used term for the hymen. *Kızlık zarı* would be my habitual choice if I impulsively pursued a familiarizing strategy without speculating on the political implications of the term. However, that would betray *Bekâret*'s feminist agenda since *kızlık zarı* reflects the definition of women's bodies in their subordinate relation to male bodies as the distinction between girlhood and womanhood (read: childhood and adulthood) is predicated on whether a penis has penetrated and "marked" the vagina or not. The (hetero)-normative gender script, within which *kızlık zarı* is embedded, attributes to the penis the role of a mighty gatekeeper that determines whether a female subject (or object?) can cross over into the territory of womanhood/adulthood by designating the hymen as the most fateful feature of her body—a boundary marker that assigns her to a social identity and status. *Kızlık zarı* implies the reduction of her existence to a miniscule (tangible or illusive) membrane that is imagined to make her. In this discursive frame of reference, becoming a woman is defined in terms of termination of virginity through the penile dissolution of the hymen—an identity grounded on loss and becoming less. Therefore, familiarization in this case would mean the perpetuation of a misogynistic discourse.

The Turkish word *kız* (girl), from which *kızlık zarı* derives, not only signifies age/youth and a "female child/adolescent," as it does in English, but also refers to a (supposedly unmarried) "female virgin." In fact, *kız* is used more than *bakire*, the literal equivalent of "female virgin," in both daily and official languages—for instance, medical virginity test reports declare whether the person in question is "*kız*" ("is a girl") or "*kız değil*" ("is not a girl") (Parla, "Honor of the State," 79). Also, women's premarital last name is called "*kızlık soyadı*," literally "last name in girlhood," which again attests to the close (inverse) relationship between virginity and marriage. In fact, it is not just the last name that officially gets changed when a woman marries a man in Turkey. The backside of her national ID card, which includes information about family registry and the location of the registry, becomes entirely different after marriage. When a *kız*/girl is married (and becomes a *kadın*/ woman), her file gets automatically transferred from her father's registry into that of her husband's. Hence, her registration details change along with her official history. The use of *kızlık soyadı* shows that women's citizenship in Turkey is contingent upon the state's designation of their virginity-based marital gender status.

Another case that illustrates the hetero/sexism inherent in the conception of *kız* is offered by the online collective project called "Discriminatory Dictionary," which seeks "to problematize, rather than neglect, the discriminative language" in regard to Turkish.[28] As the project documents, numerous Turkish sayings using the word *kız* reproduce the notion of "'the-girl-to-be-married' as a property to be given away and taken, as secondary and passive." In fact, "give" and "take" appear to be the most common verbs accompanying *kız* in these phrases.[29] In this context, *kızlık zarı* sets apart a *kız*/girl (read: to be married/given/taken) from a *kadın*/woman (read: already married/given/ taken) while marking both as male possessions in reference to marriage with its legitimizing state apparatus. A striking reflection of this normative binary marking is the saying, *kız gibi* ("like a girl"), which is used to describe "unused, brand new goods." Then, *kızlık zarı* signifies the "untouched" object, "unused" commodity, and "unopened" package status of the "virginal" female body, conceived exclusively in its institutionalized submission and service to the hetero-male bodily consumption in Turkish/Turkey.

This troublesome reservoir of meanings harbored in the semantic field of *kız* is perhaps best encapsulated by the infamous comments of the former Turkish prime minister, and now president, Recep Tayyip Erdoğan, who, in 2011, deployed the *kız/kadın* binary to condemn a political protest.[30] In his upset response, Erdoğan, referring to a woman protestor whose hip was broken during the demonstration because of police brutality, said:

> This morning I see on TV this—I don't know *whether a girl or a woman* climbing a police panzer in Ankara. And as if the panzer is not enough to stop her, from there she runs and attacks with a stick in her hand our police officer standing with a shield; she hits him while the officer patiently stands there" (emphasis mine).[31]

Erdoğan's "I don't know whether a girl or a woman" remark might sound innocent or at best irrelevant or unwarranted to the English-speaking audience, but in Turkish it is right to the point and highly charged. In an attempt to cover up and justify police violence and curtail the credibility of the woman victim, Erdoğan takes refuge in the local virginity grammar by invoking the pervasive hetero/sexist *kız/kadın* vocabulary. He assumes that by simply pronouncing the words *kız* and *kadın* and implicitly calling into question the protestor's virginity status, hence her morality and social legitimacy, he can effectively debunk her demand of justice and disregard her experience of police brutality. His remarks imply that a woman deserves public attention, respect, and justice only if she is properly sexed and sexualized: That is, if she is either an unmarried virgin (girl/*kız*) or a married nonvirgin (woman/*kadın*). As the example shows, the dualistic semantic field of *kız* and *kadın* is so deeply entrenched in the sociolinguistic landscape of Turkey that Erdoğan can activate the hegemonic virginity discourse without even having to enunciate too many words. *Kız* does the trick once and for all.[32]

Given this brief glimpse into the unfortunately rich hetero/sexist repertoire of *kız/kızlık zarı* in Turkish and the collective stock of virginity knowledges it sustains, it becomes clear why I struggled with the translation of "the hymen." In order not to reenact the hetero/sexism of *kız/kızlık zarı*, I decided to translate "the hymen" as *himen*, a word obviously borrowed from English and used almost exclusively (yet inconsistently) in medical texts in Turkish. So, I defamiliarized the term. I explained the reasons for this choice both in the translator's preface and in a footnote. The *himen* use was an interventionist strategy in pursuit of my feminist agenda, but it was not without problems.

To transplant *Virgin*'s potential to disrupt the medical hymenal objectification of virginity in Turkish, I shied away from repeating *kızlık zarı* with its cultural stock of gender-normative meanings. Instead, I preferred to translate "hymen"[33] as *himen* because the term sounded more "neutral" without the immediate hetero/sexist connotations of *kızlık zarı*. This apparent neutrality was claimed partly because *himen* was a medical term with associations of scientificity, but more importantly because it was an alien word lacking a history of sociolinguistic circulation and saturation through interactions with other local hetero/sexist grammars. That is, *himen*'s defamiliarizing potential was exactly what made it an appropriate choice.[34] Thus, in a project trying to dismantle virginity's medical construction, I ended up using a medical term for the sake of creating a nonsexist discourse and perhaps even contributing to the medicalization of virginity. Although I believed my *himen* choice made the book's critique more powerful since it disrupted the connection between virginity and the vaginal membrane identified as *kızlık zarı*, it could also be argued that it contradicted the larger goal of my translation for further medicalizing virginity. So, some might interpret this textual exercise of demedicalization, where virginity is reformulated as anatomically nonexistent, as an act of remedicalization simply because of my use of *himen* over *kızlık zarı*. How would I respond to this perfectly sound argument?

The claim of apparent neutrality does not mean that *himen* was a thoroughly disinterested word that "can belong to 'no one'" because as Bakhtin notes, "there are no 'neutral' words and forms . . . language has been completely taken over, shot through with intentions and accents. . . . Each word tastes of the context and contexts in which it has lived its socially charged life; all words and forms are populated with intentions" (*Dialogic Imagination*, 293). My claim of relative neutrality was based on the fact that *himen* had not lived "a socially charged life" in everyday Turkish and was not used consistently even in medical literature where it occasionally appeared. For instance, in the Turkish Medical Association's (TMA) virginity-related statements, *himen* usually appeared next to *kızlık zarı*. In "Kızlık Zarı ('Himen') İncelemeleri," the ethics committee's 2009 resolution on virginity tests, while both terms were used interchangeably, *kızlık zarı* appeared more often.[35] In other TMA documents, such as 2010 "Kızlık Zarı Kontrolü ve Onarımında Hekim Tutumu Bildirgesi" [Declaration on the Doctor's Attitude about the Control and Repair of the Girlhood Membrane], which was the resulting publication of the 2009 resolutions, *himen* was not mentioned at all; *kızlık zarı* was used exclusively.[36]

As a term that did not enjoy a consistent usage even in the accessible and influential TMA documents *himen* was obviously not thoroughly inhabited by local accents and thus seemed convenient for critical recapacitation. If as Bakhtin argues, "the word is born in a dialogue as a living rejoinder within it," *himen* was a term that lacked a history of engaging in dialogues with the entrenched constituents of Turkey's sociocultural locale, where it could now navigate through existing discursive terrains and become a meaningful "living rejoinder" (*Dialogic Imagination*, 279). Thus, through its subversive deployment and circulation in and through *Bekâret*, a popular history text that was less intimidating and more accessible than medical texts, *himen* would get a chance both to be absorbed in the local virginity grammar and talk back to its hegemonic enunciations. It was indeed this function of talking back that invested *himen* with the capacity to contest Turkey's virginity regime. That is, when *himen* entered into a dialogic history through its critical deployment in *Bekâret*, its infiltrating move potentially started the process of the reader/s' owning it and making it "ours." In Bakhtin's words, a term "becomes 'one's own' only when the speaker populates it with his [*sic*] own intention, his [*sic*] own accent, when he [*sic*] appropriates the word, adapting it to his [*sic*] own semantic and expressive intention" (293). Such reappropriation of a word to disrupt hegemonic intentions is never guaranteed, but rather difficult, particularly because relations of ruling hold the control of discourse-making and validating apparatuses. Yet, this control is never absolute, and resignification attempts at least leave subversive traces on the living word, if not generate a full-scale transformation in its semantic field.

Moreover, the scientifically endorsed term "hymen" was so depoliticized and dehistoricized that it did not reveal its *history* of medicolegal fabrication. In Turkish, this historical background was far more invisible as the word itself was rarely heard. In my translation, I used *himen*, yet contextualized it in a historical discourse that demystified the concept. This, I hoped, would expose the biopolitics behind the scientific making of the hymen. Now, the scientifically endorsed term could get "contaminated" by *Bekâret*. Hence, I infused *himen* with the critical historical content it lacked. Unlike mainstream medical texts (such as online ads for hymen reconstruction surgeries), where *himen* indicates the anatomical proof of virginity, I resituated *himen* in a deconstructive symbolic economy of body and used it against itself. So, although there is no easy way out of the aforementioned dilemma, in the context of this project, with limited linguistic resources at hand,[37] I could not think of a better strategy than problematizing the *master's* own words to attack *his* masterful fabrication.

*Himen's* journey of being charged with subversive voices and meanings started in Turkish immediately after *Bekâret's* publication—for instance, in feminist book reviews, which consistently refrained from using *kızlık zarı* and preferred *himen*. When these reviews mentioned *kızlık zarı*, it was presented in scare quotes to highlight the sexism it inscribed. There were also several news articles, commentaries, and blog essays on *Bekâret* that used *himen*.[38] Perhaps even more important are the recent feminist publications, research reports, educational videos, and workshops on virginity that do not mention *Bekâret* at all—but clearly draw on its knowledge—and opt for *himen* contributing to its ongoing critical resaturation in Turkish.[39] The most striking example is the recently published book *Jinekolog Muhabbetleri* [Conversations on/with Gynecologists], edited by Aslı Alpar and published by Kaos GL, one of the oldest and largest LGBT+ organizations in Turkey. Following an online article series that started in 2017 with the invitation, "Write to us if you say, 'I have had homophobic, transphobic, moralist gynecologists too' and would like to contribute to the series," *Jinekolog Muhabbetleri* seeks to increase gynecologists' political awareness on gender and sexuality issues and empower marginalized people who avoid gynecologists for fear of phobic encounters (5, 7). The book includes patients' testimonials of "violations," findings of a survey on patients' experiences with gynecologists, and interviews with gynecologists. Virginity makes a major topic of discussion in the book, where there is a section titled, "*Himen*" (12–14). What is crucial about the book is that it not only contributes to the demedicalization of virginity and enhances *himen*'s circulation in Turkish, but also, by adding to the conversation issues of gender fluidity, homophobia, transphobia, ableism, etc., stretches the intersectional boundaries of the critical virginity discourse that *Bekâret* has been pushing forward since 2008. So, *Bekâret*'s use of *himen* has obviously facilitated the saturation of the term with dissident accents, whose key claims are the contestation of the virginity norm and the demystification of *himen* as the falsely assigned proof of virginity.[40] This positions *himen* as different from *kızlık zarı* as it responds to a different question, one devised in nonnormative feminist discourses and populated with disruptive intentions. That is, unlike *kızlık zarı*, which has been saturated to the point of discursive closure prescribing the misogynist grammar of the status quo, *himen* is open-ended being charged with the interrogative and deconstructive gestures and knowledges of *Bekâret*'s feminist virginity discourses.

The experimental deployment of *himen* becomes more meaningful when the reader's role is considered. Since many readers were believed to be unfamiliar with the term, it was highly likely that *himen* would interrupt the fluent reading process, which was consciously planned (although never guaranteed). My implied reader was hypothesized to reflect on *himen*'s implications when they first saw this "strange" word. The political potential of this textual disruption was strengthened by my use of paratextual spaces to activate the reader's critical engagement with the text, especially the translator's preface, where the reader first encounters *himen* and my explanation. I presented a similar explanation later in a footnote in case the reader skips the preface. So, the very alienating nature of *himen* in a way ensures that readers would refer to the preface and/or the footnote to make sense of this term and ultimately participate in the translation's interrogation of virginity as well as hetero/sexist language.

Finally, I should note that since *himen* appears a lot in the book, the translator's otherwise suppressed or silenced voice becomes regularly audible, hinting at the same time the foreign context in which the text first emerged. That is, *himen* underlines the fact that the traveling text does not exclusively "belong to" the author, as common sense dictates, but also to the translator. In doing so, *himen* marks not only the translator's feminist agency and the text's reworked otherness, but also the ensuing multicultural and polyphonic nature of translation, which allows various voices across borders to intermingle and engage in dialogues. Translation, then, is a space of polyphony, defined, in a Bakhtinian sense, as a dynamic collective of interacting voices, accents, and discourses that exist in a permanent conversational mode populated by authors, translators, readers, and all the other meaning-making agents. As Linda Park-Fuller notes, "Polyphony refers not literally to a number of voices, but to the collective quality of an individual utterance; that is, the capacity of my utterance to embody someone else's utterance even while it is mine, which thereby creates a dialogic relationship between two voices" ("Voices," 2). This means that *himen* helps prevent the illusion of monophony in *Bekâret* and instead encourages differences to encounter and talk to one another in the texture of translation.

## The Translator's Preface

I wrote for *Bekâret* a twenty-four-page-long preface titled "The 'Untouched' History of Virginity in Turkey," which discussed Turkey's virginity politics from the 1980s till the 2000s and aimed to encourage readers to build connections between the virginity contingencies of their locality and the book's western history ("Önsöz"). That is, the preface was to facilitate the cultural crossover of the book's disruptive potential. It sought to initiate a localized problematization of virginity and increase the book's activist force despite its possibly alienating identification as western. To smooth the localization process, I used various textual strategies, the first of which was to frame the preface's contents within the book's transgressive truth discourse. So, I wrote the preface in such a way that Turkey's virginity stories were modeled after Blank's truth claims and composed in the framework of *Virgin's* alternative truth regime. In this way, the preface also reveals how epistemically productive *Virgin's* cross-border travel can be when its translation is taken as an opportunity to expand the borders of feminist virginity knowledges. *Virgin* invites knowledge production by positioning itself as a partial history of a geohistorically vast topic that needs further in-depth research (256):

Anthropologists and historians have made only rare attempts to study virginity, and their attempts provide only spotty coverage: even a survey-style book like this one only skims the surface for a small portion of the world. There is a great deal of information that has yet to be gathered and many books that have yet to be written about virginity.

The translator's preface retold the book's major knowledge claims by equipping them with the local contingencies of Turkey. In doing so, it showed that no matter how irrelevant the book's western history might have seemed for readers in Turkey, *Bekâret* in fact told a very familiar and relevant story. For instance, repeating Blank's claim that virginity is a fabrication, the preface explained how virginity had been fixed in Turkey by a vigorous cooperation between the state-sanctioned institutions of medicine, law, education, military, and language. Following *Virgin*, the preface also emphasized the intersectional configuration of virginity where gender interlocked with other relations of power, particularly sexuality and ethnicity in the Turkish case. The preface was particularly informative about local virginity practices, such as virginity tests, virginity reconstruction surgeries, the use of red belts in weddings to symbolize brides' virginal status, and the deadly masculinist notion of "honor."

Also included in the preface were a riddle and a "joke" on virginity—two genres employed in *Virgin* as well. My use of these folk genres sought both to make the text more appealing to a wide range of readers in Turkey, where riddles and jokes are popular cultural idioms and could help the text resonate more with local readers, and to establish a discursive parallel between the preface and the rest of the book—another bridging attempt to make *Bekâret*'s admittance into local canons easier. I wrote the riddle myself and used it as an introduction to my questioning of what virginity meant in the cultural context of Turkey ("Önsöz," 12). Each line of the riddle spoke of a particular local virginity reality. For instance, while the third line referred to the ritual of displaying the bloodstained bed sheet after the wedding night, the fourth line suggested virginity violence. Here is a translation of the riddle:

> Can't be seen with eyes, can't be held with hands,
> White lies under the blood it sheds,
> Either a sheet that doesn't stay on beds,
> Or a loud scream at the head of graves,
> What is this malady, take a guess?

By establishing a stylistic and critical parallel between the Turkey-centered preface and the west-centered contents of the book,[41] the riddle and the "joke" helped emphasize the common ground between the two geographies and perhaps even enhanced the dialogic possibilities across borders.[42]

Another textual parallel that I deliberately created between the preface and the remainder of the book appears at the end of my preface: "Hoping that this journey on which Hanne Blank and I have set out together in order to end the bloody domination of virginity on our bodies, sexualities, and lives will reach its goal . . ." ("Önsöz," 33). Likewise, Blank ends her prologue saying, "For all these reasons, and many more, I am honored to be at the helm for this maiden voyage into a fascinating untouched history" (*Virgin*, xi). By using a similarly invitational and adventurous tone (yet in a more assertive manner) and framing the text within a narrative of experiencing the history of virginity as a journey, the last sentence of my preface offers a smooth transition from my "domestic" voice to Blank's mediated "foreign" voice and stresses once again the cooperative production of the traveling feminist book by appointing both "Hanne Blank and I" at the helm of the "maiden voyage." Finally, while reworking *Virgin*'s virginity discourses in the preface, I paid special attention to highlighting the voices of feminist scholars and activists whose works and political actions to stop virginity violence in and outside Turkey was an inspiration for me to embark on this translation. That is, I tried to make visible the feminist intertext that was already present in my voice and words before I wrote the preface.

Finally, the preface explicitly identifies *Bekâret* as a project of "feminist translation" and lets readers know that the text they are reading has been mediated by a politically invested subject, whose voice has been integrated into the text whether they hear it or not. Marking the text as feminist is key because "signature, in turn, creates context. A feminist's signature on a translation positions the reader expectations" (de Lotbinière-Harwood, *Re-belle*, 154). Hence, my "confession" in the preface is both an ethical disclosure and a political act that seeks to reassure readers that the text they are reading has not been filtered through heteropatriarchal interpretive models and assimilated into hegemonic discourses during translation. In this regard, the preface solidified the book's feminist identity and stance and perhaps even helped local feminists to embrace the book more readily and easily.

## Repackaging *Virgin*

While textual details of translational journeys receive a lot of attention in translation studies, the material transformation that traveling books go through as part of the translation process is too often neglected.[43] Yet, the visual redesign of the translation's package is vital as it resignifies the text for a different readership and gives us clues about the sociopolitical redesignation of the text in its new setting. Oftentimes, readers first encounter a book via its cover pages, strategically designed to draw attention to the book and convince readers to buy and read it. Cover pages, by visually and verbally emphasizing specific features about the book (and downplaying others), are assumed to give us clues about the text and generate first impressions, which become meaningful only in the sociocultural context in which they appear. Therefore, when a book travels to another locale in translation, the packaging is often domesticated to make it more meaningful to its new readership. In a similar vein, when physically compared to *Virgin*, *Bekâret* appears to be a completely different book.[44]

Although İletişim had a graphic designer to rework *Virgin*'s cover, I was still included in the decision process. *Virgin* had a plain cover with the title and author's name printed on an orange background (see Figure 1). Instead, my editor, Aksu Bora, and I suggested using a Renaissance image, such as a scene with a unicorn and a "virgin" woman—referring to Blank's discussion of the ancient myth about virgins' magical powers of taming unicorns (171). When we could not find that image in high resolution, the designer, Suat Aysu, created a new image: an abstract figure that looked like a pinkish flower, on the one hand, and blood spilled over the cover, on the other (see Figure 2). This "floral blood stain" or the "bloody flower" image became *Bekâret*'s conspicuous cover.

The cover image, no matter how abstract and obscure, resignified the book's materiality in ways that would be pointedly meaningful in the context of Turkey. In comparison to the previously considered option of a Renaissance ("re-birth" of the *west*) picture, which drew on western virginity mythologies, the new image ended up familiarizing the traveling text and increasing its local relevance. That is, the new cover physically turned *Virgin* into a locally consequential product that would more easily resonate with readers who shared a cultural heritage of virginity narratives that was somewhat different from the one told in the book. Since virginity is strongly associated with the bloodstained bed sheet of the wedding night (symbolizing virginity "loss") in the country's cultural imaginary, the image appeared as an irritating reminder of Turkey's blood-guilty virginity regime.

My email correspondence with cover designer Suat Aysu revealed that *Bekâret*'s material reconfiguration was guided by concerns of catering the book to local readers, visually highlighting the domestic cultural associations of virginity, and alleviating the risk of the book being perceived as "pornographic."[45] As Aysu noted, "Although the study is not about Turkey exclusively," the illustration was selected to emphasize the cross-cultural

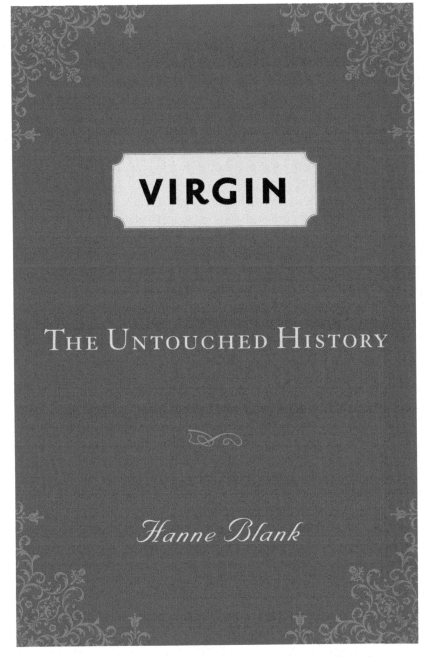

FIGURE 1: The cover of *Virgin: The Untouched History* (2007). © Bloomsbury
Publishing Plc

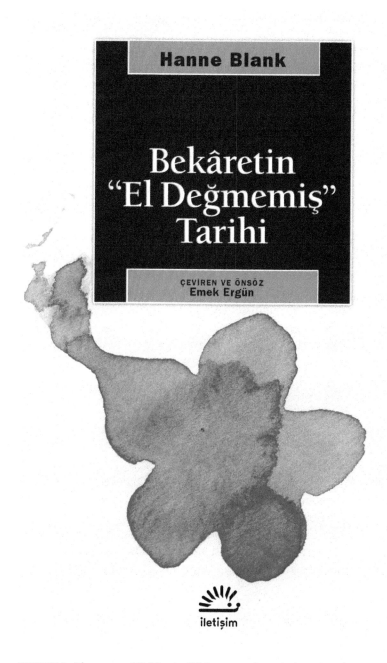

FIGURE 2: The cover of *Bekâretin "El Değmemiş" Tarihi* (2008). © İletişim Yayınları, İstanbul

familiarity of the issue in hand and evoke "the virginity realities of our geography." The cover, then, was intended to act as a bridge between the western epistemologies of the book and Turkey's virginity contingencies. Given virginity's taboooness in Turkey, the image gave *Bekâret* a more disconcerting materiality than its imageless American version. In fact, by conspicuously depicting virginity in its most "intimate" form, the cover publicly defied its taboooness and potentially turned its readers into accomplice taboo-breakers. When the image was combined with the title, "The 'Untouched' History of Virginity," where virginity was boldly named, the cover's disruptive potential, and by extension that of the book, became even more obvious.[46]

In short, while translating *Virgin*, I used both familiarizing and defamiliarizing strategies to increase *Bekâret*'s chance of being admitted into local feminist canons, provide a counter-hegemonic discourse on virginity, and expand both the local and transnational scope of feminist virginity resistance. All my translation choices, as well as the decisions of the other meaning-making agents involved in the project, intended to facilitate the "safe travel" of a feminist virginity text into Turkey's heteropatriarchal landscape marked by a heavily medicalized, taboo-ridden, violent virginity regime. However, while I wanted *Bekâret*'s readers to easily read and connect with the book, I did not want to conceal the text's translatedness and its "point of origin" in a different geopolitical setting. Such an illusion of untranslatedness would undermine the translation's potential to help build transnational feminist affinities and collectivities. When a feminist text reads like an "original," the reader's imaginative dialogues with the agents implied in the book and her solidarity-based perceptions of other feminists living in other locales might be debilitated or hindered. To prevent such transnationally disconnectionist readings, I tried to strike a balance between familiarizing and defamiliarizing strategies in *Bekâret*. However, without in-depth analyses of the imported text's receptions among actual readers, it is not possible to assess the success or failure of these politically geared translation strategies. In the following chapters, I explore *Bekâret*'s political influence among a group of situated, embodied readers starting with the most intimate readings to reveal the text's impact on feminist subjectivity.

## CHAPTER 3

# Remaking Feminist Subjectivity
# in Feminist Translation

> We must examine how experience informs political
> thinking through the medium of narrative because we
> generally encounter, discuss, and invoke experience in
> narrative form. We must also examine the social practices
> by which narratives circulate, for experience becomes
> public knowledge through an exchange of stories in which
> specific people, in the context of historically specific social
> and cultural institutions, relay their views of events in a
> particular rhetorical style to a specific audience.[1]
> —Stone-Mediatore, *Reading Across Borders*, 5

What happens to feminist subjectivity—an ever-changing and contingent operation of discursive and material forces—when the subject encounters a translated text that speaks against their experiential, embodied reality? That is, what happens to feminist readers when they engage with subversive theories and stories traveling from far-away places, yet now speaking to them in their own language—"foreign" theories and stories that were rewritten to disrupt their familiar (memorized?) narratives of gender and sexuality? How is feminist subjectivity transformed in and through contact with translated transgressive texts, which are themselves transformed in the process of crossing borders? This chapter explores those questions about the co-constitutive relationship between political subjectivity and reading translation by drawing on the reception study conducted with *Bekâret's* feminist readers. As noted in the previous chapter, *Virgin*, by debiologizing and demedicalizing virginity, encourages its gendered and sexualized readers to reimagine themselves in relation to the hegemonic virginity ideology, which I called "re-vision" in Adrienne Rich's words: "the act of looking back, of seeing with fresh eyes, of entering an old text from a new critical direction," which "is for women more than a chapter in cultural history: it is an act of survival" (*Lies, Secrets, and Silence*, 35). In fact, by providing readers with critical epistemological and analytical tools, the book helps them rearticulate their experiences and break the ideological and material hold of virginity over them. Here, I explore whether that interventionist potential of Bekâret's materialized in its cross-border encounters with readers.

Taking a closer look at the transformative role of translation in the remaking of feminist subjectivity, the chapter reveals that "translation is a significant medium of subject re-formation and political change" (Apter, *Translation Zone*, 6). In our intensely, and disastrously, globalizing world, where situated subjectivities are too often forged through animosity-ridden and fear-driven differences, it is even more crucial to study this connectionist power of translation—a textual encounter with the allegedly threatening other. I argue that only in light of such recognition we can practice ethical encounters—or "strange encounters"[2] in Sara Ahmed's words (*Strange Encounters*, 137–60) and "hungry translations" in Richa Nagar's words (*Hungry Translations*)—that take place among differently situated subjects who do not personally know each other but touch one another in the symbolic contact zone created by translation. The chapter illustrates how that cross-border textual touching is accomplished while reading translation—an expansive form of rewriting, wherein the printed text, in the process of being signified by several subjectivities, becomes much larger than a book with a fixed number of pages and extends beyond its material boundaries and its alleged ending, which is only prematurely and tentatively announced. So, instead of celebrating "the birth of the reader" or mourning "the death of the author," the chapter attests to the cooperation of the subjectivities of the reader and the translated text that in/form one another in reading (Barthes, *Image/Music/Text*, 148).

My analysis rests on two entwined theoretical premises: (1) that reading is a subjective operation of meaning-making, wherein the reader is an active participant in the rewriting of the text; (2) that reading is a subjectivity-making operation, wherein the text is an active participant in the rewriting of the reader's self—a unique entanglement of the corporeal and the discursive. And both of these acts of rewriting take place in an interpretive and material context that affects, even regulates, the course and consequences of the hermeneutic acts. If subjectivity, as Teresa de Lauretis argues, is a product of continuous semiosis, then reading is a significant discursive act of subjectivity-(re)making (*Alice Doesn't*, 14–15). This is precisely why she argues, "strategies of writing *and* of reading are forms of cultural resistance" (7, emphasis original). In this regard, reading not only activates inter/textual and corporeal meaning-making operations in the reader's self already inhabited by other inter/textualities and corporealities, but also provides them with opportunities to reinterpret and alter their embodied subjectivity. Hence, both the text's and the reader's agency co-perform reading, as a result of which the reader's political consciousness may shift, "that consciousness in turn being the condition of social change" (184). The reading subject's agency is in their re/interpretation, re/writing, and re/enunciation of the text of the book and the text of their embodied self. The agency of the text, which in the case of *Bekâret* is a cross-culturally subversive one, lies in its capacity to activate reflective (re/think), suggestive (re/member), interrogative (re/question), and disruptive (de/re-construct) acts of reading. Hence, the act of reading indicates the simultaneous expansion of both the traveling text and the reading subject, whose historically contingent encounter and engagement mark only the beginning of a potentially infinite cycle of interpretive, enunciative, and performative inter/textuality.

Based on those two theoretical premises, in this chapter, I explore, on the one hand, the ways in which a group of feminist readers inscribe and expand *Bekâret*, through their preformed repertoires of discourses and experiences. On the other hand, I analyze the ways in which those readers' political subjectivities are imprinted by discourses and experiences provided by the imported text. Such an analytical framework helps us both recognize the discursivity and the materiality of subjectivity and reveal the inseparability of those two dimensions. The multilayered methodological design of my reception study reflects this interconnected theorization of reading and subjectivity since the reading diaries, focus groups, and interviews uncover readers' narratives of meaning-making experiences as well as their renewed sense of self as feminist subjects after reading the book. Although the unfinality of reading and the instability of the book are expected in this model, it is still crucial to study the cross-sections of (incomplete) readings as they enable a closer look at the textually mediated trans/formation of political subjectivity—what the book's new critical insights add to the reader's subjective repertoire of political discourses and actions, and how the reader reacts to those epistemic challenges by the book.

In the next section, I analyze the readers' inner dialogues with *Bekâret*, which as a translated and edited text speaks through multiple mouths and is populated with numerous voices and accents, although on the surface, the act of reading seems to be done in the solitude of the reading subject. The section frames reading translation as a dialogic encounter where the reader's locally in/formed subjectivity engages with the "alien" discourses of the traveling text. The next section, conceiving reading as an embodied act, asks how the readers responded to a text within which they were bodily implicated while being situated outside its geopolitical compass. While these two sections highlight the discursivity and the materiality of subjectivity separately, this is only an analytical plot as those dimensions constantly re/configure each other in an endless play of possibilities called subjectivity.

## Translation as Dialogic Expansion

Reading is a dialogic interaction during which two interlocutors come into contact and co-create meaning. While such an encounter can culminate in an egalitarian relationship between the reader and the text, it could also bear witness to the domination of the meaning-making operation by one of the two agents. That is, instead of talking and listening to one another, the text or the reader could subdue the voice of the other by refusing to hear what it says and miss the opportunity of being transformed by it. Also, while on the surface this dialogic process seems to take place between two voices only, texts are made up of numerous echoes (discursive traces, ideological articulations, and textual signs of consciousnesses), which may not always be discernible. The polyphony of texts exists not only because texts are made of multiple voices, but also because, as Bakhtin argues, words carry meanings left by earlier utterances (*Dialogic Imagination*). So, words have histories composed of numerous speaking subjectivities. This crowded nature of words is the reason why, during translation, the semantic fields harbored in the text expand, shrink, and shift as the text crosses linguistic, cultural, and subjective borders entering new semantic collages (Shread, "Metamorphosis").

In this section, I examine how *Bekâret's* readers responded to the numerous subjectivities harbored in the traveling book. I ask whether they unconditionally yielded to the (western) text's epistemological scheme giving up on their preformed truths without any doubt or force-fed their own truths to the text without giving it a chance to dispute. This question on the dialogics of reading translation is important for a couple of reasons. First, I envisioned my translation of *Virgin* as a project of facilitating cross-cultural dialogues between differently located and constituted feminist subjectivities summoned and implicated in the course of reading. Second, I intended *Bekâret* to intervene into Turkey's virginity regime, which necessarily begins with the reader's transformative interactions with the text. Since the way the reader relates to the text determines the meanings they make, in order to investigate the text's political effects, it is necessary to study how the translated book was signified.

Reading translation is an encounter between the self and the other, which could take the form of assimilationist othering or rejectionist othering—both echoing the oppositional logic of "us versus them," using different non/engagement tactics, yet serving similar ends of self-preservation. Or it could be an encounter defined by generosity and hospitality, which, Ahmed argues, necessarily involves some degree of assimilation but still contains an element of surprise that emerges in the process of an open, intimate dialogue (*Strange Encounters*, 150, 156). It is in this sense that Antoine Berman designates the aim of translation as "to open up in writing a certain relation with the Other, to fertilize what is one's Own through the mediation of what is Foreign" (*Experience of the Foreign*, 4). That is, "the essence of translation is to be an opening, a dialogue, a cross-breeding, a decentering" (4).

The sense of foreignness that appears in reading is greater in the reception of translated texts because translation is always already marked as a foreign text, originally made by a foreign writer for a foreign audience. In this sense, translation is by definition an encounter with an other. That is why in translation the stakes are higher with regard to whether readers engage with the text with an open-yet-critical mind since reading translation is not just any psychosocial experience of signification, but also a cross-cultural act of sharing—"an act that contains the possibility of becoming radically vulnerable. It is impossible to 'know' where the sharing might lead us without having taken the risk of exposing that intimate fragment that can only be translated inadequately" (Nagar, *Muddying the Waters*, 46). Then, unless the reader relates to the traveling text in ways that turn both the text and themselves vulnerable, translation's indeterminate potential to bridge across borders would be wasted.

An analysis of my participants' reading narratives reveals that in the face of the translated text's foreignness, they assumed neither an entirely submissive nor a completely dominant role. Rather, they formed intense, productive engagements with the book in which they were "able to integrate past experience with the experience created by the text through critical evaluation of the interwoven signs encountered in the process of reading" (Flynn, "Gender and Reading," 270). In other words, the readers did not silence the alien text or their own subjective stocks of meaning but engaged in mutually enriching dialogues that transformed both signifying parties. They achieved such mutuality by simultaneously listening and talking to the book—by commenting on it, arguing with it, asking it questions, responding to its questions, sharing intimate experiences with it, quoting it, criticizing it, disputing it, and learning (with) it. So, they built an egalitarian relationship with *Bekâret* by living in and through it, during which the book became alive with an ever-expanding subjectivity.

The mutual discursive remaking of the text and the reader is clearest in the participants' diaries, several of which display intense conversations with the book.[3] These diary dialogues not only retell the book's truth claims and theoretical arguments, but also are full of positive remarks that indicate the readers' incorporation of the book's ideological stance. For instance, the main claim of the book, "virginity does not exist," was embraced by all the participants. This was not an act of passive compliance with the authoritative (western) voice of the text, but rather a product of active negotiation with it, which was described by many readers as a process of "convincing"—a term that was not used in any of the research questionnaires. The word choice is meaningful since "virginity does not exist" is not an easy statement to accept given the strong hold of the medically cloaked virginity ideology in Turkey. Indeed, virginity is so forcefully medicalized in Turkey that an outright denial of its existence comes at first glance as an impudent claim. The reader constituted in Turkey could, thus, experience a disjuncture and resist this statement, which seems to erase both their subjective testimony to the troubling "existence" of virginity and the high social recognition granted to it. Hence, to agree with the assertion, the reader needs to be recruited (convinced) into an epistemological stance that is against their habitual disposition reinforced by their local stock of gender knowledges (particularly that the hymen is a "scientifically reliable" sign of virginity). This is exactly what *Bekâret's* readers seem to have experienced. The following extracts illustrate this process of owning an alien epistemic account—a major shift of consciousness that was previously molded on the basis of medicalization:[4]

> Dilan (interview): Even the author's "virginity doesn't exist" claim itself changed my view on virginity. . . . Indeed, I, too, used to think that virginity was just about the presence or absence of the hymen. I mean I knew about the types of the hymen, etc. but other than that, the way she refuted these ["medical facts"] through her claim that virginity doesn't exist—my mind significantly changed on that matter.

> Pembe (diary): In the beginning of the book, it seemed like a too assertive statement. But after I've finished the book, I now think, no other idea should be advocated.

> Deniz (diary): The claim that virginity is an abstract concept and abstract concepts can only be proven with evidences that point at their existence is convincing. When we consider that the hymen displays structural differences and that the vagina-penis intercourse is not the only form of sexual relationship, as well as the function of the virginity institution, virginity turns into a strange, meaningless idea.

These and numerous similar remarks show that the readers approached Blank's claim with a skeptical yet open mind and let it alter their views on virginity (even when they held well-established and seemingly trustworthy medical knowledge, as in the case of Dîlan, who was a medical student). Instead of dictating their preformed opinions or suspicions on the foreign text, they situated themselves as conversation partners and listened to what the book had to say about "nonexistent virginity."

Many of the participants also noted their "conditional" approval of the book's aforementioned claim by saturating it with their own arguments or explanations:

> Ece (diary): Virginity does not exist in the sense we have defined it, yes. It is definitely invented by the human mind. In a way, it is like the concept of soul. It is not something we can hold in our hands and show. But virginity this, virginity that; we don't stop harping on about it. It exists as much as we believe in it.

> Bilge Su (diary): [Blank] thinks that virginity exists as an abstraction . . . She simply emphasizes that its indicators are highly variable and frail (although they are not perceived as such). It doesn't exist in that sense. I agree.

Ideologically, these accounts do not diverge from Blank's truth claims; however, they are not the exact same narratives either. In the act of repeating the author's claim in their own words and through their own subjective reasoning, the readers own a claim rooted in "western history" (read: "not theirs"). Such cross-border epistemic metabolization is the very act of learning, which highlights translation's role in enabling transnational exchanges. Without such exchanges, there is in fact no transnational.

The readers reworked *Bekâret* also by extending its arguments to address their own realities and by merging the narratives of the book with those of their locality, which resulted in new, hybrid narratives. An example is in Çise's diary, which provides some of the liveliest reading accounts in the study. In her diary, Çise's intense dialogues following direct citations from the book exhibit intimate discussions on feminist politics of virginity, body, sexuality, marriage, and so forth. In one such case, Çise first writes down a quotation about the link between identifying the paternity and legitimacy of children and women's virginity conceived as "men's prerogative" (Blank, *Virgin*, 27). Taking off from the quotation, she discusses the "bizarre" postmarital practice of "transferring" women to their husbands' household, to which they are expected to devote themselves utterly. Then, she adds:

> Çise (diary): You know what, during the first days of my marriage, when I had my ID card renewed, I couldn't look at its back.[5] Because all that was familiar had been displaced. Thanks to the new [civil] law, I had managed

to put my maiden name in front of my new last name, but the back of my card . . . indicated a brand-new city, town, neighborhood, and numbers.

By linking *Bekâret*'s argument to her own reality, Çise turns the borrowed material into an owned one and shows that during reading the translated text is resignified in relation to the particularities of the reception context. It is in such interpretive acts that the reading subject and text both get transformed.

The dialogics of reading during which the readers actively engaged in conversations with the text were also evident in their disagreements with the book. These disputes did not indicate failures of communication. Neither were they grounded in disjunctures caused by the text's alienness. On the contrary, they were cases of intense dialogues, wherein the reader articulated a clear understanding of the text's truth claim and then critiqued it by refuting its validity through her subjective experiences and knowledges. One such objection came up with regard to the aforesaid assertion, "Virginity does not exist." While all the readers accepted this claim, some found Blank's following statement in the final chapter contradictory: "To paraphrase P. T. Barnum, there's a virgin born every minute" (*Virgin*, 218). In the group session, Şeyma brought up this issue of conflicting assertions:

> Şeyma (focus group): At first, the book says that virginity is fiction. But then it says, whatever happens, we are still all born virgins. I didn't understand here if "we're born virgins" emphasizes its fictionality or is it to emphasize that we are born sexually inexperienced?

In response to this inquiry, a lively discussion takes place on the incompatibility of the two claims: While attempting to eliminate virginity's essentialist load and highlight its social constructedness, the text at times seems to reproduce the very problematic load it contests. So, the book is criticized for falling into the same essentialist trap that it defies. Yet, even such a serious disjuncture does not result in rejection of the book or its argument of nonexistent virginity. Rather, after they identify the dilemma and find the narrative "partly flawed," the readers move on to agree that the text's larger mission of "deciphering myths," in Bilge Su's words, is politically momentous and well-substantiated enough to adopt. This example illustrates that in their critical assessments of the validity of the book's truth claims, the readers manipulate, or take advantage of, those moments of epistemological failures to repair the traveling text so that it now attends to the theories and realities of its new readership.

*Bekâret*'s readers did have such dynamic reading experiences because they trusted the text well enough to become intimate with it, no matter how alien its stories appeared to be. One key reason of this trust is the book's apparent subversive take on virginity. The readers' subjective mental frames, or "horizons of expectations" in Jauss's terms, shaped by both local gender and sexuality codes and their feminist agendas, facilitated them to form a specific anticipation from the book—to provide a theoretically sound, analytically reliable, epistemologically rich, and politically useful feminist discourse (*Aesthetic of Reception*). When this counter-hegemonic expectancy was greeted by a similarly voiced and equipped dissident text, hinted in the translator's preface that explicitly ascribes a feminist agenda to the book, the readers seem to have entered the text with trust, or "a peace of mind," in Ayşe's words.

Indeed, when asked if the translator's openly declared feminist standpoint affected their relationship with the book, all the participants said it made it easier for them to connect with it:

Selma (interview): Knowing that you are a feminist reassured me from the beginning. . . . So, I trusted you; I thought the upcoming thing was going to be a good thing.

Milena (diary): If the person who translated the book and I share opinions, that makes the book much more pleasant. She too is a feminist like me . . . So, the book evoked in me the feeling of gaining new experiences in a pleasant conversation.

Yasemin (diary): I can summarize my experience of reading this book like this: It was as if the translator, the author, and I were having a conversation. Nobody's voice was silenced; not one voice was suppressing the other.

As these remarks show, the initial feeling of trust that the readers felt for the translator was extended to the feminist author and the book, regardless of its origins in a distant geography or its exclusive western focus. Thus, the co-performance of a feminist identity by both the translator and the author helped build a common political ground between the reader, translator, and author, which enabled the reading to ensue as an egalitarian exchange of ideas—familiar or unfamiliar, alien or domestic—and result in a hybrid text, despite being positioned on the opposing poles of "west vs. east."

Considering that translated texts may present additional dialogic challenges since their otherness is more pronounced, readers of translations might experience serious trust issues (especially in our world of intense boundary-marking and enemy-making paradoxically escorted by growing cross-border contact).[6] In this context, the translator can play a crucial role in facilitating ethical encounters with the other by mediating the voice of the imported text in ways that do not intimidate the reader into a submissive position or assimilate the text into a tamed standing. That is, the feminist translator's signature in the text, where the other is treated as a "significant other," can function as a dialogic model of hermeneutics and facilitate connectionist readings. In fact, most of my participants explicitly noted that my feminist translation strategies, especially my use of non-hetero/sexist language and the translator's preface, played such a constructive role in their encounters with the alien book:

> Ayşe (diary): The fact that the translator presents herself as a feminist certainly made a difference. . . . This enabled me to surrender to the book with a peace of mind.

> Deniz (diary): That the translator described herself as a feminist enabled me to get much closer to the book. Her voice didn't bother me at all; if anything, it enabled us to build a stronger relationship with the book. Because the book was about the western culture—a culture that is foreign to us—I needed that help.

These and similar remarks suggest that, when combined with the book's subversive voice and amenable tone, my self-reflections as a feminist translator, largely in the preface, helped readers ethically and responsibly engage with *Bekâret*. This is why we need to ask more often, how do we translate to accomplish such ethical engagements with traveling texts? What sorts of cross-border feminist hermeneutics do we need to facilitate more egalitarian transnational readings and connectionist meaning-making operations across all geopolitical directions?

These questions on forging ethical encounters between differently situated feminist subjects and subjectivities point out the urgency of bringing translation to the center of our discussions on transnationality. Confronting the translation question in the context of transnational feminism invites us to have deeper conversations about how to engage with differences ethically and how to accept each other's stories into our political subjectivities. Transnational connectivities and assemblages of resistance cannot be achieved without ethical translation and reading practices that turn cases of encountering differences into cases of cross-border learning and cooperation, during which our political subjectivities get the chance to grow with each other, rather than against one another.

## Translation as Embodied Encounter

Here, I explore the ways in which *Bekâret* was textually orchestrated to produce a feminist reader who is invited to experience the subversive discourses of the text through her own embodied—gendered and sexualized—subjectivity and the ways in which the actual readers who bring different experiential repertoires to the reading process respond to this textual arrangement. In its facilitation of embodied reading practices, *Virgin* in fact does what Kathy Davis says about *Our Bodies, Ourselves*: by "imaginatively situating the reader in her own body," the book "instructs the reader to remember that her body—as well as the bodies of other women—has a specific history and is located in the specific circumstances of their lives" (*How Feminism Travels*, 162). *Virgin* accomplishes that primarily because it questions a normative concept dis/owned by women's bodies and in the process pulls the reader's gendered body in to be resignified.[7] In this section, I examine what happens at those encounters between the body of the text and that of the reader and what sorts of re-embodiments follow.

Texts' interpretive schemata facilitate certain subject positions for the reader to take up (or reject), and, during such textual activation, the text performs its ideological stance in and through the reader's embodied memories and experiential knowledges. *Bekâret*'s interpretive scheme is a mixture of feminist her/story, social constructivist epistemology, and counter-hegemonic re-vision. The primary subject position offered for the reader to adopt is a transgressive one, wherein the reader is summoned to dismantle the assumed scientific factuality of virginity (and other similar gender/sexuality codes designed to alienate and usurp her body), to reconfigure it as a misogynistic invention devised to discipline, possess, and control her body, and to rewrite her preformed virginity knowledges and experiences within the semantic field of this new alternative truth discourse.

The way *Bekâret* is composed facilitates intense engagement with the reader whose gendered body is directly implicated in its virginity stories, even when they seem to be speaking of disparate geohistories. First, aside from focusing on virginity, itself an embodied concept, the book avoids heavy academic language and uses a more colloquial tone, which diminishes the risk of textual alienation (after all, *Virgin* is a popular history text). Second, the book's persistent use of an all-embracing "we," discussed in Chapter 2, directly implicates readers, including those located in Turkey, in its stories. Third, and perhaps the most effective instrument of *Bekâret*'s textual activation of an embodied reading subject position is its strategic use of self/reflexive questions located at the beginning and end of chapters. The first example appears in the very beginning of the book when Blank asks, "How do we define virginity? How have we defined it in the past? How do we tell who is and isn't a virgin?" (*Virgin*, 4). These questions invite the reader to remember her preformed virginity theories before hearing the book's alternative theory. They are, then, followed by a supposedly straightforward question, "Are you a virgin?" This is the moment when the book starts reminding the reader that they have a gendered and sexualized body and are already assigned a subject position in the binary discourse of virginity.

Then, continuing the dialogue with explicit questions that indicate the ambiguity of virginity, the book highlights the gendered reader's body as a contested site of meaning-making: "What if he only put it in a little bit? What if she didn't bleed" (4)? These questions draw the reader into the text's fabric as an embodied subject with experiential virginity knowledges, which she is then invited to reevaluate, revise, and even discard. For instance, one of the participants, Deniz wrote:

> Deniz (diary): I think it was with whales [where] the function of the hymen was to drain water like a filter and prevent infection from developing inside. For years, I presumed, or I was made to presume, that this was also the case with women. When I went on a vacation with my family [and because I wasn't a virgin], it was a nightmare for me to swim in the sea. I would think that I could catch a disease and then everything would come out; I would have to go to the doctor's and explain everything. For a while, I thought of it ["not being a virgin"] as keeping a secret from others; whereas now I think I don't have to explain anything to anyone.

Deniz is responding to Blank's discussion of the hymen's protective function in whales and seals, as opposed to humans' hymen, which does not serve any anatomical functions. Her remarks illustrate the importance of self-revelations on how our bodies are inscribed by regulatory discourses since it is only through those self-reflexive moments that readers can embark on the journey of reinscribing their bodies and bodily experiences in ways that alleviate the strong hold of virginity over their selves. Indeed, using the book's feminist gestures, Deniz now refuses to explicate her sexual status and have her body implicated in the virginity regime, which defines her body as the communal responsibility, property, and domain of family and state control. She later states in her diary, "This [being sexually active] used to be a situation that I had to hide but now I think of it as a situation I don't have to explain/announce; it's my business only." Deniz rewrites the narrative of her body by using *Bekâret*'s theory. Then, although the book denies virginity's embodied existence, it does not cancel out bodily experiences (e.g., "first sex"). On the contrary, while women's experiences are recognized as legitimate topics of critical inquiry, their bodies are reclaimed from the disciplining grip of the virginity regime.

Given the normative force of medicalized virginity in Turkey, *Bekâret*'s debunking of scientific virginity claims has a direct bearing on the ways in which the reader re-imagines and re-experiences her body in light of the book's knowledge. *Bekâret* pursues such an effect of re-embodiment by first inviting the reader to reflect on medical virginity claims (e.g., "the hymen is a reliable source of data on women's sexual past") and second, by scientifically discrediting them and reframing them as politically motivated, yet epistemologically false claims. The text then replaces this destabilized medical discourse with a feminist one that affirms and elevates the reader's own truth about her body:

> What are we to do, then, if we want to know whether a woman is or is not a virgin? Where can we turn for an answer, if the doctors cannot tell us? The only honest answer is that there is in fact nowhere to turn, and nothing that can give us anything more ironclad than a maybe. In truth, if for some reason we care whether someone is or was a virgin, it would seem that the best solution is simply to ask (Blank, *Virgin*, 94).

As a result of this counter-reframing of virginity, medical virginity tests appear problematic not only because they have no scientific basis, but more importantly because they deny women's statements about their sexual histories. That is, virginity tests become more than misuse of power by doctors. In *Bekâret*—most explicitly in the translator's locally focused preface—they are resignified as an exercise of state power that endows doctors with the authority to designate women's sexual statuses. In fact, the preface shows that Turkey's history of virginity is at the same time a history of the state. Therefore, far from being the innocent enterprise it claims to be, medical knowledge production appears in the book as a *political* project and the reader is now invited to talk to her body without the coalescing voices of the state and medicine interfering. That is, *Bekâret* gives credit and currency to its reader's own words rather than to the state-sealed medical verdict and holds her experiential knowledge above scientifically acclaimed, state-sponsored medical knowledge. This is a powerful discursive gesture in a sociopolitical context where virginity tests remain largely unchallenged on the grounds of epistemic validity. It gives the reader a legitimate way out of the heteropatriarchal "sentence" of medicine whose diagnostic authority, no matter how strongly endorsed by the state, is now undercut in regard to virginity and enables her to gain the control of her body (Treichler, "Escaping the Sentence," 70).

Interestingly, *Bekâret* enables not only the (hetero)sexually active reader to feel at ease with her decision to have male-partnered sex, but also the sexually inactive reader to reconceive her sexual status outside the phallocentric virginity discourse and feel at ease with her decision to refrain (temporarily or permanently) from sex. No matter what sorts of a/sexual experience the reader brings into the reading process, they are encouraged to feel "at home" in her body. For readers who identify as sexually inexperienced and/ or indifferent, *Bekâret* accomplishes this bodily affirmation by pursuing a nonnormative and nonprescriptive approach to virginity (refusing to frame virginity as a matter of right or wrong) and telling historical stories about "virgin" women who were paradoxically empowered by the virginity regimes of their time. In doing so, *Bekâret* allows its readers "an imaginative entry into the experiences of different women" (David, *How Feminism Travels*, 138). One interesting case of such self-affirmation activated by the book's empowerment stories is Kırmızı, who wrote:

> Kırmızı (diary): In the book, the women who took a sacred virginity vow affected me greatly. I could identify with them. I felt as if I was a derivative of them. I mean, I felt like I shared the sacred virgins' ideology, as if I were following their traces. The book helped me realize that I have been trying to build a lifestyle in line with this ideology. Apparently, vestal virgins[8] appear even among contemporary women.

Kırmızı, who said that she had been struggling with the virginity idea for a while now and that critically reflecting on this issue constituted "the starting point of [her] feminist journey," identified with Rome's vestal priestesses. She believed that her "asexual status" (Kırmızı herself never used the term "asexual" but implied it several times while explaining that she did not feel any sexual attraction or desire to engage in sexual relations) similarly gave her power, although she was not sure why or how:

> Kırmızı (interview): I am not fully sure but this [book] has just started my self-reflection. I can't exactly give it a name, but it has fostered in me some awareness and my beginning to question virginity has helped me take a step forward.

By gaining an imaginative entry into vestal virgins' lives through *Bekâret*, no matter how distant the story appears to be, Kırmızı engages in a deep self-reflection during which she asks herself whether she is shying away from sex because of the social pressure surrounding her (unmarried) body, or because she feels empowered by sexual disavowal, refusing to participate in the heterosexual economy.

One of the most recurrent themes of *Bekâret* that stimulates some of the most intense embodied self-reflections is "losing" virginity, which, as Blank notes, should not surprise us as "virginity is invariably defined in terms of what it is not" (*Virgin*, 96). Since the existence of virginity and the moment of its termination are both defined in terms of bodily practices and signs, while reading *Bekâret*, "the reader cannot help but recall her own stories": What is *her* virginity story and how does *she* feel about it? (Davis, *How Feminism Travels*, 162). In fact, the reader's understanding of the book depends to a certain extent on the particular "virginity story" she brings into the book.

Vaginal bleeding as the (alleged) physiological mark of virginity "loss" was at the very center of the narratives that the readers read into and out of *Bekâret*. For instance:

> Leylak (diary): Reading this book encouraged me to think of my first [sexual] experience. There was no [vaginal] bleeding in my first experience. Of course, neither my partner nor me worried about this or questioned it. I knew there was a chance that it might not have happened, but I still used to go back in time from time to time and think, what if I was raped during my childhood and didn't remember it?

The medical virginity discourse is so powerful that the lack of its main bodily sign—vaginal bleeding—compels Leylak to doubt her body and memories rather than the discourse itself. The book, therefore, puts her at ease by defying the medical association between hymenal bleeding and first vaginal intercourse and ruling out her theory of rape.[9] In light of this epistemological shift, Leylak rewrites her sexual experience as "truthful" and designates the medical "fact" as "suspicious." On the other hand, even when a woman is sure of her "virginal status," lack of bleeding during first intercourse may lend itself to a sense of "disappointment" in one's body or a sense of being "betrayed" by it:

> Bilge Su (diary): The bafflement/disappointment I felt due to the lack of bleeding during my first sexual experience! My partner supposed that I had not had sexual intercourse before (and it was so), because we had not had penetration in the first month [of our relationship] as I was a little afraid. Although I wasn't fully ignorant about the hymen, my lack of bleeding baffled/disappointed me and although he didn't care about "virginity," the feeling that I had "lied" to my partner upset me.

It seems that regardless of her preexisting knowledge of virginity's shaky anatomical ground, Bilge Su still had to confront the psychic force of virginity's fictionality while reading *Bekâret*, which encouraged her to question virginity's regulating and incarnating effect on her and fully disown it.

Reaching such an acute awareness of the biopolitics of virginity and its role in self-discipline is a crucial step in re/gaining ownership of one's body (though not in absolute terms). Several readers extended this realization to other examples of women's experiences with sexual embodiment (e.g., having difficulty with reaching orgasms during heterosex, refraining from masturbation and sexual self-exploration, and struggling with vaginismus,[10] all of which, the readers argued, had to do with the virginity pressure put on women in Turkey). Illustrating this critical force of the book, Ayşegül noted,

> Ayşegül (focus group): I think this is in fact a very serious problem because as we are raised—due to the virginity nonsense, our sexual parts, I mean, our "bikini area" is constantly [policed] by our families when we are just kids; you know, "oh be careful, don't let your underwear show; don't touch that." You know, we grow up with so many advices like that and we are incredibly estranged from our own sexual parts and we don't know it. You know, we don't touch there. . . . We can't look at our own sexual parts. I mean, we can't get a mirror and hold it [there]. Really, that moment of getting to know your self—we need to hold a mirror [to ourselves/our bodies].

As seen in this comment, *Bekâret* not only helped its readers reimagine their bodies and sexualities in relation to the local virginity codes, but also encouraged them to problematize the ways in which women's bodies were turned into objects and public properties serving heteropatriarchal enterprises and to search for ways to reconnect with their estranged bodies. In fact, Ayşegül's comments are remindful of the renowned photograph in *Our Bodies, Ourselves* that depicts a woman looking at her genitals with a mirror. It seems that *Bekâret* achieves a similar interpretive activation without visuals. Given such evoking of feminist body politics in *Bekâret*, it is not surprising that the participants often referred to a widely used slogan of the feminist movement in Turkey: "My body is mine." In Deniz's words, "I consider the book feminist since it gives women their bodies back." Hence, the imported book fit well into the existing feminist agenda of resignifying and repossessing one's body, resulting in a case of local discursive cohabitation that invited the readers to question the virginity norms of their embodied habituation and loosen the habitual grasp of such self-regulation on their subjectivities.

Another example of reading *Bekâret* into the local feminist discourses of embodiment is seen in the unique case of Müjgan, whose troublesome history of incest by her father made her engagement with the book, with its intimate narratives on first sexual experiences and "virginity loss," challenging and exhausting, to say the least. Müjgan's life story, in which, she narrated, she "neither embraced nor discounted virginity" (focus group) was so entwined with sexual abuse that, unlike the other participants, she could hardly identify with the textually implied figure of the woman whose body was irrevocably marked by the virginity norm. Thus, it was difficult for her to readily accept the book's invitation to reflect on its virginity discourses through her own experiential knowledges:

> Müjgan (diary): Since the first years of my childhood during which I believed that when it was night, it was night everywhere and that those people in planes that I waved at waved back at me, the taboos of the society in which I live stand side by side with hypocrisy in my mind. In my story, virginity has slipped through the cracks among a bunch of other traumas. It is neither something whose presence I owned, nor something in whose absence I felt a deep loss.

Despite this and several other entries illustrating Müjgan's struggle with embracing the self-reflexive overture of the book, she still manages to connect with *Bekâret*. She does so by framing virginity as one form of violence against women amongst others (honor-based violence, domestic violence, etc.), in which she is always implicated as a gendered body, and by positioning the book as a political act of resistance in which she participates as a woman who has "gotten her share of gender violence," but regardless has survived it. Then, in order to deal with the embodied distress triggered by *Bekâret*, Müjgan draws on the local feminism's most vocal discourse (struggle against violence against women), which acknowledges her pain, yet does not disempower or isolate her as "a *victim* of a male villain." By situating virginity as part of a larger political arena, wherein she is both a survivor and a feminist activist, she makes the book hers even though she experientially does not partake in its virginity stories. Rewriting *Bekâret* as history of women surviving misogyny, she manages to let her embodied self into the text and welcome its stories into the collective resisting "us." In her words, "our stories are those of a survival struggle." Müjgan reads her survival narratives into those of the book and reads those empowering meanings back into her narratives, in the process of which both her body and the book unite against violence against women, resulting in a pool of experiential knowledge of and for women's survival. It is in this sense that "reading is an act of survival" (Kaufman, "That, My Dear," 234).

Some of the participants also used the traveling book to question the normative implications of local feminist discourses by rewriting their sexual attitudes in light of *Bekâret*'s nonprescriptive take on virginity. An example appears in Dîlan's diary, which she starts (before she reads the book) by telling her struggle with the "paradox" of self-identifying as a feminist and advocating for sexual liberation, on the one hand, and "being a virgin" and "having a hymen," on the other:

Dîlan (diary): I was asking myself whether the fact that I had not been [sexually] involved with a man was because of the fear I felt due to the existing [social virginity] pressure despite all the [feminist] values I advocated for. I had experienced frivolous affairs (kissing, cuddling, etc.) but I had never had intercourse. Especially when I was pleading for the cause of sexual liberation in front of my friends who knew I was a virgin, I started to feel seriously disturbed by their flinging my virginity up in my face. The critiques were about that I didn't maintain action-discourse integrity. . . . I was literally being crushed under the weight of the hymen's presence. At times I would plan on getting rid of the hymen myself, but I knew that it wouldn't eliminate the hymen obsession that I had created in me. And eventually, I had a one-night stand with a man I liked. . . . Then, I noticed that nothing had changed in me.

Dîlan's expectations from *Bekâret* were shaped by this embodied dilemma, which she did not fully resolve until reading the book, although she no longer identified as a virgin. She continued questioning her decision to have sex with a man not only to defy patriarchal norms and assert her "sexual freedom," but also to prove her feminist identity. She added in her diary, "I think I'll find in this book the answer to, 'Is my being a virgin an obstacle to my being a feminist in practice?'" Reflecting the intimate nature of this expectation, Dîlan's reading eventually culminated in her negation of both patriarchal and feminist normativities: "I am sure that if I had read this book before my [sexual] experience, I wouldn't adopt such a solution" (diary). This comment may at first appear as a simple act of regret, but Dîlan is, in fact, using *Bekâret*'s claim of nonexistent virginity to redraft the narratives of her sexual status and experiences outside the two local normative discourses—patriarchal and feminist—that created her dilemma to begin with: "Now, I don't want to use the term 'virgin' for a woman who has not had sexual intercourse. I mean, I want to refrain from using the word 'virginity' altogether" (interview). Hence, upon reading the book, Dîlan articulates a new discourse that refutes virginity and reconstitutes her embodied subjectivity within that non-normative discourse of sexuality.

Similar "What if?" and "I wish" narratives were also articulated by other readers (Ayşe, Selma, Milena, and Ece), who engaged both in retrospective imaginative exercises about *Bekâret*'s potential effects on their experiences of "virginity loss," and in recuperative acts of redrafting of those past experiences by drawing on the book's argument of virginity as nonexistent. Then, what happens to the reader's subjectivity when she re-embraces an inherently embodied notion as bodily nonexistence? How does the reader de-embody virginity? The following diary entries could provide an answer:

Ayşe (diary): Reading this book added a lot to me; it made me realize how I articulate my virginity experience. Virginity is something that doesn't exist as long as we "don't lose it." I wish the book had been written when or before I had my first sexual experience and I read it at that time. I'd have gotten over that thorny process faster.

Nil (diary): Before I read the book, there was a doubt in me that I was trying to suppress. But I now think that those certain things that I assumed I lost are not in fact lost because it [virginity] is nothing! I am at ease. Because I know that my body and the responsibility of my body belong to me. Not to my father, mother, boyfriend or anyone to judge me! I am very happy that now I haven't let remain in me even a bit of those nonsense conventions that have been going on for centuries.

Within *Bekâret*'s new ontological feminist framework of virginity defined by "nothing to have, nothing to lose," Ayşe and Nil revise their "first sex" narratives by rejecting its association with bodily, psychological, and social loss. Their adoption of nonexistent virginity does not eradicate their bodies, but erases the implied deprivation, depletion, and expiration from their narratives of self. In doing so, they replace their previous "loss" experiences with a new embodied sense of "gain" by rescripting their sexualities as "under my control" and bodies as "in my possession."

Such acts of narrative restoration and reimbursement of past experiences that emphasize the readers' redesigned embodiments in light of their ideological "self-cleansing" also has important implications for the readers' future interactions with others:

Ayşegül (focus group): My younger sibling is starting college this year and I've given her the book as a gift since she hasn't had sexual intercourse, but I don't want her to conceive it as losing. There is no such thing anyway; something that doesn't exist can't be lost, and I recommended it to her for that.

Yasemin (diary): While reading the book, I had a few conversations with my friends by referencing the book. One of them was a woman friend who had the virginity taboo. I talked to her mostly about virginity's medical aspects. I explained to her the truth about the medical lies/nonsense told us and recommended her the book.

This statement, echoed by several other readers, illustrates that *Bekâret* mobilizes readers both to retrospectively revise their sexual embodiments and to prospectively prefigure their yet-to-come sexual embodiments (and of those they may impact). This is why the interpretive act of reading is never finished when the reader runs out of pages. As Michel Foucault notes, "The frontiers of a book are never clear-cut: beyond the title, the first lines, and the last stop, beyond its internal configuration and its autonomous form, it is caught up in a system of references to other books, other texts, other sentences: it is a node within a network" (*Archaeology of Knowledge*, 23). The contingent embodiment facilitated by reading is never absolute, but rather is a continuous process of experiential rearticulation:

> Defne (interview): The book hasn't ended in me yet. I mean, we keep saying that the book is finished but it hasn't for me, it's still continuing in me. Yes, I opened it last week, but I don't know when it will be closed, if it'll ever close, and I honestly don't want it to close. Because even when I sit down and talk to my friends about it, the book continues in me. I mean, it doesn't have a last word.

> Müjgan (interview): I'll take the book home, I'll look at it over and over again, the conversation will end, I'll leave, but the book is always with me. I can give it to my friends. So, it is living on; it's a living thing. It doesn't stay where the author left it.

By virtue of its reciprocally transformative encounters with the readers, *Bekâret*, in which, according to the participants, the author and the translator jointly spoke with them in pursuit of their common feminist agenda, takes on differently meaningful lives—an infinite form of "living on"—and becomes more than its apparent materiality on paper (Benjamin, "Task of the Translator;" Derrida, "Living On," 62). Such textual fluidity continues in and through the fluidity of the reader's embodied subjectivity and lasts so long as the reader beholds it. So, in the course of crossing borders through translation and reception, *Bekâret* gets embodied differently—even more subversively—as it engages with a different sexual economy that has its own unique virginity regime, a different feminist legacy, and a different constituency of feminist readers. This points at translation's power to transform our political subjectivities (and eventually political movements) when we read it with generous hospitality and radical vulnerability—that we grow with each other's alien stories precisely because they are alien.

How come *Bekâret*'s readers did not give in to seemingly irreconcilable cultural differences or geopolitically dictated animosities assumed between Turkey and the book's "birthplace" and managed to hear the book, even when its stories seemed incompatible with their lived realities, subjective embodiments, or experiential truths? This is an important question on the politics of translation and reception inviting us to "see the labor of ethical translation as one where the possibilities of what the text can do for justice are in fact created in and through responsible receiving and interpretation" (Nagar,

*Hungry Translations*, 153). Also, what can we do to change the oppressive, and repulsive, global culture of textual flows and reception so that translation becomes a way to "host the other" in our own dwellings and connect with one another across our differences, no matter what the direction of the flow is, because, as Susan Guerra once beautifully said, "I am because we are. Without expecting sameness" (quoted in Keating, "El Mundo Zurdo," 519)? In the next chapter, by expanding the analytical scale from the subjective to the local to focus on the encounters of the traveling book with Turkey's buzzing feminist reserve, I provide another layer of responses to this urgent question.

CHAPTER 4

# Local Politics of
# Feminist Translation

Strategies of writing and reading are forms of cultural resistance.
Not only can they work to turn dominant discourses inside out
(and show that it can be done), to undercut their enunciation
and address, to unearth the archeological stratifications on
which they are built; but in affirming the historical existence of
irreducible contradictions for women in discourse, they also
challenge theory in its own terms, the terms of a semiotic space
constructed in language, its power based on social validation
and well-established modes of enunciation and address. So well-
established that, paradoxically, the only way to position oneself
outside of that discourse is to displace oneself within it—to refuse
the question as formulated, or to answer deviously (though in its
words), even to quote (but against the grain).
—de Lauretis, *Alice Doesn't*, 7

Translation, as a form of cross-cultural contact and exchange, has always
played a major role in the configuration, rejuvenation, and expansion of
the feminist movements in Turkey by providing feminists with theoretical
frameworks, analytical tools, activist models, and epistemic resources that
have been produced and proved politically effective in different localities. By
relocating such resources within the discursive fields of Turkey, translators
have enabled the cultural crossover of numerous critical theories and knowledges that have helped enlarge the epistemological and political repositories
of feminisms in the country. Yet, the contributive and corroborative effects
of translation on the local feminist politics remain understudied in both
translation and feminist studies in Turkey. This chapter partially intervenes
in that knowledge gap by analyzing the ways in which the subversive virginity discourses of *Virgin* traveled across the Atlantic through my feminist
translation, *Bekâret*—as well as the mediating practices of other key actors
(such as the main editor, the publisher, and the cover designer)—and settled
in Turkey with its mission to unsettle its cultural economy of virginity.

The chapter reveals translation's locally catalytic and transformative impact by illustrating the particular ways in which *Bekâret* has informed Turkey's feminist virginity politics. I argue that the translation project has enhanced and expanded feminists' political repertoires in terms of epistemology and political action, including raising critical awareness and building feminist vocabulary. These two fronts of encounter between *Bekâret* and local feminists form the analytical sections of the chapter. Although these categories are intertwined and implicated in one another, I analyze them in separate sections only to highlight some specific areas of interaction between the imported text and local feminisms. Hence, the categorical markings should not be taken as mutually exclusive or jointly exhaustive, but rather read in relation to each other and only as themes with blurred boundaries.

Translations of feminist texts (particularly groundbreaking ones that blaze a trail by forging new epistemological, theoretical, and political paths) bring us into cross-border contact with a diverse range of feminist discourses. They help us recognize and confront the fact that we lack the discursive repertoires necessary to analyze and critique our locally grounded gendered experiences and worldviews. In doing so, they accelerate the political discovery process. That is, feminist translation helps us imagine otherwise and invites us to fill the gaps in local discursive fields through our own makes and remakes. By facilitating our confrontations with numerous faces and interfaces of patriarchy with other systems of domination, every act of feminist translation becomes a local political intervention because it prompts us to detect and replace heteronormative, male-centric "terms, themes, conceptions of the subject and subjectivity, of feeling, emotion, goals, relations, and an object world assembled in textually mediated discourses and from the standpoint of men occupying the apparatuses of ruling" (Smith, *Texts, Facts, and Femininity*, 1–2). Considering that patriarchies are multiple, unfixed, mobile, intersectional, and locally situated yet globally connected, the importance of translational exchanges among different feminist movements and agents responding to different patriarchal arrangements and practices around the world becomes evident. Indeed, translation can stimulate critical dialogues on issues that have received little or no attention from local feminist agents. For instance, translation can help break silences on taboo issues (e.g., issues of sexuality) by importing thought-provoking "foreign" discourses and encouraging locals to question their realities through the traveling knowledges and experiences of the other. Such borrowings from a cultural outsider would facilitate not only a formative dialogue with the other, but also a transformative dialogue with the self. Translation, thus, offers a contact zone where the self can encounter the other—an encounter that has the capacity to help us face ourselves (and the other) as well as the sociocultural habitat we inhabit (and that inhabits us) in ways that we have never before. Such translational, transformative encounters are political and activist in their forms and effects, and need to be recognized as such.

This chapter argues that without in-depth studies that bring translation under the spotlight as trans/local activism, feminists anywhere remain insufficiently equipped to fully identify their transnational histories and build inclusive collective memories on women's liberation struggles. The history of feminisms can, and should, be told "without relegating the generative mechanisms of translation and contributive labor of translators to the margins and without reiterating the hegemonic discourse of 'originality,' which only conceals the epistemologically and politically rich and telling processes of local creative appropriations, hybrid formations, and cross-cultural dialogues that constantly take place via translation among feminists around the globe" (Ergun, "Translational Beginnings," 51). Virgin *Crossing Borders* in general and this chapter in particular seek to provide a narrative example on how to do that and highlight translation's key role in the formation of feminist politics. Since my focus is on a single translation and its encounters with local feminisms, my study cannot provide an overarching picture of translation's cumulative effect on the evolution of feminisms in Turkey. Yet, it is my hope that by presenting an extensive case study tracing the cross-cultural trajectory of a specific text, it can inspire and equip scholars with a theoretical and analytical model to study the mass border crossings of feminist discourses and their localization processes at a larger scale.

## Feminist Translation as a Site of Knowledge Production

In *Black Feminist Thought*, Patricia Hill Collins cites an insightful story that illustrates the power of the epistemic reconfiguration of "the truth" and the discourse through which that truth is validated (251):

> A small girl and her mother passed a statue depicting a European man who had bare-handedly subdued a ferocious lion. The little girl stopped, looked puzzled and asked, "Mama, something's wrong with that statue. Everybody knows that a man can't whip a lion." "But darling," her mother replied, "you must remember that the man made the statue."—As told by Katie G. Cannon

The story, initiated by a child's confusion over the fact that the truth told by the statue is not validated by her situated knowledge, ends with her mother's intervention into the very discursive regime that creates the truth and upholds it as such. The mother's intervention is remarkable not so much because of her rejection of the truth claim, but because of her reconceptualization of the statue itself as an inventive product that has been naturalized (and naturalizing) but could in fact be imagined and materialized otherwise. What we see in the story is the seemingly simple act of articulating that what we take as the truth, whose existence is assumed to be outside the human social and whose production and ideological maintenance are erased from its very existence, is actually "man-made." The story resonates with the feminist mission of *Virgin* and *Bekâret* because both reveal the disruptive power of revealing truth regimes that fabricate and validate truths whose discursive and material effects are of domination. Throughout patriarchal histories, which are many, virginity has been one such invested regime with truth claims functioning to discipline, control, and exploit women and their bodies. *Virgin*, by revealing that the "statue" of virginity is man-made and unfolding its constructedness, challenges that domination. In this section, I analyze the readers' responses to this unsettling potential of *Bekâret* to see whether and how its transgressive knowledges intervened in local virginity politics.

First and foremost, *Bekâret* legitimized virginity as a serious topic of knowledge production, taking it outside the supposedly petty terrain of women's everyday ("personal/private") experiences. Aware of the epistemic trivialization that so many of women's experiences receive, Ayşe wrote,

> Ayşe (diary): I think the book will take virginity into a different dimension because now that it exists as a published scholarly text in Turkish, virginity will stop being a topic of "restroom talks" in middle school and become a topic that can be spoken about in academic language.

Through *Bekâret*, virginity is elevated to the status of a legitimate subject matter that is worthy of researching, writing, publishing, translating, reading, and discussing. Indeed, several participants expressed in their diaries surprise and concern about the book's length, so, even when it is deemed a valid field of critique, virginity may not be expected to command a large epistemological turf:

> Milena (diary): As it turns out, there was so much that could be said about virginity.

> Defne (diary): When I see the book's page count, I ask, "What is told in so many pages?" It is important for me that a book does not repeat itself. I will find that out when I finish the book.

These comments point at the underlying initial assumption that virginity has a narrow epistemological field that could easily be told in a small book, which explains the readers' astonishment. The initial belief in virginity's limited epistemological yield is partly facilitated by the scarcity of critical, reliable sources on it. When persistently faced with absent or scant literature, it becomes easy to suppose that there are not many sources on virginity because there is not much to know or write about. In fact, even Hanne Blank herself talks about her gradual transition from a state of "there is not much to be known about virginity" to that of "there is too much to be known about virginity" during her investigation (*Virgin*, ix–x). Moreover, when something is conceived exclusively as a private matter and naturalized into "common sense," it becomes even more difficult to see the need to question it or expect other sources to do so. So, the lack of critical literature on virginity might not only reinforce the epistemological triviality of the subject and foster initial suspicions towards new sources on it, but also play into the very hands of a vicious circle that ensures its commonsensical acceptance.

*Virgin* claims that it is the first comprehensive source on the history of virginity, although its scope is confined to the west. As Blank says in the preface, "Even though my interests were limited to virginity and virgins in the Western world, it was rapidly becoming obvious to me that if I wanted to read a comprehensive survey of virginity, I was going to have to write it" (ix–x). More than half of the participants mentioned this "one of a kind" status of the book as a big advantage that increased its potential to intervene in Turkey's virginity politics. While some pointed out the value of the book "as a first" based on Blank's claim as such, others noted that they themselves had never come across such an encompassing, critical text on virginity. The quotations below illustrate this appreciation:

> Müjgan (focus group): This is actually the first book that I have read on virginity and whatever it said I needed it.
>
> Yasemin (diary): It is an indisputable fact that this comprehensive one-of-a-kind study is an important source both for Turkey and for other countries.
>
> Yasemin (interview): Of course, before this book, virginity was being discussed and examined in the feminist movement. But, after all, the fact that there is a now written source on it registers a concrete visibility [to the issue of virginity] and implies a different kind of progress.

In addition to applauding *Bekâret* for being the first comprehensive feminist book on virginity, several readers also mentioned its nonnormative standpoint as increasing its epistemic and political potential:

Ayşe (diary): I find this book feminist because unlike patriarchal narratives, it doesn't judge or prescribe rules by saying, "this or that is bad and forbidden."

Defne (interview): There is nothing in the book that says, "from now on ladies should think like this" and this is the best part because after reading it, you begin questioning with the book.

*Bekâret* is praised not only for offering a new critical repertoire on virginity, but also for intervening into the very discourses that sustain and naturalize it as a norm. It equips readers with transgressive knowledges that could enable them to challenge virginity's normativity. The book's title, especially its claim of telling an "untouched" (read: fresh and nonconformist) history of a very "touched" matter, which in the Turkish version is emphasized more by quotation marks, was also interpreted by several readers as attesting to the fact that, unlike male-centered virginity discourses, the book would take a nonprescriptive stance. These observations illustrate that the readers did recognize *Bekâret*'s potential to help forge an alternative subversive discourse in the cultural landscape of Turkey by simultaneously negating and dismantling the grounds of hetero/patriarchal discourses that validate virginity as a norm.

All the participants, even the ones who criticized the book, described their reading process as a *learning* experience during which they gained new, concrete, in-depth knowledges on virginity. Many readers also articulated their expectations from the book in terms of finding new insights on virginity:

Deniz (diary): I want to learn about why and for what need virginity came into existence. And I also want to learn about the changes it has undergone and the pace of its change.

Ece (diary): What I expect from the book is to expand my knowledge, change my ideas, resolve the questions that I have about my personal [sexual] history, and perhaps give me confidence on a topic that can still be regarded as a taboo.

Given the epistemological mission ascribed to *Bekâret*, it is not surprising that "knowledge" and "learn" were two of the most frequently used words in the participants' reading narratives:

Nil (diary): I've never come across anyone on TV or in my family that seriously examines the sociological, psychological, and scientific aspects of virginity. That's why it is interesting. I've learned about the historical and scientific dimensions of virginity from a trustworthy source.

Milena (diary): First of all, one doesn't learn a lot from every book. But this is not one of them because I've learned so much from this book.

In terms of being epistemologically "nourished, illuminated, informed, confirmed, enriched, supported, reinforced, clarified, substantiated, refined, grounded, ensured, and crystallized"—terms that were used by the participants to describe the book's benefits—the first section of the book "Virginology" (and particularly Chapter 3, "Hymenology") appears to be the readers' favorite:

> Çise (diary): Especially the first part dissolved a good deal of my ignorance. Of course, the history in "Virgin Culture" was also quite interesting but the fact that the first part contained detailed information on the nature of the hymen and that it was the very first part of the book made me appreciate it like the first glass of water drunk by a thirsty person.

> Ayşegül (diary): Virginology was the part that I really enjoyed reading and where I learned so many things that I didn't know. And I ended up establishing, just like the author said, that most of what we think we know about virginity is actually a bunch of lies.

Interestingly, like Ayşegül, several other readers also agreed with the message of the alternative title that Blank humorously ascribed to the book in her preface: "Everything You Think You Know About Virginity Is Wrong" (*Virgin*, ix). For instance, Defne wrote in her diary, "Virginity, which I thought existed but in fact I realized I knew nothing about, now has a solid foundation that I can build on." Such epistemological realizations suggest that the book both equipped the readers with new virginity knowledges and encouraged them to question their preformed knowledges and face the fact that they did not know everything about virginity contrary to their initial assumptions of their full, accurate epistemological command. In this sense, reading *Bekâret* was not solely a *learning* exercise for the readers, but also an exercise of *unlearning* their "memorized" commonsensical knowledges.

The problematic practice of virginity tests in Turkey made *Bekâret*'s first section particularly relevant for the readers due to its direct focus on the hymen myth. Interestingly, even the readers who initially noted that they were already informed about the variability and unreliability of the hymen were impressed by the richness of the book's contents as it equipped them with more in-depth knowledge on virginity. For instance, the third focus group had a long conversation critiquing doctors as well as the medical institution for perpetuating the myth of the hymen and medicalizing virginity under the cloak of scientificity. In the end, they all agreed with Bilge Su saying, "Nothing I read in this book is completely new but in regard to its demonstrating how and how much my experiences have been defined by that foundational construct, you know, it is like 'oh my gosh' all over again." Regardless of their previous knowledges on the hymen, *Bekâret* seems to have triggered in all the readers a similarly shocking confrontation with the immense disciplining power of the hymen:

Ekin (interview): I didn't know much about the hymen and as it turns out, the things I thought I knew were wrong anyway.

Müjgan (interview): [Before reading the book,] I knew—but of course this was memorized knowledge—I had the knowledge that somebody bled this much, another bled that much but I thought everybody would bleed. Obviously, I was wrong.

Dîlan (diary): I too thought that the virginity exam done by the gynecologist yielded an absolute result in terms of [determining] virginity and the book changed my take on that.

Kırmızı (interview): I had some knowledge about the hymen; I knew that not all women experienced bleeding in the first intercourse. . . . But I learned from the book that the hymen itself was also something made up. I realized that the hymen was invented and given a name.

These remarks on discarded and newly acquired knowledge on the hymen and virginity testing reveal the greater epistemic potentiality of *Bekâret*'s first part for Turkey's truth regime on virginity.

The locally situated emphasis on the book's first part was also visible in the media reviews, which focused mostly on *Bekâret*'s disruption of the hymen myth and hence expanded its epistemological reach by repeating its key truth claim that the hymen is not a reliable proof of virginity:

The hymen, which is nothing more than a tiny spot in regard to women's biological existence, whose structure varies from woman to woman, and which does not have an absolute medical quality, is given a meaning that walks around being escorted by the state's permanency, the nation's integrity, and the family's sanctity. . . . No matter how much [or how hard] you measure it, even if you put all the people of the world up against the woman in order to measure it; that is, even if you convince everyone that it can be measured, that does not mean virginity exists (Kurnaz, "Bedenden Öte").

Ergun underlines the fact that because the hymen's structure varies among women and also because its structure changes by itself over the years, the hymen can under no circumstances yield any absolute, "scientific" answers (Gülen and Eren, "Bekâret Kavramı").

Virginity, which all in all is a leftover piece of flesh, or, an object of desire, doesn't actually exist. When observed as an object, one cannot see anything other than an amorphous membrane; only when seen "from a specific angle," it acquires obvious qualities. . . . An object that is postulated as such by desire. In a similar vein, the hymen is also perceived in a distorted way because it does not have an existence "in and of itself" outside that distortion (Öğüt, "Yamuk Bakış").

Hanne Blank has gathered information on the hymen by drawing on several medical literatures. What is repeatedly highlighted in the book is that doctors cannot find and see such a membrane in everyone and that, even if it exists, it has no anatomical benefit for the human body. The misleading nature of the signs of the existence/absence of the hymen—and, here, the most widely known and apparent sign is bleeding—is explained in every possible way (Günyüzü, "Ve Tanrı").

These media excerpts clearly illustrate that within the cultural landscape of Turkey, where virginity is firmly medicalized and endorsed by the state, *Bekâret* is ascribed the crucial mission of transforming the local epistemological repertoire on women's virginity and the hymen.

As opposed to the book's second section, "Virgin Culture," which is concerned with the cultural aspects of virginity, particularly its configurations in Christianity, the first section is geopolitically more apt to border crossing due to its focus on the "universal" discourse of science. In other words, while the religio-cultural contents of the second section may generate a cross-cultural gap that seems epistemologically harder to bridge for readers living in a locale where Islam is at the center of religious concerns, the scientific scope of the first section facilitates its travel and conversion into Turkey, where virginity is framed and understood within the same scientific truth regime of medicine.

*Bekâret*'s translation was welcome for also revealing a serious gap in the local feminist literature:

Sezen (diary): The book arrived right on time into a field of inquiry that had a gap. Although there are partial knowledges on virginity in fields like medicine and history, *Bekâret* both brought them together and critiqued them accurately.

Dîlan (diary): The publications I read before generally talked about mechanisms that limited women's sexual freedom. While in some sources the word "virginity" was never mentioned, in others it was discussed in 3–5 paragraphs. When I first saw *Bekâret*, it drew my attention because it exclusively addressed the virginity issue. And I think it has filled this deficiency.

*Bekâret* is praised for fulfilling an urgent epistemological need and deemed useful for helping raise critical awareness on virginity violence. Yet, the readers also highlighted that there was still no such source that focused on Turkey's or "eastern" history of virginity. Thus, while closing one gap in feminist literature, the book generated (or made visible) another locally or regionally defined epistemic gap, which reveals translation's pivotal role in encouraging feminist knowledge production. In Anna Tsing's words, "globally circulating knowledge creates new gaps even as it grows through the frictions of encounter" (*Friction*, 13). Yasemin noted this transnationally generative role of translation saying:

> Yasemin (interview): In the group discussion, we all came to agree on the need to undertake such a study for Turkey. . . . When we read the history of the west, we saw that virginity was much more deep-seated and got shocked. We grasped what we were up against much better. So, a question emerged on how it actually is in Turkey, or how it has developed in eastern geographies, especially in the context of Islam. . . . A gap that we had not noticed before arose.

Hence, *Bekâret*, by not only carving an exclusive discursive field on virginity, but also admitting its limited geopolitical focus, inspired the idea of expanding the epistemic borders of the existing virginity literature. In Müjgan's words, "Virginity gap! Virginity that has been fretted about so much and yet disregarded so much. It is us who must fill the gap" (diary). Hanne Blank's self-reflexive remarks about *Virgin*'s shortcomings seem to have contributed to this effect. For instance, in the epilogue, calling her book a "limited treatment," Blank stresses the exigency of studying various geohistorical formations of virginity and invites researchers to take it on themselves to expand the cross-cultural repository of virginity studies (*Virgin*, 256). It appears that *Bekâret*'s readers heard this call and positioned the book as a beginning of an emerging critical field. Indeed, several readers described the book as a starting point or a preliminary source to be followed by other subversive virginity projects:

> Çise (diary): Of course, virginity is a very large field of inquiry; its history is old, and it is a condition defined differently by many cultures. Covering many more aspects of virginity would require writing not one, but several books. I think *Bekâret* makes a great start.

> Yasemin (interview): I think the book is the beginning of something else. Yes, it has filled a gap, but it is more like a beginning, and other things that emerge around it will be even better.

> Ece (diary): It is as if the book just uttered the first word and is now waiting for the next word.

> Bilge Su (interview): For someone who will conduct a study on virginity in Turkey, the existence of this book is critical with regard to both help-

ing them grasp the problematic and enabling them to do a comparative study. . . . So, in regard to how the book would benefit feminist debates in Turkey, I can say that here we have a book that points at a problem, that unfolds and deciphers it, and opens up a data field on the basis of a specific cultural and historical background; a book that says that you can talk/debate it out in that data pool.

*Bekâret* is interpreted as laying an epistemological foundation for future scholars, providing them with a preliminary analytical framework and offering them a "reference book" to enter into conversation with. Given that what we call scholarship is an intertextual and dialogical form of epistemological accumulation, such a reference attribute symbolizes the inception and potential growth of a feminist virginity scholarship in place of which there used to be no such distinguished body of knowledge.[1]

In fact, almost all the readers called *Bekâret* a "reference book." Ece, for instance, described it as "the source that we want to reach when we want to read on the subject" and added, "it is nice that one of the reference books that will support the feminist movement has been written and translated" (diary). Readers also treated *Bekâret* as a reference book by marking its key statements. For instance, Defne, who had already lent her copy to a friend by the date of the focus group, said: "I took notes on the book, you know, I underlined it so that I would pay attention to those parts if I read it again, and also so that others would pay attention to them if they read it" (diary). Others wrote quotations in their diaries and discussed them in detail. These quotations were often accompanied by accentuating remarks like "I should not forget this" (Ekin), "This is one of the most highlightable sentences" (Pembe), and "This should certainly be kept in memory" (Çise). Some also mentioned taking notes on pieces of paper and posting them around so that they would not forget those critical insights.

Designated as a reference book, *Bekâret* enriched the readers' epistemological repertoires and provided them with a legitimate, reliable source that they could use in their debates on virginity:

Gülümser (interview): This is like a source book, you know, I can always look at it, I can give references to it, and that is very empowering and precious.

Leylak (interview): This is a book that people involved in the feminist movement could seriously benefit from, a book they could use to provide evidence for their arguments."[2]

Ayşe (diary): Reading this book has not changed my opinions on virginity but enabled me to get hold of a source that will help me defend my ideas more effectively and that I can show people when they ask me, "How do you know that?" And this is so crucial. Unless you reference a scholarly work there is a big chance that what you say will not be taken seriously.

Ayşe further explained in the interview,

> Ayşe (interview): I don't know if there is another comprehensive study on virginity in Turkish. I mean this is probably a first even in the west. That's why it is so important to have this source in Turkish because when I say that virginity doesn't exist, when I present this argument, people say, "how do you know?" Now I have a chance to show them the book and say, "read it."

Clearly, the readers established *Bekâret*'s value not solely in subjective terms (for epistemologically nourishing and affirming them), but also in inter-subjective terms (for being a tool of critical dialogues and exchanges). Since virginity is both a private and political matter, the readers expected *Bekâret* to be both subjectively and collectively interventionist and empowering, and only when both of these expectations were met, they elevated the book to the status of a *feminist reference book*. Ayşegül highlighted that at the end of her diary saying, "I once again saw that the personal is political," which points at another well-known feminist discourse that is rooted in acts of translation.

Because many readers positioned *Bekâret* as the reference book of virginity, their assessments of it were grounded on the degree of epistemic persuasiveness. On the one hand, they expressed that while their perspectives on virginity were not radically transformed by the text, they still felt politically confirmed. On the other hand, they themselves were so firmly convinced by its knowledge claims that they were sure of the book's achievement of similar effects on other feminist or pro-feminist readers. In fact, "convincing" was another frequently used word in the study. The readers discussed the book's persuasiveness especially with respect to its potential impact on non-feminist readers. For instance, Deniz, speaking of friends who were under the hold of the virginity ideology, noted in the interview, "It seems to me that the text would convince them. That is beyond me, but I believe the text could accomplish that." However, not all participants agreed on the book's persuasion ability for a conservative or relatively "less educated" audience. Some thought the text's "academic" language could hinder its reach to a larger audience, particularly readers who were not familiar with feminist discourses. This was a major discussion topic in the first focus group, where two participants, Leylak and Dicle, argued that the book would cater to a limited group of people, while the other two, Lorin and Gülümser, were more optimistic about its potential transformative impact on "lay readers."[3]

The book's potential outreach was a key concern for the readers precisely because they wanted the book's knowledges to spread out. Because they believed that the text's critical insights were powerful enough to disrupt Turkey's virginity regime, some interpreted its density and "academic" quality as potentially self-defeating. Yet, other readers, like Deniz, interpreted the same quality as enhancing the book's political potential. Given that academic discourse connotes "objectivity" and carries more credibility in our "age of science," these readers viewed the book's tone as empowering.

Interestingly, as opposed to the identification of *Bekâret* as a "scholarly" book in Turkey, *Virgin* was deemed by some reviewers as falling short of scholarly standards in the US. For instance, its lack of academic-styled references was criticized even though the book was mark(et)ed as popular history and did not claim an academic status. Then, it seems that in its travel from English into Turkish, *Virgin* transformed into a different genre, "upgrading" into an academic text. There could be several factors and actors involved in this transformation. First, the fact that English and Turkish—languages that exist in a hierarchical relation in the global order—are unequally equipped with scientific terminologies and discourses, enjoy asymmetrical levels of abstract language, and have achieved uneven degrees of popularization of academic discourses—with English holding the upper hand—seems to have increased the text's density in Turkish.[4] İletişim's reputation as a publisher of scholarly, social sciences books could also be a factor in shaping the readers' perceptions of the book as academic.

My reading and rewriting of the text as a translator immersed in academic discourses might have also unconsciously seeped into the text through my lexical and syntactical choices, although I consciously tried to create a text that would appeal to a broad range of readers. Finally, my preface seems to have accentuated *Bekâret*'s academic discursivity through its passionate and radical tone as opposed to the more "restrained" and distant style used in the rest of the book. Almost all the readers described the preface as a striking, angry introduction whose enthusiasm was contagious. In contrast, they depicted the rest of the book as laid-back, unemotional, and unassertive. In Ece's words:

> Ece (diary): The author's style is less assertive than the translator's in the preface. I think the author presents the biological and historical data and instead of highlighting her own critique, she wants it to occur by itself in the reader's mind; she wants the conclusions to emerge from the data. The translator's language in the preface was radical and revolutionist.

While the translator's preface was intended to call readers' attention directly to the book's demedicalizing framework by substantiating it with the facts of Turkey's geohistorical virginity regime and populating it with feminists in Turkey, Blank leaves more room for readers to make their own conclusions. This contrast between the preface and the rest seems to have unintentionally caused a disjuncture for some readers who expected, but could not find, the preface's enraged and enraging tone in the rest of the book. This was a major source of disappointment and irritation for those readers. Dicle, for instance, found Blank's textual attitude "too relaxed" and not activist enough. Selma similarly said in the interview, "The preface was very enthusiastic. It perhaps somewhat disappointed us when the book became so academic afterwards." Ekin also reported experiencing a preface-related disjuncture; yet, unlike the other readers who criticized the book for not living up to the stylistic standard set by the preface, Ekin critiqued the translator for hindering an exciting reading process:

> Ekin (interview): I think your preface was very good, but it also gave away some of the things in the book. So, when I read them in the book, I couldn't read them with the same excitement.

It seems that the epistemological guidance deliberately aimed by the preface caused a disjuncture for Ekin as it cut back the thrill that she could get from the book had she not known in advance what to expect from it. I had assigned this guidance task to the preface to ensure readers' grasp of the book's key claims so that it could more easily generate an unsettling impact. Yet, I realized in the course of the study that it also raised the risk of setting limits to readers' interpretations. As Milena explained,

> Milena (diary): The preface is positive in terms of providing readers with some foreknowledge about the book. But I don't know if it could cause a situation where the translator's sharings [of her views] would restrict readers' impressions of the book, so readers end up content with the translator's imagination and proceed only to the point where the translator takes them.

Milena is rightly concerned about the possibility of the preface generating a restraining interpretive effect on readers. Although I wanted the preface to highlight the book's key theoretical claims by providing signposts, I did not want it to shape the readers' interpretive journeys altogether. As far as my research findings go, the preface seems to have emphasized *Bekâret*'s epistemological potential and motivated the readers to engage with it more attentively, but it did not fully command or dictate their reading experiences in any deterministic ways. On the contrary, in the context of the reception study, the main outcome of the preface appears to be facilitating geopolitical connections between the readers' local experiences and the book's traveling knowledges. The preface certainly misguided some readers by stirring up the expectation of a passionate discourse throughout the book and eventually caused affective disjunctures (be it experienced as occasional boredom or disappointment with the text), but these disjunctures did not keep any of the readers from continuing reading the book.

Also, not all the participants who noted the stylistic incongruence between the translator's preface and the rest of the book evaluated the distant and unassertive language of the main body of the book as a weakness. In fact, some thought it could potentially enable the text to reach a larger audience across a wide political spectrum and generate destabilizing effects beyond already established feminist circles. Şeyma explained this in the third group session saying,

> Şeyma (focus group): I said earlier that I had expected a bit of more force-fulness [from the book] but the lack of such force could make it easier for women whom we've just called "accomplices"[5] to get closer to the book. . . . I actually find the book efficient in that respect. I mean, because it doesn't try to predicate a very assertive viewpoint; we can say that it doesn't try to impose its own opinion. Therefore, I believe it can help people who don't think in this [subversive] way understand its points more easily or to think more critically about virginity.

Şeyma suggests that the lack of a loud, politically sided tone in the book could prevent some readers, particularly those keeping their distance from manifesto-like feminist discourses, from experiencing a debilitating disjunc-ture in the reading process. Since it could easily lead to the reader's rejection of reading the book, such a disjuncture would fail *Bekâret*'s ultimate goal of reaching out to different constituencies of readers and opening a transgres-sive discursive space on virginity. Indeed, an online comment about *Bekâret* implies that this possibility of alienation due to "forceful" language might be real for some individuals who are not used to (or keen on) reading and engaging with assertive feminist texts: "Thankfully, the translator's excite-ment in the preface is not present in the book."[6] Then, perhaps, the preface's harsh, even confrontational tone, by spotlighting the mild tone of the rest of the book, might have helped some non-feminist readers engage with the rest of the book more easily.

Despite causing some affective disjunctures, almost all the participants evaluated the preface positively for epistemologically complementing the book, informing them about the local history of virginity oppression and feminist resistance, intensifying their desire to read the book, helping them connect with the book's western contents, and enabling them to trust it. In fact, even the readers who experienced an affective disjuncture saw the preface as forming a coherent unity with the rest of the book. Then, it seems that the preface increased the book's epistemic capacity. Moreover, while inadvertently inducing a stylistic disjuncture, the preface appears to have prevented another—geopolitically defined—disjuncture by playing the role of a bridge between the book's western scope and the reception context that is ambivalently yet oppositionally positioned in relation to the west.

The preface's bridging function was intentional on my part because I was concerned that the western outlook of the book could cause obtrusive disjunctures for readers and undermine the critical goals pursued by *Bekâret*. The preface aimed to help readers comprehend the book's truth claims by providing them with an analytic model on how to adapt its western epistemologies to their own locality and add more to them. In doing so, the preface showed that the book's contents were highly relevant for them despite the fact that they were geopolitically framed in a category that excluded Turkey:

> Ece (diary): I think the translator's preface is necessary. The book was written by an American, so the preface plays an orientational role as the book crosses over from one culture to another.

> Nil (diary): The preface provided me with good introductory knowledge and enabled me to look at the knowledges that I'd gain in the upcoming pages from Turkey's viewpoint as well.

The preface achieved this interpretive bridging by applying *Virgin*'s main truth claims to Turkey's geohistorical particularities in the 1980s–2000s and reframing the key *institutional*—medical, legal, and sociolinguistic—virginity practices of Turkey/Turkish in Blank's subversive discourse:

> Dîlan (diary): Through this introduction, I came to understand how I have been boiled down to a hymen by all these institutions in a way that made my blood run cold.

I also discuss in the preface findings of some important medical studies that were conducted in Turkey to assess the validity of virginity tests,[7] which confirms Blank's later claim that virginity does not have any provable materiality. The readers seem to have found this aspect of the preface very useful:

> Pembe (diary): It is very striking to present a fact that is underlined several times in the book in Turkey's concrete reality. Honestly, this is a reference that I can always use about virginity.

Echoing this comment, several participants applauded the referential quality of the preface for providing them with detailed information on Turkey's virginity regime. For instance, the preface offers a legal analysis and demonstrates that virginity tests violate not only the penal code and constitution, but also the international declarations and treaties ratified by Turkey. This analysis seems to have made quite an impact on the readers. As Dicle, a middle-school teacher, told me,

> Dicle (interview): You discuss international treaties and I can easily—for example, if something like this happens at my school—though I've never experienced it—but if an administrator wants to take a student to a virginity test, I can immediately object to it. I can say, "Look, in terms of law you are committing a crime." Otherwise, I would react differently, like "it is not ethical" and stuff. So, it was really useful to learn about the legal grounds of virginity tests.[8]

Several readers praised the preface's epistemological bridging by noting that without it the book would be "deficient" (Müjgan, Dîlan, Ayşegül, and Çise) and "less effective" (Ece). They added:

> Yasemin (interview): You know, in the end, I live here. And virginity is experienced very differently over there although there are of course similarities. In order to get inside the book, I need to be able to flow from here to there. Therefore, such an introduction seems necessary.

> Sezen (diary): I think this separate introductory text is necessary and important because it is able to build a connection, a bridge between the western culture where the book was written and the partially eastern culture where we are reading it. . . . In fact, I don't think I could build such a close relationship with the book if this preface had not been added to the book.

The comments suggest that my intention of invigorating readers' cross-cultural connections with the book and facilitating an easier transactivation of its western epistemologies was fulfilled by the preface. Yet, this does not mean that the readers were fully satisfied with the book's exclusive focus on the west. On the contrary, although they knew one book could not do it all, several of them still reported having expected some coverage of virginity politics outside the west. The book's focus on Christianity particularly seems to have created some curiosity about the cultivation of virginity in Islam:

> Yasemin (diary): I knew the book was going to tell the western virginity history, but I still expected it to touch on the eastern geography at the very least. Or a serious need or curiosity was awoken in me in this respect; maybe that's why I thought that. When I see that Christianity harbors so much culture regarding virginity, I necessarily wonder about that in Islam.

While the preface met the need to expand the borders of the book's virginity knowledges to a certain extent, the readers (and media reviewers) emphasized the need for a more comprehensive study that focused on different geohistories, including that of the Middle East and Turkey. Also, because Islam was not discussed in the translator's preface, the readers' expectations of reading a critical analysis of Islam and virginity remained unaddressed. For instance, in our interview, Dîlan said:

> Dîlan (interview): I definitely wish the author talked about non-western cultures. I actually felt its lack a lot, although your preface on Turkey narrowed that gap a bit. But I expected the book to mention Islam at the very least because it is one of the biggest religions in the world.

Such disappointments once again suggest that *Bekâret* both created a geo-epistemological curiosity and further emphasized the need to expand critical knowledge production on virginity beyond the western and Christian world. Yet, the readers and media critics seemed hopeful about such epistemic expansion. As Bayraktar noted in her review, "The need for new initiatives on virginity is actually a signal of that more feminist researchers will analyze this as a subject in and of itself" ("Bekaretin"). This is why the readers proposed that *Virgin* should be translated into more languages so that it could travel to other geographies, increase awareness, and inspire the creation of politically similar but geohistorically variant virginity knowledges. Only then, they believed, a collective feminist resistance against hegemonic virginity regimes could grow across the world. In the next section, I further analyze this connection between *Bekâret* as a feminist knowledge project and as a call for feminist action.

## Feminist Translation as a Call for Feminist Action

In the previous section, I discussed that *Bekâret* contributed to the local feminism by providing an alternative truth regime on virginity that disputed Turkey's regulatory virginity discourses. In addition to informing, confirming, and refining the readers' perceptions of virginity, the book also seems to have solidified and substantiated their critical consciousness about virginity in particular and body politics in general. Raising critical consciousness especially on a taboo subject (read: forbidden from questioning) has significant political implications because, as Jane Mansbridge writes, it "prepares members of an oppressed group to act to undermine, reform, or overthrow a system of human domination" ("Making of Oppositional," 4–5). Critical consciousness requires ideational resources such as conceptual tools, analytical frameworks, and theoretical lenses that facilitate recognition of injustice, claims of legitimacy, demands of correction, affective motivation, belief in solidarity, and political commitment to a cause. It is a preliminary and necessary mental state that prepares individuals for collective action to challenge, transform, or abolish a system of oppression. In bell hooks' words, who describes the process of coming to critical consciousness as "politicization," "if we do not change our consciousness, we cannot change our actions or demand change from others" ("Feminism," 675).

The formation of critical consciousness is a key element of resistance and social change because as Patricia Hill Collins explains, "A changed consciousness encourages people to change the conditions of their lives" (*Black Feminist Thought*, 117). Critical consciousness is not a fixed, unitary state of mind that one has or does not have, but rather a historically contingent, continuously changing continuum. And its composition, maintenance, expansion, and mobilization are achieved both individually and collaboratively. As M. Jacqui Alexander says, "no one comes to consciousness alone, in isolation, only for oneself, passively. . . . [S]hifts in consciousness happen through active processes of practice and reflection. Of necessity, they occur in community" ("Remembering," 100). As discussed in Chapter 3, reading is one such communal reflection because, although it seems to take place in isolation, the interpretive processes involved in reading are intertextual, citational, translational, and dialogical. Indeed, when we read, we communicate with others—not just with the author. And when we communicate with others, especially those who offer us subversive knowledges and theories, our critical consciousness expands. This chapter argues that the extent of such cognitive and affective expansion—which lays the foundation for political action—can be greater in translation because the text in question is a product of a different cultural landscape, semantic field, historical buildup, and doxa. Then, did *Bekâret* shift the participants' critical consciousness and yield any political actions?

Most of my participants seem to have come to *Bekâret* with some sort of critical consciousness on virginity. As seen in the first section of their diaries, which they wrote before reading the book, most of them were already aware of virginity constituting an oppressive gender norm, a form of gender discrimination, a source of violence against women, and a taboo matter intertwined with the local honor/shame codes. Yet, the feminist knowledges they gained from *Bekâret* still transformed their critical consciousness enabling them to develop a more complete or "full-fledged" consciousness on virginity (Mansbridge, "Making of Oppositional" and "Complicating Oppositional").

*Bekâret* achieved this transformation, first, by providing its readers with alternative interpretive frameworks on virginity that they did not have within their immediate reach before. That is, the book supplied conceptual tools "that allow members of a subordinate group to draft a definition of just treatment and just distribution that challenges the definitions of the dominant group" (Mansbridge, "Complicating Oppositional," 240). The central conceptual tool that the participants borrowed from *Bekâret* was its alternative interpretive schema: "Virginity is a myth/construct/fiction." This claim was also noted in all the book reviews. Kızılarslan, for instance, repeatedly used the term "invention" in her article as well as the phrase "virginity does not exist" ("Utanç"). Similarly, Öğüt wrote in her review, "Blank writes the history of this radically changeable and moldable cultural notion, which, far from being a rigid, universal, and ahistorical fact of humanity, has a vivid and largely hidden massive history" ("Yamuk Bakış").[9] The claim was deemed crucial because it meant that virginity was historical (its definition changes over time), cultural (it is geopolitically variable), and thus, not written in stone but *changeable*. The participants noted that *Bekâret* substantiated this claim of changeability well by revealing the rich history of virginity tests preceding the medical advent of the hymen, which was "discovered" only in 1544 by Flemish anatomist Andreas Vesalius (Blank, *Virgin*, 50):

> Kırmızı (diary): What most stood out to me were the tests used to materialize virginity in women's bodies until the hymen was invented. . . . *Bekâret* is a feminist work precisely because it unfolds the constructs of the patriarchal ideology of virginity. . . . Like any sort of social deed, virginity is also a constructed thing, a fiction. So, nothing is unchangeable.

> Bilge Su (diary): The fact that *Bekâret* questions virginity's "unchangeability" by stressing its historicity is of course a clear sign of a feminist concern.

It is crucial that *Bekâret* reconfigures virginity as changeable, unlike the hegemonic discourse that perpetuates the illusion of its fixity, since no political action can be taken against a "fact of nature," particularly one that is anchored in women's "biological bodies," unless it is first deemed changeable.

Second, *Bekâret* transformed the readers' consciousnesses by raising their awareness on the gravity of the issue—revealing the systematicity and the colossal gendered history of violence behind its construction and thus, underlining the exigency of building organized feminist resistance against it:

> Defne (interview): Virginity is one of those issues that we always brush aside, but it is in fact one of the most important things that we need to fight against.

> Yasemin (diary): Throughout the book, I was shocked to see that virginity had such a deep-rooted history. . . . The final feeling that remained in me

[when I finished reading] was a hurtful, well-grounded, and rightful feeling of rebellion in the form of "we need to fight against this."

Yasemin further explained this impact of the book in our conversation:

> Yasemin (interview): Having read the book, I now recognize what I am exactly up against much better and I see that virginity is something that needs to be taken more seriously. After all, I'm 22 years old; I only have 22 years of experience with living with this norm. But seeing that its creation goes so far back in history and that it doesn't lose force but continues only by changing form gives me goose bumps. I can say that seeing all that has inspired me in my participation in the women's movement.

In a similar vein, Müjgan noted,

> Müjgan (diary): This and other similar books are particularly valuable and very necessary because they show us our history, how we have survived that history, and what we have been struggling against. . . . *Bekâret* constantly made me think of this: Over so many years, issues like virginity have been passed on like a recipe from Avicenna to the Pope, then to the Minister of Health here. They have come to this day by systematically being nurtured by religions, patriarchies, nationalisms, and other similar conservative thought climates, which have closed ranks in ways that cannot be achieved in anything else. So, this will not change in one stroke. However, although everyday women among us lose their lives in the wheels of this system that grinds women, it is empowering to know what we are up against because that knowledge sheds light on our search for solutions.

These insightful remarks highlight that by reframing virginity as a transculturally and transhistorically systematic and persistent form of gender injustice, *Bekâret* provided its readers with "coherence, explanation, and moral condemnation," a key element of a full-fledged critical consciousness (Mansbridge, "Making of Oppositional," 5). In doing so, it helped them redefine virginity as a non-trivial issue that required urgent collective and cross-border feminist attention.

*Bekâret* appears to have transformed the readers' consciousness also by complicating it with a somewhat intersectional approach and thus changing the parameters of feminist discourse and action against virginity. Although Blank's analytical framework is not consistently intersectional, since her virginity narratives are mainly centered on gender, her occasional discussions of the interweavings of gender with sexuality, class, race, and religion in the symbolic configurations and material appearances of virginity seem to have opened the readers' eyes to previously unnoticed faces of virginity. Among these discussions, which are also highlighted in my preface in relation to Turkey, virginity's interconnections with heteronormativity and capitalism seem to have impacted the readers the most:

> Selma (diary): What interested me the most and suddenly turned on a light in my mind was the part that revealed how virginity normativized heterosexuality. I had never thought that. Also, the part that argued that virginity was a parameter measuring a woman's value in the capitalist marriage market turned my attention once again to the necessity of refuting virginity.

Then, although *Bekâret* did not drastically transform the readers' consciousness, it obviously encouraged them to see virginity in intersectionally complex and nuanced analytical frameworks.[10]

Building on the ideational tools supplied by *Bekâret*, the participants began questioning the massive ideological hold of virginity also on their selves. In fact, several of them realized during the study that they had wrongly assumed to have subjectively defeated or overcome the virginity norm:

> Bilge Su (interview): Seriously, it almost doesn't single out any class or "intellectual progress" but seizes everyone from somewhere. This virginity terror is something that we absolutely encounter; you know, something we can cope with, but also something we have to cope with.

To put another way, *Bekâret*'s readers noticed that even women who had built up feminist sensitivities about patriarchal biopolitics were not exempt from the tight grip of the virginity norm:

> Selma (blog): Although I believed that personally I had already solved the virginity problem, I realized while reading the book that I had not solved anything. There was so much about virginity that I didn't know or was misinformed about.[11]

*Bekâret* activated the readers' confrontations with the fact that they had internalized the hegemonic virginity ideology so deeply that even if they intellectually defied it, they were still not immune to it experientially and affectively. In Defne's words, the book "woke me up from my sleep and brought me to my senses" (diary). These realizations about virginity's strong hold over the readers' psyches, which further emphasized the gravity of the problem, were also facilitated by Blank's strategic, frequent use of thought-provoking questions, as discussed in chapter 3. This stylistic feature of the book functioned to raise readers' curiosity and draw them into the narratives. For instance, Ece said,

Ece (diary): I frequently underlined the exploratory questions that Blank asked before beginning new topics. For example, "even if we could define virginity, this takes us to another, more interesting question: why we care about it so much."[12] Questions like this were exactly what I had missed to ask [about virginity].

It was in reference to this self-reflexive effect of the book that several participants noted the book's potential to raise critical awareness on virginity, encouraging its readers to imagine virginity otherwise (e.g., as non-existent or non-normative). Moreover, *Bekâret* goes on to ask, "how can we change it?" and invites readers to devise concrete strategies of action to reform or overthrow the virginity regime:

Nil (diary): The book brought up some questions, the most important of which was, "how can we prevent this?" I'd thought about this before, but I had not dwelled on its answers so much.

Bilge Su (interview): I have very few ideas in mind regarding what can be done against virginity violence but now I certainly know that we need to think about it much more.

Defne, who emphasized that political struggles could only begin with one's understanding of the history of a problem and their subjective positionality within that history, pointed out,

Defne (interview): I seriously realized how much value has been attributed to virginity and what a huge problem it has been turned into in Turkey. Honestly, I've begun thinking how I'll help demolish this.

These remarks suggest that by stressing the magnitude of the problem and presenting the massive history behind its making, *Bekâret* encouraged readers to prioritize virginity in their demands of social change. In this process, their initial recognition of virginity as a problem became replaced by a more complete understanding of it as a pressing issue that required immediate organized political response.

While *Bekâret* revealed virginity's gravity, some readers critiqued it for failing to incorporate in its historical narratives western women's strategies of resistance and not providing repertoires of action to help them devise local resistance. Although the book equipped them with subversive knowledges and inspired them to fight against virginity, it did not offer them tangible plans of action. Given the sense of urgency that comes with Turkey's virginity politics due to the country's high rates of femicide,[13] this gap seems to have curtailed the book's political power in the readers' eyes. For instance, Selma, who was disappointed with the lack of an explicitly activist agenda in the book, said:

> Selma (interview): I was expecting the book to be also about political methods. . . . I was expecting it to pump us up and say, "Go girls!" So, I felt like the book wasn't written with that kind of enthusiasm, but it is actually up to us to produce political strategies, to develop activisms from it. I realized [in the focus group] that mine was a little bit of laziness in thinking.

Even though some readers reported discontent with the book's lack of repertoires of action, they also noted that it provided them with a much-needed, discursive groundwork—symbolic repertoires of knowledges and interpretive frameworks—upon which actions of resistance could be built. As Selma explained in her blog, "Blank's claim that 'virginity doesn't exist' offers a useful ground to destroy the control and self-control that virginity brings on women." Similarly, Dicle and Müjgan, who were curious about how western women achieved such a big social change added:

> Dicle (focus group): Of course, there are still lots of problems in the west; Blank does present those up-to-date examples. But eventually there has also been a big change in the west. I mean, Blank could have perhaps presented that struggle more vividly. Then, somebody who reads this book could say, "I too can do this and that." . . . There isn't much in the book that is directly related to political struggle. But I think there is quite a bit in the form of critical knowledge from which people who are already fighting against virginity violence could benefit from.

> Müjgan (focus group): By writing this book, Blank has tried to swim against the currents, to go against a brick wall that everybody has been swiftly bonding around us for centuries. . . . In a world where men have been eagerly laying bricks and imprisoning us in it, she has given us a formula about the mortar that keeps those bricks together so we can rip apart the bricks.

In appreciating the book for providing an epistemological ground, or a "recipe," upon which tangible political strategies can be produced, *Bekâret*'s readers seem to agree with Blank saying (*Virgin*, 256):

> Books like this one . . . are a crucial element of change. Information about the full spectrum of virginity issues and their history, even the awareness that one can study it at all, that virginity *has* a history, is an indispensable weapon when dealing with a social principle that is most often asserted as an irreducible fact of nature.

In fact, in her review, Bayraktar cites this very sentence concurring that *Bekâret* equips us with discursive tools of resistance against virginity violence ("Bekaretin"):

> What needs to be done is to resist with this weapon patriarchal society's values that generate virginity violence against women . . . and to start the process of redefining virginity in our cultures. Emek Ergun initiated this process by translating with a feminist consciousness Hanne Blank's book and it is up to those who oppose patriarchal configurations reproduced through virginity discourses to ensure the continuation of this process and prevent wrongful deaths.

In addition to finding *Bekâret* useful for providing an "actionable" discursive groundwork against virginity violence, several readers proposed general tactics to address Turkey's virginity issue, among which creating a large-scale critical awareness and public opinion seemed to prevail—and *Bekâret*, particularly the translator's preface with its local focus, was deemed invaluable in this process. Yet, devising such far-reaching and indeterminate actions did not alleviate questions regarding the specifics of "what to do." For instance, Çise talking about the paragraph on the reasons of why some hymens bleed and others do not during the first penetration said (Blank, *Virgin*, 36; *Bekâret*, 87–88):

> Çise (diary): Now, this is a very important sentence. . . . We need to spread out this knowledge but how? We need to reach people who would be transformed by this knowledge, who would question themselves . . . But how?

Similarly, Bilge Su, who underlined the necessity of carrying out more systemic interventions—for instance, into the curriculum design and execution of medical education and training—but was skeptical about the use of top-down (read: potentially arrogant) "raising awareness" methods, said:

> Bilge Su (interview): We need to create a "public opinion" on what virginity is or is not and prioritize the question how to do that . . . The thing we call "honor murders" is already in the feminist agenda. But we need to do more steady work on virginity. We need to do more about it but how? What to do; how to do it? . . . I think some people need to make this their job.

Several readers shared Bilge Su's stance that something had to be done on virginity in Turkey, but it was precisely the missing what's and how's of that something that seemed to have brought some to a temporary mental state of political standstill. While some of the participants remained optimistic with regard to such a major question and found hope and confidence in the sheer existence of the book, in the somewhat "progressive" history of the west, and in their commitment to and faith in Turkey's feminist movement, others reported feeling worried about the slow pace of social change on virginity politics, fearful or overwhelmed in the face of virginity's massive ideological power, angry about the violent history of virginity, and powerless due to not being able to stop it themselves. Although some of these affective states, especially hope and anger, are essential for political action, others, such as fear and sense of powerlessness, could work against it if not accompanied or replaced by feelings of courage and belief in collective power. The participants who experienced such debilitating effects drew on three sources to get through the standstill and feel more ready to act: (1) the book's geopolitically collective voice that emphasized virginity politics beyond borders; (2) the translator's preface, which provided readers not only with epistemic and affective motivation through its ardent voice, but also with practical policy propositions, such as initiating large-scale training programs on virginity (and the hymen) for medical personnel; (3) the focus group discussions, which solidified the participants' belief in feminist solidarity and helped them feel "not alone":

Bilge Su (diary): Although the preface didn't add new questions to my own questions, they got more refined and more ideas emerged in my mind in regard to "what to do and how to do it."

Gülümser (focus group): I really liked the part in the preface saying, "We need to begin somewhere—not to remain silent, to ask questions, to criticize, to make the invisible visible, to destroy and rebuild."[14] I mean, to me *Bekâret* means exactly that.

Dicle (interview): I felt the same sense of unity while reading the book as well and it made me feel good. . . . And as it turns out, I was right from the beginning; the focus group gave me this feeling that I wasn't alone in this. This is a positive thing. It arises in one the desire to fight.

Ayşegül (interview): The group discussion both solidified my knowledge and made me realize that I wasn't alone. I mean, there are women who think like me and we have been through similar experiences. In fact, we can get the same feeling while reading the book too.

Gülümser (diary): The book made me so angry. You can't help but get angry. . . . But it also made me happy. I felt that I wasn't alone, and I felt empowered by that.

The sense of "I am not alone," which is emphasized in numerous diaries and is an essential affect of political collectivity, appears to have been initially triggered by the readers' interactions with the feminist translator and author, whose distinct, yet cooperatively coalescing voices created a sense of conversation among women brought together in their common pursuit of virginity resistance. Moreover, inspired—or "pumped up" as several readers described—by this emotive effect and invested with greater epistemological and political confidence on the issue, the readers not only felt eager to share their new subversive stances on virginity with others, but also reported incidents of initiating constructive dialogues with romantic partners, friends, family members, acquaintances, and even strangers. Lorin, for example, mentioned a conversation she had on the plane with a male gynecologist (a stranger), who was also a faculty member at a major medical school in Turkey:

> Lorin (diary): I explained to him that doctors have a big responsibility to raise awareness about the fact that virginity is nonsense. I told him, "Since it was medical scientists who back in the day shot us all women to hell, it is now your job to clean this mess up." He agreed with me.[15]

Ayşegül and Defne also noted *Bekâret's* "restless," dialogic energy that facilitates its readers to act:

> Ayşegül (diary): While reading the book I felt the need to share everything I learned. I was beginning every conversation with "Did you know that . . . ?" and then the topic would take over at home. In this sense, it became a book that entered my life, enhanced it, and made me share.

> Defne (focus group): I think it is up to us whether this book will become politically transformative. You know, when I talk to my friends, recommend the book to them, and when they read it, their thoughts will necessarily change. It has changed many things in me as well. . . . So, it is not that somebody will come up and create a reform. It is me, my friends, the people whom I tell about the book that will together make this social change.

In the follow-up interviews, the participants shared other similar cases of sharing *Bekâret's* insights, which shows that the book's dialogic energy continues even years after the readers' first encounters with it. Moreover, by now, the book—currently in its 7th printing—has been taken up in numerous college courses and feminist reading and discussion groups (e.g., the İzmir branch of Amargi held such a meeting in May 2010), which has expanded the book's political reach—or its life beyond its textuality:

> Nil (interview): You know, after reading some books, you leave them behind. It did not happen with this one. With this book, there is no notion of "Yes, I read it and now it is finished." This book inflames you, prompts you to do something so there is no "the end."

*Bekâret*'s "moving" effect overflows its pages because it activates in readers the desire to act. That is, the book turns a private taboo subject into a public matter that now calls for political action. This catalytic force becomes *Bekâret*'s "truth" as Rosi Braidotti explains it: "The 'truth' of a text is somehow never really 'written.' Neither is it contained within the signifying space of the book." And she adds, "the 'truth' of a text resides rather in the kind of outward-bound interconnections or relations that it enables, provokes, engenders and sustains" (Braidotti, *Transpositions*, 171).

Indeed, *Bekâret*'s "dialogically invitational" quality was regarded as invaluable by most participants particularly because of the difficulty of talking about virginity, which constitutes a major taboo in Turkey. For example, Şeyma, who described the book as "a book woven with taboos," said that thanks to the book, she "could talk about things that under usual circumstances she could not so easily." Yasemin said in the interview that the book enabled its readers to put such a "private and intimate" matter into words and in doing so facilitated conversations about it. Defne also noted,

> I noticed that I hesitated to open up about virginity even when I talked to my friends. I realized that nobody would actually bring up this topic in our conversations. Then I realized that I myself never brought it up either. I took notice of my fears, of my prejudices like, "how would they judge me?" But after reading the book and bringing the topic up in discussions with my friends, I saw that they responded to it really well because it was their problem, too. You know, we have a problem here that is related to our gender and this pressure that the society puts on us doesn't look fair to us. And I realized that my friends saw it in the same critical way.

Both the readers and reviewers' frequent use of "taboo" in their reading narratives illustrates that *Bekâret* has subverted virginity's taboo status by turning it into an openly speakable issue. So, the book has intervened into the very plot of public secrecy that has been hatched around the concept. *Bekâret*'s taboo-disruption seems to have been regarded by the readers as an inspirational act of defiance and as an opportunity, which, they reported, deserves to be continued with other critical epistemological projects (e.g., books, articles, and pamphlets), consciousness raising practices and alternative cultural products (e.g., workshops, documentaries, and art projects), and subjective and collective forms of protests. In other words, the participants believed that the book would contribute to the development of large-scale resistance with its "ripple effects" on multiple fronts of taboo breaking. This process was perhaps best described by Gülümser, who in the first focus group session said,

I think *Bekâret*'s effect in Turkey will be great. Even what we are doing right here, right now is a political effect of the book and what we do when we go home and talk about it is also the rippling of its waves. It is a similar thing when we recommend the book to our friends. This critical consciousness spreads little by little. It is a long, difficult process. So, each of us is like a seed; it will gradually spread out in this way. . . . For example, *The Vagina Monologues* was first written in English and then its Turkish translation was done, and recently we created a Turkish book on the sexual experiences of women with the title, *İşte Böyle Güzelim . . .* [That's How It Goes My Sweetie . . . ].[16] . . . I mean it spreads out like that. You know, perhaps Emek will take this book and write a book about its appearance in here. Then, someone in India will read the book and write its Indian version. It will grow in this way like a chain. That's why it's important.

Here, Gülümser is highlighting that translation is indispensable to feminist politics not only because it enables cross-border exchanges of stories and theories of resistance, but also because it provides models of epistemic resistance and inspires more knowledge production, particularly on taboo subjects that are closed off to questioning. Similarly, *Bekâret* seems to stimulate epistemic crosspollination—or "ripple effects" in Gülümser's words—despite, or perhaps because of, virginity's tabooness.

In fact, virginity's taboo status appears to have created an opportunity for the book to stand out and arouse curiosity in Turkey. *Bekâret* defies the tabooness of virginity not only by speaking of it and inviting others to do so, but also by its very material existence. By "material existence," I refer to two corporeal, performative aspects of the book: first, the symbolic value of its sheer physical existence as a book on virginity, and second, its visual display of subversion on its cover page with the ambiguous flower/blood image and the salient title containing the word "virginity."

Indeed, the participants often discerned *Bekâret* as a traveling cultural artifact breaking a local taboo and perceived the person holding the book in *her* hands as an unruly taboo breaker:

Milena (diary): For conservatives . . . forget about discussing this topic, even the fact that a book has been written and published on virginity is alarming.

Ece (diary): For some people, even the fact that a book has been written on virginity is disturbing—for instance, my mother! She wasn't happy at all when she saw me reading the book. So, the book doesn't in fact have to do much to disturb!

The disturbance materially caused by the book also came up in the second focus group session, where Ayşe, who deliberately displayed the book in public places and received "gazes of disapproval," said,

> Ayşe (focus group): I think the book would contribute to the feminist movement even if it stayed on a bookshelf and we did not come together for this project, but then it would certainly do it more slowly.

*Bekâret*'s substantiality performs in readers' hands—especially women's—a textual embodiment and articulation of (inferred) intervention into Turkey's normative landscape and takes on a life of rebellion against virginity. The very possession of the book by a gendered body whose sexuality is assumed to be under control of the virginity regime seems to generate discomfort among bystanders precisely because the embodied connection between her body and the book symbolizes the fact that the untouched and untouchable concept of virginity is being shamelessly touched now. This is why several participants and reviewers described the book's materiality as "ironic." The Turkish title, *Bekâretin "El Değmemiş" Tarihi*, [The "No Hands Touched" History of Virginity] not only invites, perhaps even entices, the readers into touching that history, but also itself presents physical evidence to having been touched. Moreover, this forbidden act of touching is perpetrated by subjects who are systematically expected to be properly sexed and gendered, part of which requires their submission to virginity's tabooness (do not question it) and normativity (comply with its rules). In this sense, the (imagined or real) act of touching involved in reading *Bekâret* is threatening for the heteropatriarchal economy that upholds virginity. So, to achieve the above-mentioned "irony," the book does not really require an actual person holding it, as even the *imagined* daring touch of a woman can be sufficient to upset.

The first disruptive effect of *Bekâret*'s materiality is closely related to the second one involving its cover page. First of all, it seems that the title, by piecing the word "no hands touched" together with "virginity," functioned as the most immediately noticeable clue for the book's subversive stance. In fact, it is in response to the provoking title that Deniz, for instance, asked in her diary before reading the book: "Are we embracing an institution that we actually don't know?" Others also noted:

> Çise (diary): What a great title, isn't it? The adjective, "no hands touched" that is both arresting and appropriate is so ironic! Doesn't it give us clues about the spirit and contents of the book? Isn't it a sign that the book will question taboos and shake the foundations of our knowledges?

Lorin (focus group): I actually bought the book with the expectation that it had a critical view on virginity, which was implied by the title's "no hands touched" emphasis.

Perhaps the most intriguing illustration of the title's embodied subversive force is seen at the end of Gülümser's diary, where she draws the contour of her hand and signs her name under it, as if rebelliously declaring, "I have touched my hands on the no-hands-touched history of virginity."

Several readers also noted that the "no hands touched" reference aroused their curiosity and interest in the book, especially when combined with the flower/blood image on the cover:

Nil (diary): The image is critical and impressive. It makes me ask "What is in a drop of blood that makes it so important?"

Dilan (interview): I was carrying the book around in my hands all the time. And because of its cover and title, it was drawing everyone's attention. These were not long conversations. They usually ended with the question, "would you lend me the book when you finish it?"

This dialogic potential of the cover is precisely why some participants reported strategically displaying the book in public spaces. Milena, for example, narrated that she first heard about *Bekâret* from a fellow conference participant who "placed the book, which she called her reference book, deliberately on the front row of her bookshelf in her office on campus so that everyone would see it."

Although almost all the readers reported that the cover image indicated "virginity blood," their interpretations of and emotional reactions to it varied. While some took it as the blood associated with "virginity loss," others mentioned its association with the blood of honor-based violence against women—blood emanating from the absence of the "first blood." Yet, correlating with virginity's configuration as "woman," they all thought in unison that the image represented "women's blood." Variably, the image was found horrifying, irritating, sad, brave, realistic, and striking depending on the subjective and/or social contingencies it reminded them of. Ayşegül, for instance, wrote,

Ayşegül (diary): I first saw the book at my sister's. Initially, its title drew my attention. As I reached for it, I noticed the blood on it. My hand hesitated for a few seconds. It was as if that blood would smear on my hand, but just two seconds later I held the book in my hands, and it aroused great curiosity in me. So, it's a very brave cover. It really is our *untouched* history.

Implied by this remark is that virginity's tabooness is so strong in Turkey that it can even generate a bodily reflex to not touch the book—and by extension the counter-history it tells. Ayşegül later added:

> Ayşegül (interview): That hesitation is in fact a reflection of the problems that we all have generally experienced. You know, regardless of the fact that we identify as feminists today, virginity is unfortunately part of the codes that our families have instilled in us and no matter how much we claim that we have surpassed those codes, they still remain in us a little bit.

*Bekâret*'s taboo defying face was actually so prominent that several participants reported refraining from reading it in public spaces (including home when shared with parents); covering up the book around others; and feeling embarrassed, irritated, or angry due to the reactions they received:

> Leylak (diary): I liked the cover image very much. But when I took the book with me to school so that I could read it while supervising exams, I realized that I was a bit embarrassed by it. . . . I really wanted some of my friends to see it. But the fact that after seeing the book, some of them giggled, got surprised, and pursed their lips embarrassed me; I got mad at myself.

> Ece (diary): I was careful not to read the book around others. For example, I couldn't read it on the bus, on the ferry, or at work. This was more because of the possibility of getting negative reactions than actually having gotten any. It is nothing other than my own biases.

Similarly, Ekin, who visited her parents while reading the book, wrote,

> Ekin (diary): I am with my family. Last night, I realized that the book I am holding in my hands is titled *The Untouched History of Virginity*. But what if my father sees it?! Forget about reading it in sight, even if I stay in my room and read it there, my mom will bring fruit to my room and see the cover and then ask me numerous questions mixed with fear . . . although she knows that I am not a virgin. I had to tell her because of an illness. It was a big crisis for her. . . . That's why yesterday I decided to cover the book. For a while I couldn't find anything to cover it with and now the book is in my hands covered with a paper bag. . . . If my dad realizes that the book is covered, he will just say, "Ah she's reading *The Communist Manifesto*, or so." I hope.

This unsettling effect of the book's cover was also discussed in the first focus group, where the participants mentioned that carrying the book was understood as a public proclamation of "I am sexually active" or "I am not a virgin." These anecdotes suggest that *Bekâret*'s materiality defies not only virginity's tabooness, but also the virginity norm itself. Such defiance took its toll on some readers who, in addition to the cognitive labor of meaning making, also had to cope with such an affective burden while reading *Bekâret*. Therefore, opting for "camouflage" or "eschewal" to concentrate on the book is both an understandable and a retaliatory move since these readers strategically avoided the dialogic repercussions of the book's materiality to enhance their political consciousnesses on virginity. As Müjgan, who read the book mostly on the bus on her way to work and back home, explained,

> Müjgan (interview): The cover was drawing people's attention, especially men's. . . . You know, a cover like that draws a lot of attention. It has a very striking visual. So, I was like, "I can't deal with you right now, I'm very busy," and I put the book inside the notebook [diary]. . . . I was like, "Back off, I am reading here the story of ages; go away, I can't argue with you right now about the cover. You know what, I'm reading the history of what you have done to me!"

Obviously, even the seemingly passive and evasive act of concealing *Bekâret* and guarding against public confrontation was actually an act of covert but willful resistance in the face of a hostile social setting that did not welcome any critical consciousness on virginity, which, however, continued to develop precisely because of that act of evasion. In Sara Ahmed's words, "a dismissal can be an opportunity. It is because willfulness is assumed to stand out, to be so striking, that it becomes possible to act willfully by not standing out at all. She might be plotting" (*Feminist Life*, 83). Then, regarding its disturbing materiality, *Bekâret* either itself became a "feminist killjoy" through public display or secret reading—providing its readers with alternative virginity theories and knowledges, enabling them to confront its systematicity and gravity, stimulating the readers affectively, facilitating critical self-reflections and dialogues, and preparing them to devise and take political actions to end virginity.

Finally, *Bekâret* has also indirectly called for local political action by confirming and boosting preexisting feminist protest discourses on body politics. Indeed, many of the readers drew on the prevailing "my body belongs to me" and "end violence against women" rhetorics of Turkey's feminist movement in their discussions, which were infused with terms like *erkek egemenliği* (male domination), *cinsiyet ayrımcılığı* (gender discrimination), *ataerkil denetim* (patriarchal control), *eril dil* (masculine language), *hetero/seksizm* (hetero/sexism), *cinsel özgürlük* (sexual liberation), *kadınların metalaştırılması* (commodification of women), etc.—many of which, by the way, are linguistic products of translation. These terms are well entrenched in local feminist vocabulary and are regularly repeated in both written and oral accounts of the readers. The following diary entry by Sezen illustrates several elements of the local feminist discourse and their interactions with the critical insights offered by *Bekâret*:

> Sezen (diary): The existence of virginity, I mean the existence of this word and this notion has always bothered me because it is attributed only to women and it always finds an equivalence in masculine language; that while [initially] not feeling any insecurities about and alienation from their bodies, women are pushed by masculine language and this concept into such psychological states; and that only men have a say in it. When I think about a woman living her life without this concept, I feel like she wouldn't be possessed by any hesitations or moral dilemmas about her body because virginity is nothing but a concept that has been "made up" by manhood, by the patriarchal system to make women docile and keep them under control.

The comment shows that *Bekâret*'s readers not only merged the linguistic and discursive repertoire of local feminism with that of the imported text, but also questioned the political power of hetero/sexist language and asked: What if virginity did not exist in language and thought, both of which are embodied and experienced by gendered/sexed bodies as real? This is why, while incorporating *Bekâret* into the local feminist canon, the readers also demanded social change in the domain of language:

> Deniz (interview): Language is really, how to say it, quite cunning if you will. It makes us learn so many problematic things by heart without our being aware of their falsity. It actually is something that shapes us. That's why I certainly think that language should be changed as well.

These critiques of "male language" seem to have been particularly facilitated by the translator's preface, where I discuss my specific linguistic interventions during translation and raise issues with the patriarchal vocabulary of Turkish (for instance, my translation of "the hymen" as "*himen*"):

> Kırmızı (diary): The translator is rightly using the word *himen* against the hegemonic heterosexist and patriarchal discourse. But I believe we fall in the same trap when we use the word "virginity." Hegemonic ideologies establish their domination in our minds through the words they define. And when we speak with its words, it is like we think in that way.[17]

> Bilge Su (diary): What we see in the translator's explanations, that is, critiquing terms that are covered under the mask of "neutrality" and legitimated by the guise of "expertise" is very important for resisting the "normalization" pressure of hegemonic discourses.

Dicle (diary): *Bekâret* is definitely a biased book and it should be so. I think unbiasedness serves nothing but the dominant. These terms must be critiqued so that we come to understand why we think what we think the way we think it and throw off these hegemonic templates.

Interestingly, several readers described *Bekâret*'s translation as "biased," which, however, was construed as "a positive prejudice" and a source of political reassurance and anxiety-relief for them. These readers repeatedly noted that the feminist translator "made a big difference" and enabled them to "trust" and "embrace" the traveling book, to "surrender" it, to feel affirmed rather than disregarded or turned invisible by its language, and to focus on the epistemological discourses of the book instead of lingering on the linguistic details looking for a hidden hetero/sexist agenda behind every word. And the same readers, following the translator's interventionist sociolinguistic stance, also highlighted the significance of undermining hetero/sexist language and cultivating a feminist language that did not disregard, alienate, and misname women's bodies and their gendered embodied experiences.

In short, despite its apparent exclusive focus on the western configurations of virginity, *Bekâret* has managed to nourish its feminist readers epistemologically and politically and engage with preexisting local feminist (and mainstream) virginity discourses. So, the translation has provided readers with a transcultural contact zone, where their encounters with a traveling other have encouraged them to see their situated selves and conditions of embodied existence with a different critical lens. Indeed, after learning about "what has happened to us?" in regard to virginity, the readers can now not only answer it with legitimate historical knowledges, but also further ask "what to do now so that we end it?" Both questions have serious implications of gender justice and social change.

Moreover, due to the strategic localization practices involved in the feminist making of *Bekâret*, the book's political capacity to intervene in the local virginity politics seems to have increased. Several factors and actors enabled that: (1) the traveling book's fascinating topic, which not only carried substantial sociocultural weight in Turkey as a taboo, but also had already been problematized by local feminists to a certain extent; (2) the book's non-confirmative virginity focus, which fit readily into the existing feminist discourses of body politics (and femicide) that constituted one of the top concerns on the contemporary feminist agenda; (3) the way Blank wrote and composed the book, which apparently made it relevant and relatable for the feminist audience in Turkey; (4) the translator's explicit claim of a feminist identity both for herself and for the book, which forged an immediate political link between the imported book's contents and locally embedded feminist discourses; (5) the translator's preface, which performed the first cross-cultural epistemological activation of the book's feminist discourses and secured trust among feminist readers; (6) the cover design, which drew on local virginity codes and made the book directly appeal to readers in Turkey. In short, the multi-agentic project of remaking *Virgin* in Turkish seems to have achieved its initial goal of forging in Turkey a more "mature" feminist discourse, consciousness, and repertoire of action on virginity through its subversive knowledges, deviant materiality, and transgressive language. In the next chapter, I explore whether the transnational goals of the translation in regard to building cross-border connectivities of resistance were similarly accomplished in the traveling book's encounters with the feminist readers.

## CHAPTER 5

# Feminist Translation as a Praxis of Cross-Border Interconnectivity

In knowing differences and particularities, we can better
see the connections and commonalities because no border
or boundary is ever complete or rigidly determining. The
challenge is to see how differences allow us to explain the
connections and border crossings better and more accurately,
how specifying difference allows us to theorize universal
concerns more fully. It is this intellectual move that allows for
my concern for women of different communities and identities
to build coalitions and solidarities across borders.

—Mohanty, *Feminism Without Borders*, 226

In her much-acclaimed book, *Friction: An Ethnography of Global Connection*, Anna Tsing asks, "Global connections are everywhere. So how does one study the global" (1)? This chapter attends to this foundational, yet understudied question of transnationality and further asks, how do feminists practice transnational connections, eye-to-eye dialogues, and egalitarian collaborations across and beyond borders that are infused with racial fears, nationalistic defense mechanisms, orientalist arrogances, and colonial cruelties? Conceiving translation as a key site of "friction" between the subjective, the local, and the global, the chapter argues that it is in those messy, unequal, unpredictable, and creative interactions across differences and borders navigated, negotiated, and mediated in/by translation that transnational feminist connectivities materialize. The analyses here illustrate how ethically accountable and politically empowering translational feminist connectivities can be established along the colonial fault lines of the "west vs east" order, despite its fantasies of irreconcilable differences, uncompromising oppositions, and insurmountable gulfs. In an intensely antagonistic world, documenting the possibility of such justice-driven connectivities is even more urgent. This is what the chapter offers: post-oppositional lessons in/of cross-border inter-connectivity.

By shifting the analytical gear from the local to the global and exploring the translational travel of a western feminist text as a case study of cross-border contact, the chapter explores the potentials of transnational feminism. Hence, examining the ways in which the feminist virginity discourses of a substantially US-American book have crossed the Atlantic and landed in Turkey in translation, the chapter reveals the crucial role that translation plays in inspiring transnational feminist solidarities. The chapter addresses the question, how did the feminist readers in Turkey relate to a book that had been written for western women about western virginities? In other words, how did *Bekâret*'s readers manage to build bridges between the virginity stories of the west and their own locally grounded virginity narratives and realities? Did they experience any geopolitical disjunctures in the reading process? If yes, how did they deal with the alienating effects of such disjunctures and overcome the geopolitical chasm? The first section argues that the readers first engaged in a comparative and accretive gesture of meaning making by reading their own virginity realities into the text to compensate for its limited geopolitical focus and build connective dialogic bridges between Turkey and the west. The readers critically compared the book's western contents with Turkey's virginity codes and practices and added that subjectively experienced local history into the text expanding its geopolitical boundaries. In the process, they both learned about western virginity regimes and critically reflected on their own. The second section discusses another reading strategy that the readers deployed to relate to the book's western contents—a two-tiered textual move that I call "differential universalization." This complex act of geopolitical bridging enabled the readers to imagine a common ground of virginity oppression and resistance across times and spaces. At the same time, the universalizing gesture is combined with a clear recognition of differences among women and their gender/sexuality realities. In doing so, the readers seem to have performed Hannah Arendt's vision of "commonality within difference" that manages not to replicate the hegemonic gesture of ethnocentric western feminisms, often captured in the catchphrase, "sisterhood is global" (Allen, "Solidarity," 106).

## Lesson 1: Comparative Accretion in Transcultural Bridging

*Virgin*'s travel from the United States to Turkey as *Bekâret* was marked from the very beginning by a geopolitical divide: the supposedly unbridgeable gulf orchestrated between the seemingly homogenous geographical entities of the east and the west. Given Turkey's disadvantaged position regarding the "west versus east" binary of the global imaginary as opposed to the United States' privileged status as the new empire, *Bekâret*'s production and receptions in Turkey provide a great opportunity to analyze the potentials and pitfalls of transnational feminism. As a book on western virginities written by a US-American author for an English-speaking western audience, *Virgin*'s Turkish feminist translation was a geopolitically risky project. The book's exclusive western focus could easily lend itself to immediate rejection in Turkey on the grounds of being a culturally irrelevant text[1] or an imperialist product disseminating western values (potentially "immoral" ones given the book's taboo-ridden theme and the dominant perception of western women as "sexually relaxed" and "promiscuous" in the dominant Turkish imaginary). Such dismissal would indicate the failure of my translation, which was envisioned not only as a feminist intervention into the local virginity codes, but also as a facilitator of transcultural contact and feminist dialogues. How did *Bekâret*'s readers respond to my feminist translation strategies, particularly my preface on the virginity politics of Turkey, which was designed to help them not only learn about the virginity realities of the west, but also reimagine their own virginity realities through the voice of the other, and in the process connect with the other in ways that were defined by neither assimilation nor self-silencing? In this section, I discuss a specific meaning-making strategy that the readers employed to achieve such transcultural bridging against all odds.

In the first focus group discussion, Leylak, raising a critique of *Bekâret*'s exclusive geohistorical focus on the western cartographies of virginity, said:

Leylak (focus group): I had really wanted to see the historical evolution of virginity. And I liked seeing that in the book but of course it only talks about the west. I would have liked to see a comparison with Islam, with the culture of Islam, because we live here, so I was also curious about the perspective from here. That's why I drew my own conclusions, you know like, it is such and such there, and such and such here.

In the second focus group discussion, Defne responded to another participant's critique of *Bekâret* for its lack of coverage on "eastern virginities":

Defne (focus group): We said that the book didn't talk about the east. Yes, correct, it doesn't speak of the east. But I already know the east; I recognize it from my own life. And I saw that although the west has overcome some chains [of oppression], they still continue on with these [norms]. As Ayşe just said, this [virginity terror] has continued collaterally [across cultures].

In the same group discussion, Yasemin added:

Yasemin (focus group): The book directly brings you to self-reflection. I mean, I don't want to perceive this book as—ultimately, yes, it is telling the history of the west and it can, and it is already precious just doing that. I mean it doesn't need to include absolutely everything. In this respect, it is also precious because it brings us to ask questions within/among [ourselves].

Finally, in the third group session, Deniz responded to the debate on whether the western scope of the book was an "orientalist reflex" on the part of the American author, or whether it was an unavoidable consequence of the limitations of her expertise or research area:

Deniz (focus group): I read this book as one perception of virginity created in another culture, in another geography, under different conditions, through other religious, sociological lenses etc. . . . I read it as a work of cultural transfer, and I wanted to do that [comparison] with other societies. I think seeing the difference was just as negating for virginity as anything else.

These comments point at the most common strategy that *Bekâret*'s feminist readers used to make the book's seemingly distant narratives meaningful, relevant, and useful in the sociocultural context of Turkey. The readers deployed the book's debiologizing gesture to relate to the western virginity narratives and eventually, in Deniz's words, negated virginity both "at home" and "abroad." Indeed, as a result of the cross-border activation of that debiologizing gesture, neither the west's virginity narratives nor those of Turkey remained untouched. With that comparative and connectionist gesture, *Bekâret* turned into a common critical ground where the virginity stories told by the book and added by the readers had the opportunity to meet, facilitating cross-cultural association as well as repudiation.

I call this method "comparative accretion," during which the readers not only accepted the book's invitation to attend to the distinctive virginity history of the west, but also invited the book to attend to the virginity realities of their own cultural landscape, be it defined as Turkey, the east, or the Middle East. Leylak's "drawing her own conclusions" about the east, Defne's "recognition and addition of eastern virginities" to the book, Yasemin's "self-reflection within" through the book's critical gaze, and Deniz's "negation of virginity" by both reiterating the debiologizing gesture and underlining the cross-cultural differences in virginities across borders all illustrate that the readers dealt with the book's geohistorical shortcomings by embracing its subversive epistemological stance and comparatively expanding it with their own virginity truths framed in the semantics of local feminism. In other words, by comparing different virginity regimes, the readers revised their frame of reference and added their locally grown virginity epistemes to the book, which is the politically transformative moment of "defamiliarization" in Susan Stanford Friedman's terms ("Why Not Compare," 38):

> To learn through comparison that others see things differently is to rec-
> ognize the constructedness of one's own frame of reference. Such defa-
> miliarization of "home" through engagement with the "other" is often the
> cornerstone of transcultural political analysis. In other words, one effect of
> comparing cultures is to call into question the standards of the dominant
> precisely because it is unveiled as *not* universal (emphasis original).

This reading strategy is like the expansive reading practices discussed in Chapter 3. Yet, here, the expansive post-oppositional gesture is geographically outlined, as the readers, who are surrounded by discourses that foster distrust between "people of the east" and "people the west," are working to cross that divide. The fact that the western identity that is textually declared and epistemologically performed by *Bekâret* acts as a signifier of foreign (read: not of "us" and possibly against "us") makes the comparative reading strategies of *Bekâret*'s readers all the more fascinating because instead of giving in to the usual homogenizing antagonistic gesture of comparison resulting in the establishment of one party's superiority, theirs manifests the connectionist attitude of "wanting to learn from 'other' experiences that are not one's own" (Friedman, "Why Not Compare," 16–17).

A striking example of such a comparative accretion strategy is seen in Pembe's diary, which begins with her comments on her expectations from the book:

> Pembe (diary): I am curious about how virginity is experienced in the
> west, or more accurately, what kinds of experiences women are made to
> go through there due to virginity. Until now, the stories of women being
> stoned to death, the backwardness of countries practicing female circum-
> cision have been told in capital letters. I think now I will read about the
> sins of the west.

Pembe's comment, seemingly framed within the confines of the "west versus east" binary, sarcastically emphasizes the scarcity of critical knowledge
on western practices of "barbaric" gender conventions as opposed to the
abundance of imperialist and orientalist (feminist or not) discourses on such
violent practices taking place in non-western societies.[2] Yet, Pembe's compari-

son is not aimed at repeating the conceited cultural superiority complex of hegemonic western feminisms. That is, unlike orientalist discourses, Pembe's comparative reading strategy does not reproduce the hierarchical gesture of the west/east binary that puts western feminisms/women on a pedestal. Instead, she critiques that gesture and remains "open-minded and willing to learn from others" without presuming "*to know our politics; she waits to hear us articulate our politics in our own words, on our own terms—whatever those terms might be*" (Keating, *Transformation Now*, 41, emphasis original). Pembe welcomes the opportunity to learn about the west's virginity injustices so that she can imagine a relational, more complete global picture of violence against women, by adding the newly acquired virginity narratives of the west to those of the eastern geohistory that she has experientially accrued. Her comparison, then, is a destabilizing act of "transcontinental connection," as Rita Felski and Susan Stanford Friedman call it (*Comparison*, 1–2):

> Comparison, it is often said, is never neutral; it develops within a history of hierarchical relations. . . . Comparison can indeed be insidious, buttressing complacent attitudes in individuals or cultures while inculcating feelings of inadequacy or shame in others. But acts of comparing are also crucial for registering inequalities and for struggles against the unjust distribution of resources. Comparison is central to the analysis of world systems, transcontinental connections, and interculturalism, not only in the current phase of globalization but throughout human history. Moreover, comparison does not automatically authorize the perspective of those doing the comparison, but can also serve as a jolt to consciousness, initiating a destabilizing, even humbling, awareness of the limitedness and contingency of one's own perspective.

In her comparative reading of *Bekâret*, Pembe disrupts colonial narratives that too often recognize gender violences of the east yet fail to acknowledge those of the west. As a result of that interventionist cross-border meaning-making strategy, in Pembe's reading, the imaginary geographies of the east and the west become more similar than different, more connected than separated.

Clearly, then, when the west admits its own "sins" of violence against women, particularly with regard to issues designated as "of the east"—e.g., virginity violence or "honor-based violence"[3]—it helps alleviate the epistemological chasm forged between "the oppressed oriental woman" and "the liberated western woman." Such transcultural connective bridging is exactly what Pembe expects from *Bekâret* and she actively participates in that bridging by adding critical geopolitical questions and locally formed feminist insights into the text. The impact of this critical self/reflexive gesture, which undermines not only the global illusion of the "post-feminist west," but also the imperialist supposition of the "pre-feminist east," is also illustrated by Dicle's following diary comment:

Dicle (diary): [After reading the book] I've seen that we are not just the Other, that our problems have also been experienced in the west in very, very similar ways. I've come to understand that with the right kind of struggle it is not that difficult for us to overcome these issues and the way to do this is to fight against ignorance [about virginity].

Following her comparative reading, which reveals cross-cultural similarities as well as lessons to learn from, Dicle underlines epistemological activism ("fight against ignorance")—e.g., disseminating *Bekâret's* theories and knowledges that demedicalize virginity—as a necessary strategy to disrupt Turkey's virginity economy. Comparison, in this context, appears as a contact zone where words and ideas are exchanged and the potential to imagine otherwise is explored along with the epistemological accretion materializing in the process of reading. Hence, the immense political value of epistemic contact zones created by feminist translation and cross-border reading, where not just gender regimes but also local geographies and transcultural connectivities are imagined otherwise.

Following the diary entry quoted above, Pembe later adds:

Pembe (diary): Right now, I am reading Chapter 9. As I read on, I get more curious about the history of virginity in eastern societies. For instance, Blank says, in the history of Christianity, the convent and thus virginity could be a way of escape for women from enslavement that came along with marriage. Plus, the convent could even give women the opportunity to learn to read and write. But we know that such a situation would not be possible in eastern societies; I mean there are no convents. In fact, in the old times of Judaism, women were even forbidden from learning the Old Testament. So, did virginity oppress women more in Muslim and Jewish societies? This question is constantly on my mind and [as I read] I get more curious about it.

At first glance, Pembe's question on whether virginity oppressed women more in Muslim and Jewish societies might seem to replicate the orientalist logic that positions eastern/non-Christian women as more victimized by virginity in opposition to the western/Christian women. In fact, some may interpret the question as a moment of "self-doubt" in which Pembe turns the orientalist gaze back at her "eastern self" asking, "Perhaps I should reconsider the orientalist claim that casts the east as more violent and victimizing? Perhaps there is some truth to it?" Such an impulsive reiteration of orientalist convictions could indeed be easily triggered by the book's western identity, which is defined in and of itself in opposition to the east. However, Pembe's question, underlining that we do not know whether virginity regimes of eastern societies are more or less oppressive, highlights an epistemic gap and demands a response that is articulated outside the methodological habits of the orientalist imaginary.

In other words, Pembe's question does not reproduce an orientalist reflex because it is not a definitive statement, but a question—an invitation to transnationalize our epistemic repertoire on virginity. Her comparison does not engage in the colonial exposition of "quasi-masochistic self-denigration ('We will never be as good as you!')" (Stam and Shohat, "Transnationalizing Comparison," 124). Pembe asks for historically substantiated answers to her question, not ready-made orientalist claims packaged as innocent truths. When considered together with her earlier sarcastic comment about "reading the sins of the west," the question mark tactfully deployed in this second comment appears as an act of critical curiosity which invites cross-border comparisons that escape "the arrogance of centrism" (Radhakrishnan, "Why Compare," 23).

Pembe's remarks also indicate a pattern seen in several other diaries: that *Bekâret*'s in-depth analyses of "Christian virginities" trigger the emergence of a local feminist curiosity about the formulations of virginity in or in relation to Islam. The fact that *Bekâret* hardly ever mentions Islam (or religions other than Christianity and Judaism) seems to have made it challenging for the readers in Turkey to connect with the book's religious analyses. Leylak, for example, mentioned this challenge:

> Leylak (diary): I wish the book analyzed and interpreted the virginity issue within the history of Islam as well. Then, we could understand better the overall contemporary virginity perception, its views on women, and our [virginity] taboos.

However, instead of dismissing the traveling book for being "irrelevantly centered on Christianity," the participants took that challenge as an appeal to their locally demarcated analytic imaginations and epistemic repertoires and managed to build discursive bridges between different religious virginity realities while reading. *Bekâret*, then, also seems to have facilitated readings that challenged the conflation of religion and culture often elicited by secular western modes of thinking, whose orientalist motives are typically eager to conflate religion and culture, particularly those of the east, as if they are one and the same. In that regard, the readers' inquisitive remarks on Islam also reflect back to the west asking western feminists to rethink their coalescent understandings of culture and religion.

The readers could achieve such on-site bridging between different religious virginity codes partly because they perceived the male-centric logics and practices of institutionalized religions as shared across borders. Pembe, for instance, noted in her diary that all three monotheistic religions were born in the same heteropatriarchal geography, and thus, it was only reasonable that they shared many male-centric features. Yet, while the readers could draw broad parallels and general conclusions across religions and their gender norms, they remained curious about the epistemic particularities of Islam's take on virginity. And it is this curiosity that generates a cross-border feminist connectivity:

> Lorin (focus group): All these issues of virginity and sexuality, our relations with our bodies etc. are—yes, right, they have different cultural aspects. . . . So, it is all cultural, but this virginity issue is in fact very universal. The first sexual experience has been important everywhere in the world and in every religion, I mean in all monotheistic religions. . . . Indeed, this is universal, and we already know what's happening in Islam. I mean, actually, we don't of course know specifically; e.g., what was this and that prophet's [response on virginity], what was Ayşe's [one of Prophet Muhammad's wives]. We don't really know these. . . . But we could perhaps do some research about them to see what has been going on in these parts [of the world], in the east.

> Dîlan (diary): I expected the book would talk about the topic of virgin women in Islam and *houris* too [the beautiful virgins promised to Muslim men or male Muslim martyrs in paradise according to popular belief][4] and evaluate the standing of virginity in Islam.

In her diary, Dîlan even cited—but did not elaborate on—an unspecified religious source:

> Dîlan (diary): "Each of the Chosen Ones will marry seventy houris in addition to their wives on earth. Whenever he sleeps with a houri, he will find her a virgin. Besides, the penis of the Chosen One will never slacken."

Equipped with some knowledge on Islam, *Bekâret*'s readers cultivated a justified curiosity about different religious configurations of virginity beyond Christianity. They believed that revealing those would both help them gain a comprehensive, deeper understanding of the gender regime of their locality and help outline a more complete picture of virginity politics. Also, the readers added their commentaries—such as Dîlan's entry on *houris* that even included a quotation from an unidentified source—to the book's epistemological repertoire and stretched it out beyond its western scope.

The comparative attitude and the desire for more knowledge-making were expressed by all the participants and are clearly illustrated by the following excerpts from their written and oral narratives:

> Ece (diary): While reading about an issue that belonged to the west, I frequently asked myself, how is the situation in Turkey, why is it like that in Turkey? I think this could be written too.

> Defne (interview): So, there is a virginity concept in the book, and you learn that this and that happened in the west. But what is happening in my country? What has been forged here [about virginity] all this time or what has been done against it in my country?

> Milena (diary): As I was reading, I also from time to time found myself looking for a local language, a local example. I thought, how would this be articulated if a Turk wrote it? That is because we have numerous cases that could serve as a model on the subject matter.

While reading *Bekâret* with the comparative accretive lens, instigated by the book's limited geohistorical scope, yet epistemologically invitational tone, the readers critically reflected on the western virginity regime narrated in the book and the corresponding regime that reigned in Turkey. This simultaneous examination of the self and the other was also deliberately facilitated by the translator's preface, which pointed out both the experiential cultural differences and ideological transcultural commonalities between the virginity regime of Turkey and that of the west. In the process of such connectionist self-reflection, the readers focused particularly on two local issues that "served as a model on the subject matter," in Milena's words: the publicly proclaimed issue of "vaginismus," explained below, and honor-based violence against women, which to this day remains at the top of Turkey's feminist agenda.

While reading Chapter 5, "The Virgin and the Doctor," Pembe wrote,

> Pembe (diary): It is very interesting that a concept like "the disease of virgins"[5] that lasted till the first quarter of the 20th century has no visible effects today. As the author says, the most possible reasonable explanation [for the disease] is that the condition served a religious interest like Protestantism. Then, I am curious if the notion of "the disease of virgins" ever emerged in eastern societies. Obviously, the fact that there is not a single proverb [in Turkish] that could bring this condition to mind affirms the idea that in the larger eastern culture, which our society resembles, there has never been any perceptions like "the disease of virgins."

Indeed, Pembe is right. "The disease of virgins," which was considered a distinct medical disorder "for over five hundred years" in the west, has no known equivalence in Turkey's cultural or medical repertoires (Blank, *Virgin*, 65–70). Yet, *Bekâret*'s readers frequently spoke of another "medical disorder" that "troubled" many "virgin women" and thus could be deemed contemporary Turkey's "disease of virgins": vaginismus, which refers to "recurrent or persistent involuntary contraction of the perineal muscles surrounding the outer third of the vagina when vaginal penetration with penis, finger, tampon, or speculum is attempted" (Kabakçı and Batur, "Who Benefits," 277).[6] In popular belief, vaginismus is thought to be the case of the vagina being unable (or unwilling?) to let the penis in although in medical literature different types and stages are identified. Dogan writes, "Although vaginismus is thought to be the most common female psychosexual dysfunction in Turkey, the prevalence rate among the general population is unknown" ("Vaginismus," 186). The potential connection between vaginismus and the premarital virginity norm is well recognized in medical literature: "Vaginismus could be a culturally determined symptom of the female as a reaction against a long history of suppressing female sexuality and placing high value on female virginity" ("Vaginismus," 186).

Yet, unlike virginity, which is deemed a private taboo subject with the underlying normative assumption that women should not engage in premarital (hetero)sexual intercourse, vaginismus is perceived and handled in Turkey as an urgent public issue that threatens the institutions of (heterosexual) marriage and (heterosexual) family since it prevents male access to "legitimate" heterosex and procreation. Vaginismus is probably the most publicly acknowledged and openly examined matter of sexuality in Turkey. The topic is commonly, and sometimes quite explicitly, discussed even in daytime television talk-shows with "experts" such as sex therapists, psychologists, and family counselors trying to help married couples overcome "the problem." Given this local backdrop, it is no wonder that *Bekâret*'s readers brought up vaginismus several times throughout the study. Milena, for instance, began her diary with the following life story:

Milena (diary): Until I began college, virginity was completely a taboo for me. I guess college helped me. . . . In those years, I had many friends who lived together and had sexual relations. These were quite ordinary. . . . But I never experienced that with the man who was my boyfriend at the time and is my husband today. There was always a fear in me. This wasn't about "physical pain" that could occur during intercourse. . . . Soon after we started dating, during each of our frequent get-togethers, one piece of clothing was disappearing on me. In about 3–5 months when the last piece came off, yes, we were making love—for hours. He had orgasms 2 times, 3 times a day, and I did too. But we never went as far as that final phase. As I said, I was afraid. It was as if something would change after losing my virginity. What if I regretted it later or had a problem for not being a virgin? What if my family learned about it or I got pregnant? . . . Then, what happened? We got married. Before we got married, I went to the gynecologist for a general check-up. That day the doctor diagnosed me with vaginismus. And I experienced it firsthand in the upcoming days. 40 days later we had intercourse and I got rid of my virginity and everything else that oppressed me without me being aware of it.

This intimate story attests to the close link between the virginity pressure and vaginismus experienced by many women in Turkey. Indeed, several readers of *Bekâret* mentioned vaginismus as a common local issue directly caused by Turkey's virginity regime. For instance, Ayşegül wrote,

Ayşegül (diary): Sexual issues are always a matter of taboo for girl children. That's why there are a lot of vaginismus cases in our country. Girls from an early age see their sexual parts as "dirty" and "bad." The first "shame" they learn from their mothers' warnings is about the way they sit ["keep your legs together"]. So, a woman's genitals turn into "a thing that is shameful, that she should be embarrassed about and can never touch." She is supposed to withhold, protect, preserve, and then open her sexuality for the first time to the man she marries.

It is because of their identification of virginity as the source of vaginismus that the readers deemed *Bekâret* invaluable because, they thought, it could help alleviate virginity's hold on women's psychosexual subjectivities by shattering many of the virginity myths circulating both in the west and in Turkey. As Dogan reports, countering such myths is indeed urgently needed ("Vaginismus," 189):

It appears that cultural factors play a role in the occurrence of vaginismus. Furthermore, although the importance given to virginity has decreased, "losing" virginity is still a source of threat and pressure for women. For example, it is not unusual for doctors in Turkey to be asked by parents questions like whether riding a bicycle or climbing a tree can break their little daughter's hymen. Parents are often very concerned (because of virginity) about small injuries, even those not involving the genital area, or any physical changes in the genital area. Additionally, many young women are unaware of the existence of the vulvar opening and the elasticity of the vaginal wall. Some of them believe that they can lose their virginity if they touch their genitals. Another common misbelief is that the vagina is too small and penis too big. Furthermore, they believe that unbearable pain and excessive bleeding occur during first intercourse because the hymen is too thick and too tight.

Considering that the virginity myths mentioned by Dogan as contributing factors to vaginismus are precisely the ones dismantled in *Bekâret*, it does not seem surprising that many readers praised the book for its potential to "remedy" this "disease of virgins," which, according to them, is not a problem because of its threat to marriage and family, but because it adversely affects women's psychosexual agencies. This was the reason why when they brought up the issue, they often discussed it together with other sexuality problems that, they argued, women often encountered. For instance:

> Bilge Su (focus group): There is a ton of research on vaginismus. But on anorgasmia, I mean, being unable to have vaginal pleasure, which is almost equally a problem, there is very little good research. Obviously, vaginismus is, on the one hand, a fact of this society that values virginity very much and, on the other hand, it has the aspect of "okay enough, it's about time you give it up" [Moderator: "Intercourse is essential"]. Yes, it is essential because you need to procreate.... Standing right next to a ton of virginity myths is in fact the idea that "now you have to procreate;" the myth that a woman becomes a woman only when she is procreative.

> Müjgan (diary): It [greensickness] will pass when you get married! So, this tradition too is that old! I'd call this, "The doctor recommended sex." ... For instance, it would be told to someone who went to the doctor's for period cramps and also for any different gynecological problem: "It'll pass when you get married" (the curing phallus).

These remarks show that the readers not only engaged in self-reflections through *Bekâret*'s culturally distant narratives, but also enriched them with new locally grounded narratives. Apparently, then, even a narrative as geo-historically alien as greensickness could generate a domestically pertinent and transnationally connectionist reading when the readers engaged in the method of comparative accretion. This is not simply an act of "confiscation" that erases the story's alienness. Rather, it is a strategy that manifests Keating's (*Transformation Now*, 17) "connectionist approach" to geohistorical differences, or Anzaldúa's ("Now Let Us Shift," 568) "connectionist faculty," which "allows us to picture—via reverie, dreaming, and artistic creativity—similarities instead of solid divisions."

Another key example of this reading strategy was the readers' supplementing of *Bekâret* with the local issue of honor-based violence against women. While honor-based violence is a topic of discussion in the translator's preface (since it is also a crucial local feminist issue), it is rarely mentioned, and hardly discussed, in the rest of *Bekâret*. Blank's first mention of "so-called honor crimes" appears in Chapter 1, when, in an attempt to counter the common belief that honor-based gender violence is a matter of "nonwestern" cultures and communities,[7] she tells the story of a twelve-year-old Alabama girl murdered—"forced to drink bleach, then asphyxiated"—by her mother because she "believed that the girl had lost her virginity" (*Virgin*, 9). Despite Blank's scarce attention to "honor," there was not a single participant in my study who did not mention "honor" in their diaries or interviews. In fact, corresponding to my claim on the very first page of the preface, "In Turkey, virginity and honor make an indivisible pair," the readers constantly switched between the two terms, as a result of which "honor" became an inherent discursive component of the book (Ergun, "Önsöz," 15):

> Milena (diary): For a woman raised in this country "virginity" means value. ... And as long as virginity is seen as an equivalent to the concept of honor and not dislodged from the condition of a "social value," it is obvious that the situation [violence] will continue as it is.

> Müjgan (diary): I just remembered a slogan that we have been shouting in street protests in recent years: "I've lost my honor; I won't find it. I won't be anyone's honor." ... It just feels good to shout at their faces the worthlessness of the thing in the name of which we are killed.

Milena and Müjgan read the local feminist critiques of honor into the traveling book and tie the counter virginity stance of the text to the counter honor stance of the local feminist movement. In similar ways, all the other participants, without exception, talked about honor when they responded to questions about virginity politics in Turkey emphasizing the prevalent gender violence that concepts like virginity instigated and the sense of political urgency that came with such systematic violence.

The readers extended *Bekâret*'s claim that "virginity does not exist" to incorporate "honor" because in Turkey honor encapsulates virginity and in many cases of femicide it is hard to tell apart the operations of these two gender regimes. The normative codes they prescribe often overlap in the service of the same heteropatriarchal institutions and cause the same horrific acts of violence. By engaging in this conceptual extension, the readers transformed *Bekâret* into "a critical history of virginity *and honor*," which was already initiated by my preface. Making a reference to the slogan used by local feminists against honor-based violence, "We will not be anybody's honor," the preface further stimulated the interpretive extension from virginity to honor saying (Ergun, "Önsöz," 11–12, 15):

We never question what virginity is or is not and whose definition that is. While the question, 'Whose honor?' does not sound strange, "Whose virginity?" sounds silly. . . . Then, just like we question honor as a social construct peculiar to male-dominant cultures, we also need to stop seeing virginity as an intimate, private matter and question it as a product of patriarchy.

This invitation by the feminist translator to expand the book's geohistorical thematic scope seems to have been accepted by all the readers who constantly compared the virginity/honor regime of Turkey with that of the west and in the process came to the same conclusion:

Deniz (diary): In Turkey, virginity is a powerful institution; so powerful that it can kill.

Kırmızı (diary): In my country, women can be killed on the grounds that they didn't bleed on the first night (after getting married)."

Ayşe (diary): Unfortunately, I've realized once again that wherever patriarchal mentality exists, we will be faced with virginity. But I still wonder very much if the price of losing one's virginity is blood in the west too? Is it death?

Bilge Su (focus group): We do have more urgent problems. The problems we encounter blow up our lives; we see lives that it [virginity/honor] shatters; indeed, we see lives that it disables or ends. So, we need to come up with urgent solutions. It is not as simple as that the virginity notion is putting some pressure on our bodies; I mean, we- we are dying because of this.

These comments point out the pervasiveness of women's murders in Turkey—not that femicide is unique to Turkey—many of which are instigated by the virginity norm. Upon their comparative reading practices, the readers, thus, agreed with my initial claim (as discussed in Chapter 1) that Turkey's virginity regime, in cooperation with the well-entrenched honor codes, appeared to generate more systematic and extreme forms of violence against women. The readers, however, did not draw this conclusion within the "superior west versus inferior east" discourse as dictated by orientalism.[8] Rather, they highlighted the difference only to argue that due to its life-threatening magnitude, Turkey's virginity regime demanded more urgent interventions than that of the west, where contemporary patriarchy seemed to manifest itself in more covert [read: less immediately deadly] ways:

Bilge Su (interview): I don't think that things are smooth sailing in the west either. On the contrary, there is a very powerful refined and latent patriarchal perception over there, no matter how much women's daily maltreatment has decreased in many western countries. And these are important. I mean, I'm not going to make a hierarchy of sufferings and massacres.

Ayşegül (interview): As you read on, you always make comparisons. I mean I don't see the west as very free/liberated or very developed, but you still question religion's influence [on virginity]. It appears that the [religious] reform, Protestantism and so forth ruptured that solid religious structure [of the Catholic virginity regime] later on. I mean you try to weigh that to see what else needs to be ruptured for women to be truly free.... But of course, I don't think that all women living over there are liberated and very happy and have overcome the issue.

By engaging in the comparative accretion strategy to highlight misogyny as a shared reality across borders, *Bekâret*'s readers managed to overcome, not reproduce, the dualistic and separatist geopolitical orientation of orientalism and connect with the west in ways deemed unimaginable by imperialist standards. The strategy helped the readers recognize the cross-cultural differences in virginity codes and practices, yet in geopolitically nonhierarchical ways. Moreover, the differences were interpreted neither as indicating a lack of transcultural interconnectivities, nor as politically hindering or obviating transnational solidarities. Differences were taken for what they were—different understandings, experiences, and geohistorical realities that attested to the nonexistence of normative, monolithic universals like virginity. As Sezen explained in her diary, "My experience of reading the book was informative and astounding; it helped me think of different women in different geographies." Differences were also valued for the lessons they offered on how to survive and defeat the oppressive virginity regime and imagine otherwise. In Deniz's words, "Reading the counterparts of virginity in the western culture, in another culture helps make the foundation of *human* behavior more comprehensible, more revealing" (emphasis mine, diary). *Bekâret*, then, was seen as a source of knowledge that shed light on a *human* construct with different materializations and ramifications at different times and places for different constituencies of women. And revealing these differences as well as the connectivities among them could help feminists design and practice locally and globally more inclusive and effective activisms to do away with virginity and the violence it generates.

The following comments were made in response to my question, "Has your understanding of virginity in the west changed after reading the book?"

Defne (interview): The fact that they are in the west doesn't change anything. When I read the western virginity history, I realized that the west is not that different from the east given its current attitude of saying "virginity doesn't really exist" but then operating it underhandedly.

Müjgan (interview): Before I began [reading the book], in my mind I had created a counter-idea that said virginity would not confine them as it confined me or as it confined a woman in Yozgat [a city in central Turkey]. But then, I saw that it wasn't like that.

Yasemin (interview): To me, this appears to be a contradictory situation. On the one hand, western people are freer regarding sexuality. . . . On the other hand, there are many traces of virginity; I mean there are lots of signs of virginity. I guess the system once again conveniently exploits this [freedom]. The issue of sexual freedom perhaps moves forward in a way that further commodifies women's bodies. It seems like women, in fact, have not really attained that sexual freedom. And because of that I guess the west seems contradictory from afar.

Ayşe (interview): As far as I can tell from here, as much as I can see, there actually is a picture of virginity in the west that has been depicted for us. Based on the millions of Hollywood movies, American series you have watched, you think that it seems like virginity doesn't exist there, that it's already been overcome. But then when a study like this appears and especially when you think that it is a work of translation, then, you say to yourself, how come it was overcome? Because you wouldn't go back and study a surmounted issue in this way.

As these statements illustrate, *Bekâret*'s readers, based on their newly acquired self-reflexive and critical knowledges about western virginities, revised their preconceived notions of the west and understood their geopolitical "other" on/in its own terms. The west—and western women—became more "real" (historically situated, culturally pluralized, and experientially populated) than what it was alleged to be in the locally and globally circulating orientalist/ occidentalist discourses; it was now recognized both as a heterogeneous—not monolithic—cultural block harboring diverse (and contradictory) virginity histories and experiences and as a sociopolitical geography where the virginity regime—as well as other forms of gender oppression—*still* reigned, albeit in varying degrees and forms of violence.[9]

By now, it is clear that while reading *Bekâret*, the readers not only recognized the other for its otherness (not necessarily an act of othering), but also realized the interconnectivity implied in that otherness, repositioned their selves in relation to the other, and reconfigured their geopolitical self through the other's self-critical and self-reflexive gaze. This is an enormous transformation with considerable geopolitical implications because as Anzaldúa says ("Now Let Us Shift," 569),

When you connect to others, not as parts, problems, or useful commodities, but from a connectionist view, compassion triggers transformation. This shift occurs when you give up investment in your point of view and recognize the real situation free of projections—not filtered through your habitual defensive preoccupations.

That is, the readers' comparative accretion strategy revealed the mutual permeability of self/other through transcultural contact—during which both the self and the other were transformed from an oppositional binary into an interdependent unit. Thus, the strategy highlighted the role that feminist translation could play in fostering such relationality. In Keating's words (*Transformation Now*, 177),

We are interconnected. As Gloria Anzaldúa explains, "[t]he self does not stop with just you, with your body. . . . [T]he self can penetrate other things and they penetrate you" (*Interviews/Entrevistas*, 160). This permeable self extends outward—meeting, touching, entering into exchange with other subjects. Significantly, this outward movement is not an imperialistic appropriation, where the self-contained subject grows larger by extending its boundaries to incorporate or annihilate everyone, everything in its path. It is, rather, a mutual, transformational encounter between subjects. We are all changed through our interactions.

The following insightful words from Ece's diary summarize the point well:

Ece (diary): As the hegemonic western culture inescapably shapes our life, it is utterly necessary to read the book on the western history of virginity, if you have any trouble with the subject matter. That's why I think the book will contribute to other cultures as well if it is translated into more languages. No matter how different it is from another culture's, the virginity [history] told in the book will fulfill the role of the "other" in self-reflection for that culture.

*Bekâret*'s readers, then, could connect with the west because the west, rather than presenting itself as the superior cultural model to be emulated by "the rest," was engaging in self-confrontation. Therefore, the readers did not feel the judgmental gaze or the symbolic assault of the orientalist eye on their selves while reading the book. This gesture provided them with discursive tools to engage in similar acts of self-evaluation about their own geohistorical realities. In Ayşe's words,

Ayşe (interview): Even if the book doesn't belong to this geography, when it makes people start asking different questions and [think about] different things—I don't know how to say it, not just about different things, but when it propels us to rethink about things we assume that we know, then, it already helps us take a very big step forward.

Yasemin expressed this idea of "reimagining the self through the self-reflection of the other" slightly differently in the second focus group discussion:

> Yasemin (focus group): I wondered how it would be if the history of virginity were told comprehensively [in the book], if our geography were included. But then . . . maybe we wouldn't be able to take it. You know, eventually we don't know that culture very well, so looking at it from a little distance in this way enables us to think about virginity in a clearer, sounder way. So, the book was perhaps an introduction; it provided me with a critical framework.

By presenting a different portrayal of virginity that is geographically distant enough not to overwhelm and immobilize them, yet close enough to politically speak to them, *Bekâret* appears to have provided Yasemin with a discursive detour to critical local virginity politics. Such a detour may prove invaluable since virginity is experienced so gruesomely "at home" that any local critique directly focusing on it could debilitate local readers and lead to the collapse of self-reflexive meaning-making mechanisms.[10]

The comparative accretion strategy could easily echo an orientalist mentality since imagining the east through the western gaze is what orientalism perpetrates. Such a reading strategy could simply trigger the binary-oppositional approach of colonialism. As Keating notes (*Transformation Now*, 51–52),

> When we examine the world through this binary lens, we assume that the differences between our views and those of others are too different—too *other*, as it were—to have anything (of importance) in common. This assumption of negative difference traps us within our existing ideas and beliefs, for it prevents us from developing new forms of knowledge and new alliances. After all, if we're so busy defending our own views, where is the room for complexity, compromise, and exchange? (emphasis original)

Yet, as my reception study revealed, the othering gesture promoted by orientalism is not replicated in *Bekâret*'s readers' interpretations of the west since they practice reading translation as a connectionist, rather than a separatist, act. In this process, the assumed gap between the east and the west is collaboratively bridged by the author, translator, and readers' relational acts of meaning making geared toward uncovering and/or generating transcultural interconnectivities, not reinforcing oppositional detachments. This geopolitical bridging against the divisive force of orientalism was consolidated by the second reading strategy, "differential universalization," which I discuss in the next section.

## Lesson 2: Differential Universalization in Transcultural Bridging

While engaging in the bridging strategy of comparative accretion, during which *Bekâret*'s readers made tentative notes of differences across the virginity codes and practices of the west and the east and added their own locally molded articulations to the traveling book, they also noted:

Defne (follow-up interview): We experience the exact same stories told in the book here with a different name.

Leylak (interview): In the focus group, we talked about how universal all these issues were. We all agreed on that. When we think of the west, we usually assume that virginity is unimportant there, but a taboo here. In fact, how common it all is; it is important both here and there.

Yasemin (diary): After reading the book, I thought I had my feet more firmly on the ground [regarding virginity politics]. In general, my perspective of virginity has completely expanded. Seeing that virginity is similarly a deep, bottomless pit in western societies, which are deemed relatively more "modern" and are the initiators of the "enlightenment era," has solidified my conviction that the power of patriarchy encompasses the entire world.

Kırmızı (interview): Before I read this book, I would assume that so many issues were unique to us. For example, we always see it in Turkish movies; a bloody bed sheet is expected on the first night [of marriage]. I used to think that these were unique to Turkey; I mean to eastern societies. But when I read the book, it raised my awareness. I realized that virginity practices were not regional problems, that practices on women's bodies were not regional problems, that this was not a matter of backwardness, but a universal issue. . . . I now believe that virginity is not a norm that belongs to a specific culture. I think all over the world women are forced to experience this problem. You know, we always have this point of view that the west is more developed; the west is more modern. The book enabled me to realize that this has nothing to do with modernity or backwardness, that it is a problem of patriarchy.

Gülümser (interview): My thoughts on virginity in Turkey didn't change; I just saw that it [virginity] is more universal. The examples in the book overlap literally one-on-one with our lives and what happens here. There are strange rituals, tests, and so forth in the book. And, here too, there are killings, red belts being worn [by brides symbolizing their assumed virginity], aunts waiting at the door [of the bride-groom's room at the wedding night], etc. These are just as nonsense and upsetting as those urine stories [virginity tests] told in the book.

These quotations illustrating the universalizing strategy of *Bekâret*'s readers are only a few among many others—similar yet longer comments on the shared political force of virginity across borders, or "one of the rare things on which so many different people agree, the reality where so many different cultures converge on," in Müjgan's words. The readers could reach this conclusion of transnational commonality because *Bekâret*, with its self-reflexive analyses of western virginities, interrupted their perception of virginity as an issue that only affected women in the east. It seems that by encouraging the readers to dismantle their preformed occidentalist assumptions of "liberated western women" and discard their orientalist suppositions that virginity was a problem in and of "the relatively backward east," *Bekâret* helped remove the discursive barriers set between women from different geographies and in doing so, brought them closer under a newly discovered political commonality.

The identification of virginity as a transculturally common, thus universal, problem produced by heteropatriarchal arrangements of power was repeatedly emphasized by all the participants, regardless of their acute awareness of the (geo)political danger of such universalizing discourses.[11] Indeed, in many cases, their remarks seemed, at first glance, to replicate the problematic "sameness of oppression" narratives of hegemonic western feminisms that ground feminist praxis on the assumed universalisms of "women" as a homogeneous group undivided by differences.[12] For instance,

Yasemin (interview): The book changed my perspective on virginity in the west because I saw that such horrible things in fact happen in those relatively "modern" western societies as well. And I can say that this actually has changed the way I view patriarchy. I mean, wherever you go, it is universal—you know, I'm sure it takes place in different ways depending on the culture, but eventually, it's not less than here. It's just not less.

Milena (diary): It seems that in all societies the first initial, foundational ideas about virginity got shaped in similar ways. Although there are many differences when compared to us, I think, the similarities between perceptions of virginity are just as striking.

Bilge Su (follow-up interview): The book reveals that the foundational archetype based on women's virginity/innocence actually exists as much in the west as it does in the east.

Gülümser (interview): Of course, the experiences lived on this land are not specifically told in the book. Honor killings or other things that take place in the east, and here and everywhere as well, are not told in the book. But the examples [of the book] seemed to me as, okay, this is the way it works here and that's the way it works there; I mean it is eventually the same thing, its core is the same. You know, this is done, and it is done everywhere, and that's upsetting. I used to have a prejudice that it would be less in the west. Of course, that got shattered. I mean this exists everywhere. But the author exposed it, you translated it, we are talking about it. And that gives me hope. But of course, it is terrible that it is everywhere.

Sezen (follow-up interview): Our foundational concern is the same—although its practices or the times of occurrences of those practices are different, its essence is the same.

These comments all feature a universality claim. Yet, upon a closer look, it becomes clear that they do not exactly repeat the universalizing gesture of ethnocentric western feminist discourses where recognition of "women's common oppression" serves imperialist motives and expands "the 'universal' function of the 'West'" (Lazreg, "Triumphant Discourse," 29). That is, the readers' claims of universality are not "monologic" claims of sameness (Keating, *Transformation Now*, 136). Rather, they seem to be reflecting Braidotti's "nomadic vision" that states, "'We' are in *this* together, but we are not all the same" (Braidotti, *Transpositions*, 131, emphasis original). *Bekâret's* readers, then, do not emulate "the universalistic rhetoric of some Western feminism [that] involves a refusal to encounter, to get close enough to face the others" (Ahmed, *Strange Encounters*, 166). On the contrary, they claim such universality precisely because they encounter and hear the other and engage with the differences introduced by the other. In the process of establishing such "translational relationalities," *Bekâret's* readers simultaneously provincialize and transnationalize virginity (Stam and Shohat, *Race in Translation*, 298). Their remarks about the normative universality of virginity are not defined by an "epistemology of sameness" (Keating, *Transformation Now*, 100). Theirs is an interconnectivist configuration of universality that recognizes patriarchies as locally situated cross-border relationalities and virginity as an intersectional, transnational node among multiple patriarchal arrangements (Patil, "From Patriarchy" 863; Grewal and Kaplan, *Scattered Hegemonies*, 24). As Müjgan brilliantly puts it,

Müjgan (diary): How identical these issues have remained over thousands of years! In a world and buildup of humanity where there can be as many ideas as the total number of people, how come those that never agreed on/

came together became so likeminded on this matter? Was the same effort [of global collaboration] that was made on this issue made for anything else?

This comment indicates *Bekâret*'s crucial potential to reveal that virginity is a product of agelong cross-border cooperation among differently arranged and situated, yet interconnected, patriarchies and their co-conspiring institutions, such as religion and science. That is, itself a traveling concept that cuts across the oppositional geohistorical terrain of the west/east binary, virginity is "universal yet not uniform" and thus cannot be deemed either "purely western" or "purely eastern" because as Zillah Eisenstein argues, "global flows have always been dialectical, even if unevenly so" (*Against Empire*, 199). In that regard, we may consider virginity as a "transnational hegemonic borrowing," in Inderpal Grewal and Caren Kaplan's terms, and "what needs to be examined in light of such transnational hegemonic 'borrowings' are the ways in which various patriarchies collaborate and borrow from each other in order to reinforce specific practices that are oppressive to women" (*Scattered Hegemonies*, 24). *Bekâret*'s readers do precisely that while applying the strategy of differential universalization:

> Bilge Su (focus group): I started realizing more that wherever you lay your hands on, if you're trying to say something about a general problem through the particular, you're in fact doing a competent job. But in the end, you're limited. And you know that: "I'm limited. I'm speaking from here, but I don't forget the things concerning the big issue." This makes you competent, but it doesn't change the fact that in terms of scope you're working in a limited field. You always choose a field, a history, a situation, a perspective that is as comparative as possible.

In Bilge Su's words, *Bekâret*'s readers (or *Bekâret* itself) do not speak to the transcultural general without acknowledging the geopolitical particulars. On the contrary, they constantly recognize and emphasize situated differences among women (and patriarchies) while at the same time pointing out commonalities in their geohistorically contingent, experiential realities of virginity oppression and everyday resistance to it (or complicity with it). The gist of their repeated claims is: Virginity is an imaginary construct and a universal tool of heteropatriarchal arrangements so it is defined and put to use in different ways at different times and places and, thus, it affects diverse constituencies of women differently and needs to be analyzed and resisted both locally and globally at the same time.

This simultaneous recognition of universality and differentiality could even be seen in the readers' syntax. In the spoken setting of the group discussions and individual interviews, for instance, utterances of universality claims were almost always incomplete or choppy sentences (which makes them difficult to translate into English) because the participants cut them in the middle to insert claims of cross-cultural differences (e.g., Yasemin's diary excerpt above or Lorin's remarks below). The haste with which *Bekâret*'s readers intervened in their claims shows their open-ended understanding of universality as always geohistorically contingent and their attentiveness to differences as catalysts, not obstacles, for forging transcultural commonalities. Indeed, by underlining the dialogic and flexible relation between the particular and the general, the readers grounded their definitions of universality in cross-cultural differences and their situated "worldly encounters" with them (Tsing, *Friction*, 1).

After all, without uncovering the various conceptual and practical manifestations of virginity and rejecting the assumed singularity of virginity (and of the "virginal body"), we cannot dismantle its normative universality, nor replace it with a subversive universality that claims virginity's fictionality. In that regard, *Bekâret*'s production and reception can be seen as "a project in which the 'uni' is transfigured through the 'multi' so as to enable the constitution of new political subjects and new collective politics" (Brah, *Cartographies of Diaspora*, 248). Thus, in both the book's and the readers' renewed universality claims (or what Tsing calls "engaged universals"—universals that "travel across difference and are charged and changed by their travels"), we see "a deep irony": "Universalism is implicated in both imperial schemes to control the world and liberatory mobilizations for justice and empowerment. Universalism inspires expansion—for both the powerful and the powerless" (*Friction*, 8–9). The following excerpt deserves quoting at length since it clearly illustrates that irony and the typical zigzagging between commonality and differentiality claims seen in *Bekâret*'s readers' narratives:

> Lorin (focus group): I think all these issues of virginity and sexuality, our relations with our bodies etc. are—I mean, they have different cultural aspects. You know, in some countries, it is women's choice; in other countries there are different sorts of marriage, etc. So yes, it is cultural, but this virginity issue is in fact universal. It seems that the first sexual experience has been important everywhere in the world and in every religion, I mean, in all monotheistic religions. Here [in the book], there are very important examples from Christianity, you know, what women saints went through, what nuns went through, etc. And you know one of the critiques that is most often raised against us, against feminists, is that "this [feminism] is something that came from the west; this is a trend given to you by the west, and you have been carried away with it," blah blah. But in reality, these

are problems that deeply touch our lives and they are shared. Back in the day, I used to think that there was no such thing [virginity oppression] in Christianity; that Christians were more liberated and relaxed. There is a scene that we see on TV all the time. You know, the father gives away the woman to her husband during the wedding ceremony in the church, right? For example, I had never questioned that. I even found it modern and stuff. I never saw its patriarchal face. But in fact, this is universal, and we already know what is happening in Islam. . . . There are similar things in Islam.

These remarks illustrate both the universal status that the readers attributed to virginity and its plural and shifting nature. The transcultural commonalities mentioned in their narratives range from virginity being conceived as a human construct, a heteronormative gender norm, and a form of violence against women to a regulatory regime sustained by women's consent and complicity and a disciplinary scheme that women resist and challenge. All these themes are strategically used to forge some form of universal. Tsing calls these tentative adoptions "strategic universalisms" ("Transitions," 264) whose mission is "to form bridges, roads, and channels of circulation. Knowledge gained from particular experience percolates into these channels, widening rather than interrupting them" (*Friction*, 7).

Perhaps no other example is as illustrative of differential universalization as the readers' narratives on the Gitano, or "the Spanish Roman people," who believe that "there is a grape [in the vagina], an uva, that contains a yellowish liquid" and is "the only reliable signifier of a woman's virginity" (Blank, *Virgin*, 74). According to the Gitano, "the liquid inside the uva, called the honra, can be spilled once. . . . It is burst in a ceremonial defloration that happens as part of the wedding celebration" by an elder woman expert (74–75). The expert "is honor bound to stop if the bride should bleed, for the blood would spoil the 'flowers' made by the honra" (75). Blank presents the Gitano case in Chapter 6, "The Blank Page"—an outstanding chapter on the variability of virginity codes, tests, and corresponding methods to "fake" it. However, given the minoritized status of the Roma people in Europe adding their "unusual" virginity narrative to a book on western virginities is risky, to say the least. The narrative may easily facilitate orientalist readings, especially because it is juxtaposed with the globally authorized medical virginity narratives of the "modern" west. Blank could even be accused of using a sensational "third world" gender practice to prove a theory developed in and for the west and in doing so, reproducing the "Third World difference" (defining the "Third World Woman" as illegibly and inferiorly different) that Mohanty rightly criticizes (Mohanty, *Feminism Without Borders*, 40).

Interestingly, when I read *Virgin*—multiple times that is—I never interpreted Blank's take on the Gitano as orientalist in terms of its motives or implications. I did not perceive the Gitano's virginity practices as culturally inferior (read: bizarre, incomprehensible, shocking, abhorrent, or barbaric—terms that are generously deployed in orientalist discourse to describe non-western societies and their "culturally challenging" practices) (Gunning, "Arrogant Perception"). Hence, within the interpretive parameters of my subjective reading, I could argue that Blank discusses the Gitano's virginity code only to refute the western virginity codes as well as the western medical authority universally declared on virginity. I could contend that Blank does not portray the Gitano as the inferior other against which the west's superiority is asserted. Rather, I could argue, she negates the self-acclaimed superiority of western medicine by referring to a different cultural code of virginity, which appears just as dubious and problematic as the western one. I could even cite Blank to support the claim that my apparently nonethnocentric reading was the text's "true" intended meaning (*Virgin*, 89–90):

> When readers reared in the mainstream Western sexual ideology hear about Gitano defloration rituals and discover that the appearance of blood during the defloration ritual stops the proceedings cold, they are often surprised, even shocked, to discover that the bleeding they had presumed was universally recognized as a sign of virginity simply isn't always recognized in that way. As both Paterson-Brown's study[13] and Gitano deflorations prove, not only is coitarche (first intercourse) bleeding not universally recognized as meaningful in terms of virginity, it isn't universal, either.

It seems that Blank did anticipate orientalist interpretations from western readers and tried to prevent that by repeating her epistemological rejection of the universality of virginity across cases. In fact, she did not propose a hierarchy of virginity knowledges between the Gitano's and the west's. On the contrary, she presented both as equally inconclusive. Yet, her overall discourse in Chapter 6 implicitly positions the Gitano against the "modern west" without challenging global power structures that could activate the perception of the Gitano as "the other." Thus, the text does not facilitate readers, particularly western readers, to appraise the virginity codes of the west and the Gitano in a level playing field by reminding them of potential geopolitical risks of juxtaposing these two cultural methods (e.g., discussing the dangers of "cultural imperialism"). The following excerpt illustrates this lapse well (75):

> The Gitano may live in the modern cities of Spain but their rituals of virginity seem, to the rest of us, to come from a different place, a different time. They even seem to involve a different body.

Given that "the cognitive construction of the Western mind immediately calls forth the image of the barbarian native," *Virgin*, due to its contradictory, even reckless geopolitical discourse, skates on thin ice in a precarious semantic field of reception (Liddle and Rai, "Feminism, Imperialism," 514). While it would be unfair to call *Virgin* an orientalist text per se, it is important to see its occasional lapses and recognize the book's textual potential to trigger orientalist readings. Although I, as a (privileged) reader of *Virgin*, signified the Gitano's as a case of epistemological destabilization without relegating it to an orientalist motive, it is necessary to ask whether other readers would interpret it in the same "innocent" manner.[14] What kinds of meanings would the readers in Turkey make out of those geopolitical lapses?

*Bekâret's* readers seemed to share my personal interpretation of the Gitano's case, perhaps because their reading practices were not guided by western orientalist motives and compulsions:[15]

> Ayşe (diary): There are two things in the book that surprised me. One is the fact that the tests (like the pencil test) used to measure virginity are a bunch of nonsense. The other is the fact that the Gitano measure virginity without blood (of course, this stems from the virginity perception that is ingrained in me).

Ayşe obviously does not read the Gitano's virginity code as an inferior one compared to the hymen-centered code. Rather, problematizing her affective reaction, she emphasizes the fact that her astonishment at the Gitano code only proves how deep-seated the supposedly universal medical virginity code is in her mind. That is, the Gitano's virginity code is surprising to Ayşe only because it makes her realize that she has been misinformed and misled into believing that bleeding is the universal biological sign of virginity (or its "loss"). In fact, *Bekâret's* readers were genuinely struck by reading the Gitano's story, which they took as the ultimate disproof of virginity's assumed universal factuality:

> Ece (diary): It was very interesting for me that the Gitano tested virginity not with the bleeding of the hymen, but with honra. What the author later says is really very befitting: "The question is . . . according to the system of thought of the place and time in which the test was used, was it capable of providing evidence that would have been meaningful for people thinking according to that particular set of guidelines"(141)?[16] Just like we created virginity as well as the meaning ascribed to it, it is clear that we also created the tests to measure it with.

> Bilge Su (diary): There were many things I found interesting but so far it has particularly amazed me to see the existence of very different cultural

answers to the questions of what virginity is and how it can be broken, which is well illustrated by the Gitano example.

Deniz (diary): The case of the Gitano in comparison to that of the western doctors was quite meaningful. It was great to read the analysis of virginity tests and learn that their common feature was that they didn't give women the right to speak for themselves, while that was the only way to get accurate information on virginity, and that all those obstacles raised before women because of virginity tests could be circumvented by faking virginity with little tricks.

These comments reveal that the readers replaced the universal that claimed, "Virginity exists in women's bodies" with the subversive universal, "Virginity does not exist outside the human social." They achieve that by drawing on the different virginity codes and tests told in *Bekâret*, among which the Gitano seem to supply the most divergent configuration compared to the all-too-familiar hymen code. In other words, rather than taking refuge in the façade of universal sameness, *Bekâret*'s readers enunciate a new virginity universal that is grounded in the reclamation of differences. It is this gesture of differential universalization that makes way for their predication of transcultural commonalities—a creative border-crossing that Mohanty emphasizes in the epigraph of this chapter saying, "specifying difference allows us to theorize universal concerns more fully" (*Feminism Without Borders*, 226).

The differential universalization gesture, then, is not a move to ignore or erase existing differences, but to cross the divides built around those differences and forge commonalities that recognize them: making strategic universal claims, creating cross-border knowledges, learning from each other's experiences, and envisioning transcultural solidarities. As noted in Ayşegül's diary,

Ayşegül (diary): Women's struggles to liberate themselves from the situation of [being] "the slave's slave" have resulted in different experiences around the world, which, when shared, then enhanced their liberation experiences all over the world.

It is the potential to convey these liberation experiences across borders and enrich social justice praxes that makes feminist translation indispensable for transnational feminism. This is why *Bekâret*'s readers deemed the book invaluable for it facilitated them to see virginity as "a matter of sexism that is beyond the east-west issue," as Dicle put it. Or as noted by Öğüt in her review ("Yamuk Bakış"),

Unlike what is commonly assumed, the virginity notion is not unique to Turkey, or to third world countries. Indeed, it possesses considerable significance in the new conservative and neoliberal frameworks where the family institution is actively sanctified and endorsed. The negative commonalities among young women killed because "she wasn't a virgin" or "the bed sheet wasn't bloody" make a universal phenomenon.

Acknowledging the east-west binary's dividing effects, yet refusing to "remain locked in an embattled, us-against-them status quo," Bekâret's readers let go of their preformed "oppositional energies" that "limit our vision for change, restrict our options, and inhibit our ability to create transformational alliances" (Keating, Transformation Now, 3, 7). They cherished Bekâret precisely because it revealed the cross-cultural differences in virginity regimes, thus, dismantling virginity's patriarchal universality, which the readers replaced with a feminist universality that was tentative and open-ended enough to inspire new visions of transnational feminist collaborations—of which, in fact, the translation of Virgin and the readers' engagements with it are hopeful examples. In other words, by reclaiming the universal, Bekâret's readers staked a feminist claim to "the global stream of humanity" (Tsing, Friction, 1):

> The universal offers us the chance to participate in the global stream of humanity. We can't turn it down. Yet we also can't replicate previous versions without inserting our own genealogy of commitments and claims. Whether we place ourselves inside or outside the West, we are stuck with universals created in cultural dialogue.

In a recent issue of Signs, under the in-print symposium section titled "Translation, Feminist Scholarship, and the Hegemony of English," Claudia de Lima Costa and Sonia Alvarez claim a "translational turn" in feminist scholarship and activism, and add ("Dislocating the Sign," 557–58),

> We are witnessing an ever-growing need for feminists to engage in productive dialogue and negotiations across multiple geopolitical and theoretical borders. We propose to consider translation as politically and theoretically indispensable to forging feminist, prosocial justice and antiracist, postcolonial, and anti-imperial political alliances and epistemologies.

Indeed, this chapter illustrated this intensifying need for egalitarian cross-border conversations among feminists, particularly across geopolitical borders that are overly charged with antagonistic energies that too often hinder people on both sides from talking and listening to each other and welcoming one another as potential allies for justice. As Chilla Bulbeck notes (Re-Orienting Western Feminisms, 56),

We must walk this tightrope between similarity and difference armed with knowledge, stories told to us by the other; with honest self-criticism, asking what are our interests as opposed to those of the other; with connection, meeting and hearing the other; and with an understanding of the structures of political and economic domination which have made white voices louder and the voices of the other often muted.

Exploring that "tightrope between similarity and difference" and acknowledging the growing need for more egalitarian transnational feminist exchanges brought up some key questions in the chapter: How to transform such antagonistic border energies into transcultural affinities that seek to undermine the very systems creating those antagonisms? How to temporarily transcend, before we permanently undo, the existing hierarchical schemes of power that make us fear and hate differences and perceive them as barriers to cross-border dialogues? How to accept differences as positive forces and put them to use in our search for transcultural commonalities and flexible, open-ended, and contingent subversive universalisms? *Bekâret*'s readers' stories, revealing the transnationally transformative power of feminist translation and ethical reception practices, have presented us with a set of transgressive strategies in response to those questions. In the next section, I continue conceiving reading feminist translation as an exercise of imagining feminist solidarities and communities, and further explore the connectionist potential of translation by bringing in the question of geopolitical directionality (of the traveling text).

## CHAPTER 6

# Imagined Translational Feminist Communities

Am I not reaching out for you in the only language I know? Are you reaching for me in your only salvaged tongue? If I try to hear yours across our differences does/ will that mean you can hear mine? Do we explore these questions or do we settle for that secret isolation which is the learned tolerance of deprivations of each other?
—Lorde, *Sister Outsider*, 164

*Bekâret*'s readers, by engaging in the translational reading strategies of comparative accretion and differential universalization, managed to overcome the supposedly unbridgeable divide between the east and the west and configure feminist commonalities across borders. In this process of cross-border mobilization, the readers did not deny the presence of geopolitical borders that prescribed oppositional meaning-making schemes, nor the cultural and experiential differences accompanying those borders. However, they did not see differences as barriers to developing transcultural affinities or claiming universal political grounds. Rather, their "sensitivity to both commonalities and difference" served "as a constant reminder of the importance of comparative study and maintaining a creative tension between diversity and universalization" (Baca Zinn and Thornton Dill, "Theorizing Difference," 328–29). That is, the readers recognized and used differences, as well as similarities, as vital resources of transformative exchange to envision transculturally shared dreams of liberation and in doing so, they problematized the apparent seamlessness and fixity of divisive boundaries.

In this chapter, I first discuss that one crucial outcome of those postoppositional meaning-making strategies is that *Bekâret*'s readers imagined transcultural feminist communities bonded by an open-ended common vision of a world free from virginity oppression (and broader oppressive fronts of body politics). Thus, agreeing with Kathy Davis that translation "can create imagined feminist communities that are capable of recognizing differences among women while anticipating possible commonalities of struggle," the first section of the chapter analyzes the optimistic—perhaps even utopic—narratives of translational exchanges of critical gender discourses, especially in terms of their potential to foster imagined transnational feminist solidarities (*How Feminism Travels*, 175). So, I conceptualize feminist translation as a promising ground of ethical encounters that take place among differently situated women who do not personally know each other, but touch each other in the symbolic contact zone created by the transnational practices of feminist translation and reading.

In the second section, I draw on the follow-up interview study that I conducted with *Bekâret*'s readers in 2017–2018, where, in addition to questions that sought to update their perceptions of the traveling book and virginity politics, I also asked them the following hypothetical question: how do you think western readers, particularly western feminists, would react to a similar feminist book that dismantled virginity by examining the geohistorical realities of the east? How would you imagine the political journey and fate of that traveling "eastern" book in comparison to your own experiences with reading *Bekâret*? Would you expect silence, solidarity, or appropriation? This question, which I revisit in the conclusion, revealed some of the most intriguing responses in the study in regard to the issue of cross-border trust in the other's reciprocity, hospitality, and vulnerability (as opposed to apathy, pity, or hostility). Indeed, despite their dreams of "sisterhood," most of the participants, who persistently displayed those very affects of transnational feminist solidarity while reading *Bekâret*, articulated charity, rather than solidarity, as the probable interpretive scheme of western feminists in their hypothetical encounters with that traveling "oriental" feminist text. These geopolitical concerns of mutual ethical responsibility in encounters of feminisms raise important questions: How do you connect with an other who you believe would not connect with you in similarly non-hierarchical ways across borders? How do you travel to the other's world in/for solidarity when you are not sure if that same other would travel to your world in/for solidarity? Can we even claim transnational feminism if we believe that the other we look eye to eye would only look down on us? By attending to these questions from two different angles of cross-border intersubjectivity—one yielding a hopeful picture of post-oppositional transnationality, while the other remaining doubtful of it—the two sections in this chapter provide us with mutually complementary lessons about imagining (and building) transnational feminist interconnectivities and communities in and through translation.

In conceiving imagined transnational feminist communities, I draw on Chandra Mohanty's notion of "imagined communities of resistance" formed by "women with divergent histories and social locations, woven together by the political threads of opposition to forms of domination that are not only pervasive but also systemic" (*Feminism Without Borders*, 46–47).[1] The concept is "useful because it leads us away from essentialist notions of Third World feminist struggles, suggesting political rather than biological or cultural bases for alliance" (46). So, imagined transnational feminist communities are grounded in shared transgressive politics (rather than identity politics)— communities that derive their subversive force from both similar and different experiences with and responses to intersecting systems of domination. These are unities of allies whose provisional, solidarity-based configurations know no geopolitical bounds. This does not mean that global hierarchies play no role in such visionary collective formations. They do, but imagined transnational communities have their transformative potential precisely because they are envisioned both despite and because of those global structures of domination in pursuit of cross-border politics of liberation and justice. So, the concept is based on the promise that people from all geopolitical terrains can form communities of resistance regardless of how hierarchically positioned they are in relation to each other in the global order. What are the enabling conditions of imagined transnational feminist communities, then? What kinds of political and ethical practices of communication and collaboration facilitate their imaginative formation?

One way to respond these questions is to bring translation to the center of discussion, not only because there simply is no transnational without translation, but also because, as an analytic of alterity, plurality, and connectivity, translation enables us to address the ethics and politics of feminist community-building across differences and borders (with their regulating mechanisms such as "roadblocks and migratory checkpoints") that delineate our inter/subjectivities, inter/actions, and im/mobilities (de Lima Costa, "Lost (and Found?)," 67). Hence, my use of "imagined *translational* feminist communities." In conceptualizing this notion, I particularly draw on María Lugones's theory of world-traveling, which highlights the intersubjective experience of radically relating to the other's "world" of sense, which can be profoundly different from one's own world and thus can generate major shifts in one's ways of knowing, thinking, seeing, feeling, experiencing, imagining, and acting.[2] Lugones theorizes "world" outside the duality of actual versus imagined worlds. Her "worlds" are lived—"inhabited at present by some flesh and blood people" but they can "also be inhabited by some imaginary people" (*Pilgrimages*, 87). Lugones's worlds are multiple, heterogeneous, non-autonomous, and permeable structures that constitute and organize social life. While world-traveling can be (and often is) compulsory (for instance, for people of color, traveling to the dominant white/Anglo world is "a matter of necessity and of survival"), Lugones argues that, in order for it to facilitate justice-driven coalitions, it should be a willful act of cross-border relationality exercised with a "loving perception," rather than an "arrogant perception" whose purpose is "erasure of the other 'world'" (88, 95). It is this willful mode of ethical world-traveling that I explore in this chapter as a function of feminist translation and as an enabling condition of transnational feminist solidarities and communities. When combined with Gloria Anzaldúa's post-oppositional theory of *nepantla* ("in-between space") and *nepantleras* ("those who facilitate passages between worlds" and do not give in to the polarizing, monopolizing force of binary structures but rather moves in and out of them without ever claiming them), the significance of engaging translational contact zones—world-traveling—becomes even clearer ("Preface," 1). Indeed, translation can serve to produce and preserve "arrogant perceptions" (as in the making of colonial mobilities and relationalities), but it can also enable "loving perceptions" depending on the kind of traveling it facilitates—one that assimilates the other world, or one that takes the risk of being surprised with the unknowns of the other world and self-transformed by it. In the remainder of this chapter, by further drawing on this interplay between Mohanty, Lugones, and Anzaldúa's theories of world-traveling and world-making, I discuss *Bekâret's* readers' insights on those two modes of encountering the other as they imagine translational feminist communities.

## Imagining Oneself with the Other

Translation is a paradoxical border-space—an unpredictable in-between space of contact between the self and the other ("threshold" in Keating's words (*Transformation Now*, 10–18) and *nepantla* as Anzaldúa would call it) where colonial legacies can be sustained or contested depending on the nature of the encounters that take place in that liminal space of relationality. Translation is paradoxical because, on the one hand, it is an interlinguistic practice where a text, in the broadest sense of the term, is translocated across borders—that the practice's very existence depends on borders. Hence, translation is an attempt to negotiate differences claimed by borders. The consequences of that negotiation depend on how the border-navigation is done during translation and the encounters enabled by it. In this sense, translation, as an act of transforming the different into familiar, affirms, even substantiates the borders it crosses and reinscribes the differences declared by those borders. It is for this reason that translation can be seen as an operation of "bordering," at times recharging the oppositional energy of borders, many of which are in fact colonial legacies (Sakai, "Count a Language," 84).

On the other hand, affirming differences is also the beauty of translation. The problem with borders is not that they sustain difference; the problem is that the kind of bordering we often engage in operates within the colonial economy and recognizes difference only in essentialist, oppositional, separatist structures. Feminist translation can help us engage in a different kind of borderwork; one that welcomes difference without colonial modernity's murderous appetite for monopoly. As Lugones says, "communication across worlds is complex not because of impermeable cultural boundaries but because domination fragments the social" (*Pilgrimages*, 26). This is why we need to engage with translation with a well-grounded yet flexible enough ethics of "radical vulnerability" and responsibility so that the kinds of relationality we practice while encountering translation does not play into the very structures of domination that are designed to fragment the social, particularly the transnational social, and the cross-border resistances that grow out of that social (Nagar, *Hungry Translations*). In short, the paradox of translation compels us to ask, does it inflate or negate the colonial border? This question has crucial implications for transnational solidarities and communities of resistance. In what follows, I explore how readers responded to the oppositional charge of the border-space called (by) *Bekâret*.

The simple fact that *Virgin* was made into *Bekâret*—that it could travel across the seemingly impermeable borders that separate the western civilization from the (non)civilization of the orient[3]—and the readers in Turkey read and "owned" the book, which now speaks more dissident truths from multiple mouths, proves the falsity of assumed border fixity and homogeneity. Given that borders are "places where claims to ownership—claims to 'mine,' 'yours' and 'theirs'—are staked out, contested, defended, and fought over," *Virgin*'s translation could in fact be seen as a case of border dilution, where the implied constituency of the "original" text's "our" was reworked into a larger category geopolitically blurred enough to embrace a diverse readership across the east/west divide (Brah, *Cartographies of Diaspora*, 198). In other words, *Bekâret*'s readers accepted the book's invitation to permeate the oppositional borders it crossed and travel to its "worlds." They repopulated the text's foreign virginity narratives while simultaneously inhabiting the discursive and material locality of their "home"—which, however, is now resignified through the other's traveling stories. During those simultaneous acts of double-dwelling and border-blurring that flouted the "either/or" schemes of orientalism, the readers questioned the virginity politics of both "home" and "abroad." They allowed themselves to be textually recruited and mobilized into an imagined translational feminist community through the transcultural cooperations that took place in the making and reading of *Bekâret* "as a shared political project—a project aimed at developing empowering knowledge practices concerning women's bodies" (Davis, *How Feminism Travels*, 210). For instance, in the focus group, Defne explained how in her encounter with the traveling book's subversive knowledges, virginity became a simultaneously more intimate and more transnationally populated episteme for her:

> Defne (focus group): Before I started the book, I didn't think it would add so much knowledge to me. In fact—and I noted this at the end of my diary as well—the book woke me up to an issue about which I was actually asleep but thought I was awake. You know, what are my mother's problems? I asked myself what other things this woman deals with. I saw that virginity was also a problem of hers, her neighbor's, or of another woman who lives on the other side of the world.

As seen in this excerpt, *Bekâret* helped Defne see virginity as a political issue that affected women on a systematic basis both "at home" and "abroad." So, virginity, for her, became a "worldly" issue, not just an abstract matter. It is by making its readers aware of such transcultural systematicity and worldliness that *Bekâret* seems to have motivated its readers to imagine a global feminist community that potentially included both actual acquaintances and people they never met face to face—thus, helping them recognize that their mother, themselves, and a woman living on the other side of the world had potentially more in common than they had imagined before. It is this linking of the intimate with the global, the recognition of multiple "worlds," and the possibility (and necessity) of traveling to them that enabled visions of translational feminist communities among *Bekâret*'s readers.[4]

The transnational communities of resistance imagined by *Bekâret*'s readers were also grounded in the promise of social change held by the present and future production of feminist epistemologies that sought to dismantle virginity and liberate women from the disciplinary power of such gender norms anchored in women's bodies. Indeed, the readers often stated that the traveling book dispelled their sense of isolation when it came to undoing virginity. Even the book's presence on their bookshelves helped reduce their sense of isolation. Moreover, thanks to the fact that the book not only revealed a history of virginity resistance but also populated it with actual women while describing geohistorically shifting virginity codes, the readers reported remaining hopeful about accomplishing systemic change because now they knew that they were not alone in their struggle against virginity and that social change was possible. So, the readers' sense of isolation was broken because of *Bekâret's* epistemically subversive load, particularly its claim that virginity is a human invention, and its promise of change. As Ayşe noted in her diary, "if virginity is a fiction in the west, it is necessarily a fiction everywhere." Or in Kırmızı's words, "I recommend this book to everyone because virginity has a history. Just like every social deed, virginity is also a fiction. So, nothing is unchangeable" (diary).

The belief in the possibility and urgency of social change and the accompanying visualization of feminist collectivities of struggle against virginity terror also encouraged *Bekâret's* readers to demand more feminist knowledge (including art and media) production on virginity because they believed that would broaden the geopolitical scope of such communities of resistance and expand the reach of the book's politically unsettling effects—or "ripples" in Gülümser's diary words—to different localities while at the same time enabling world-traveling, contact zones, and transcultural bridges:

> Gülümser (diary): Dear Hanne Blank, thank you very much for dedicating your days and nights to this work. A woman (me) on the other side of the world lived with you for a while. This mode of rippling and producing gives me hope. It would be great if documentaries were made about this issue! I am interested in cinema; perhaps I will make one and send it to you.
> —Lots of love, Gülümser.

Indeed, Gülümser did produce a documentary that indirectly confronted Turkey's virginity regime.[5] Such materialization of an inspirational idea attests to the politically creative potential of *Bekâret's* translational "ripples" across borders as well as the hope it has generated among feminists who now imagine a transnational community of resistance no matter how immutable or insurmountable the borders between the east and the west might seem to be. In fact, Gülümser's "letter" to the author testifies to the communicative, connectionist, transformative potential of translation, where, instead of walls, the readers now see bridges—"the best mutuality we can hope for at the moment" (Anzaldúa, "Now Let Us Shift," 570). This is precisely why Anzaldúa said, "the bridge is both a barrier and point of transformation. By crossing, you invite a turning point, initiate a change" (557). Indeed, by enabling its readers to dismantle their preformed (self-orientalizing) assumptions about "liberated (post-feminist) western women" and discard their suppositions that virginity was a problem "of the backwards east and its desperately oppressed women," *Bekâret* helped remove the discursive barriers between women from different geographies and facilitate the feeling of transnational affinity:

Kırmızı (diary): The book gave me a feeling of "affinity." For example, it enabled me to learn that the oppressions that women experience due to virginity is not a situation unique to Turkey. I understood that keeping women's bodies under control is a universal adoption.

Kırmızı's comment closely resonates with Anzaldúa's connectionist theory of *conocimiento*: "Conocimiento shares a sense of affinity with all things and advocates mobilizing, organizing, sharing information, knowledge, insights, and resources with other groups" ("Now Let Us Shift," 571). After traveling into the "worlds" of western women and seeing their comparable gender realities, the readers' earlier views of western women as irrelevant transformed into a new vision that not only recognized their political relevance and agency, but also emphasized the potential of solidarity-building across borders previously deemed unbridgeable. It is precisely due to facilitating such "(re)encountering what is already encountered" that translation emerges as a promising contact zone (Ahmed, *Strange Encounters*, 178). In this zone of *nepantla*, ethical encounters take place between seemingly irreconcilable groups and lead to an acknowledgment of transcultural commonalities—defined not as a façade of sameness—and a vision of collaborations and coalitions across seemingly impassable distances.

The non-othering reconfiguration of differences and borders by *Bekâret's* readers is a crucial gesture since "the recognition of boundaries exposes relational possibilities and creates space for building alliances across difference" (Aiken et al., *Making Worlds*, 203). Engaging in such a connectionist move is in fact the very first step of forging feminist coalitions and communities across borders—indeed, "to bridge is to attempt community"—because we cannot embark on transnational resistance unless we first imagine such collaborative communities as possible (Anzaldúa, "Preface," 3). As Keating notes, "The attention to commonalities, defined as a woven linkage—a synergistic, alchemical combination between sameness, similarities, and difference—offers us another entry into coalition-building and transformation" (*Transformation Now*, 42–43). Feminist translation is crucial precisely for this reason because it provides us with that post-oppositional entry point into transnational feminist communities by enabling "mobile subjectivities" that "seek coalitions with other similarly situated localities: 'affinity, not identity' [Haraway, "A Manifesto," 197]" (Ferguson, *Man Question*, 153).

*Bekâret's* feminist readings demonstrate that, when practiced as subversive acts of cross-border rewriting and reading, feminist translation can be a catalyst for imagined transnational feminist communities by facilitating dialogues between constituencies that are geopolitically deterred from talking and listening to each other because of the adversarial mappings of the globe. Such translational encounters and egalitarian exchanges take place among people who do not personally know each other but who cognitively connect with one another in co-creating subversive meanings and common political visions against the global status quo. That is why translation should be considered a vital part of the transnational agenda to achieve "global cognitive justice," because without it there is no global (Santos, Nunes, and Meneses, "Introduction," xix). This connectionist potential of translation is well recognized by both Lawrence Venuti and Kathy Davis. Davis, for instance, writes, "the very act of translation . . . also partakes in a necessarily utopian desire for mutual understanding and an 'imagined feminist community'" (*How Feminism Travels*, 174). Similarly, Venuti says that translation "harbors the utopian dream of a common understanding between source and translating cultures," and by inventing a new readership for the text, it can promote imagined communities whose effects are cultural and political, domestic and transnational (*Translation Changes*, 29). He further notes (28),

> The communities fostered by translating are initially potential, signaled in the text, in the discursive strategy deployed by the translator, but not yet possessing a social existence. They depend for their realization on the ensemble of cultural constituencies among which the translation will circulate in the receiving situation.

Feminist translation, then, is a communal project because it can recruit isolated readers into an imagined transnational collectivity identified by the subversive agenda and common liberatory vision of the translation project. One of the participants, Ece, while evaluating the feminist translator's translation strategies, especially the translator's preface, acknowledged this potential saying:

> Ece (diary): I found the translator's preface immensely useful. . . . Yes, virginity is a universal issue but how its specific manifestations appear in Turkey is something that closely concerns the Turkish-speaking reader. Every day, we are bombarded with tons of [false] information on TV and newspapers; there is so much annoying news about "morality," virginity, and what happens after its loss. . . . Yet, there is still no universal response to it.

As the quotation illustrates, the diverse virginity narratives told in the translator's preface and the rest of *Bekâret* underline the commonality and political affinity between the readers located in Turkey and *Virgin*'s readership located in the west as well as the diverse group of women whose stories are told in the book. This affinity emphasis is, indeed, so powerful that Ece ends her remarks by noting the lack of a "universal response" to virginity oppression, despite its being assigned a "universal women's issue," and thus, envisioning a feminist community defined by global resistance to virginity.

The fact that the feminist translator's signature is quite visible in *Bekâret*, particularly through my preface whose use of "we/us/our" is similar to Blank's embracing readers regardless of their location, seems to have encouraged the readers to read the book in a more connectionist framework—in "a model of *métissage*, of borrowing and lending across porous cultural boundaries" (Felski, "Doxa of Difference," 12, emphasis original). Indeed, while speaking from the collective position of "we," the preface consistently shifts between "women in Turkey" and "women in the world" in its signified constituency and in doing so, facilitates a sense of togetherness among readers. Also, by including myself, a fellow "native" of Turkey, as a feminist agent in the book's subversive discourse, the translator seems to have further inspired readers to step in and reside in the western book and visualize themselves as part of an imagined community of readers whose lives have somehow been affected by virginity oppression, no matter where they live. In that regard, Davis's following account of *Our Bodies, Ourselves* as a text that empowers women by activating them to imagine feminist communities of readers also describes *Bekâret*'s readers' interactions with the book, which (*How Feminism Travels*, 138)

> . . . allows them an imaginative entry into the experiences of different women and, along with it, the understanding that each woman has her own subjective project, depending on the circumstances of her embodiment and the social, cultural, and political context in which she lives. The recognition that others—however differently located—are also involved in intentional projects is what ultimately allows for reciprocity and the possibility of collective action.

Then, my transparent presence in the text as a translator, a "boundary-crosser" or a "thresholder" in Anzaldúa's words ("Now Let Us Shift," 571), seems to have helped *Bekâret*'s readers imagine cross-border feminist collectivities of resistance against virginity violence because, by never denying or attempting to conceal the otherness of the traveling text, my mediating voice continually reminded them of the salience and relevance of the other in regard to that transnational vision:

> Ayşe (diary): The preface is very important in terms of both piecing things together and reminding us that the author and translator are coming from different cultural backgrounds. While reading translated books we often don't think of the cultural context in which it's been written because the

book we are holding in our hands is speaking in our own language. Thanks to the translator's introduction, I never forgot the fact that what I was to read was "the history of virginity in the west" and thus, while reading it, I had the opportunity to compare it with Turkey. . . . I don't see translation as a barrier between two languages/cultures. On the contrary, translation is a practice that brings people closer, that helps them understand each other.

Ayşe's comment, highlighting translation's potential to enable a sense of cross-border togetherness, brings to mind Lugones' following words: "The opportunity is one of understanding by 'translation' a much larger act, a much more faithful act, a more loving act, a more disruptive act, a more deeply insurgent act than the finding of linguistic 'equivalences'" (*Pilgrimages*, 3). It is due to this connectionist potential that *Bekâret*'s readers articulated hopes of more translations of the book. Hence, the book's locally cherished translatedness, which indicates its projected translatability for other locales, inspires further imaginary exercises of broader transnational feminist connectivities and collectivities:

> Kırmızı (diary): Above all, the book will create awareness across the world. There will be more people who will be critical of virginity and question things. Other cultures will also learn about the different [virginity] methods that have been practiced throughout history. They will have information on other cultures' virginities. This will make a big impact in terms of social change.

> Nil (diary): I believe the book will contribute to feminist movements in Turkey and across the world. The book has given me a lot of issues to critically think about. I am sure it will give that to other readers as well and this growing critical awareness will make a big contribution to the feminist politics. The awareness raised among readers will drive others to take actions, too.

> Yasemin (diary): It is indisputable that this one-of-a-kind comprehensive study on virginity is a crucial source for both Turkey and other countries. Thus, translating the book into other languages would facilitate an important [political] initiative/opening for other cultures as well.

These comments demonstrate that translation facilitates imagined transnational feminist communities not only by creating an epistemic contact zone, where political lessons are exchanged (and further saturated) across borders, but also by inspiring the formation of more such zones. Davis's description of the translational travels of *Our Bodies, Ourselves* explains this potential well: "This imagined community was none other than the international communities of readers, readers who were diversely located individuals unified not by virtue of their shared identity as women but by their shared quest for knowledge" (*How Feminism Travels*, 191). If *Virgin* is translated into more languages (particularly with a feminist agenda that seeks to facilitate post-oppositional connectivities across borders), the epistemic global network of resistance it has initiated expands to include more readers. It is this realization of "translation=transnational" that explains *Bekâret's* readers' faith in translation/world-traveling; it is the connectionist desire to grow into a larger togetherness.

Indeed, I argue, imagined transnational feminist communities among otherwise geopolitically isolated and distanced readers require feminist translation praxes because only when engaged with a feminist ethics of hospitality, generosity, responsibility, and "radical vulnerability" will translation maintain and perhaps even accentuate the feminist discursivity of the traveling text and also create bridges between cultures and readers (Nagar, *Hungry Translations*, 29–31). This is why all the participants expressed that *Virgin* should be translated into other languages because other parallel translations, they believed, could similarly help dismantle virginity norms and build more bridges of solidarity. In Nagar's words, the readers highlighted that "the journey on which we have come thus far through trust, solidarity, and self-critique cannot stop at one or two critical experiments, one or two books, or one or two institutions. It is a dialogic process that can be sustained only through continuous movement and questioning" (*Muddying the Waters*, 148). After revealing how eagerly *Bekâret's* readers imagined themselves with the other (and other others that the book might touch in translation) as partners in a transnational project of ending virginity violence, in the next section, I explore how they imagined a reverse scenario of world-traveling. That is, did the readers think the other would walk the bridge of *Virgin* with a similar spirit of solidarity if the book traveled from the east to the west?

## Imagining the Other with Oneself

The previous section illustrated *Bekâret's* readers' yearnings for solidarity-based transnational feminist collectivities—or "sisterhood" (*kızkardeşlik*) if you will, which, in the interpretive ground of Turkey's intersectionally organized feminist movement, is not a tainted term that is overgrown with the exclusionary tendencies of imperialist western feminism—activated by their encounters with the traveling book. In these encounters, the readers imagined themselves side by side (or, eye to eye) with their geopolitically defined other. That is, while they were keenly aware of the binary scheme that positioned them in opposition to the translated other, they could see beyond that oppositionality. In the follow-up interviews, I asked the participants to reverse the geopolitical composition and direction of the traveling feminist book and imagine its reception by western feminists—so that *Virgin* would become a similarly transgressive book that seeks to dismantle heteropatri-archal virginity regimes but within the geohistorical context of "the east," however the readers would define that terrain. Would western feminists similarly embrace the traveling book because of its epistemic intervention although its stories did not exactly reflect their specific gender realities? Would they elevate the eastern book's theoretical claims to a universal status while adding their local stories to it? That is, did *Bekâret*'s readers expect a "loving perception" or an "arrogant perception" from western feminists? This was a strategic question to test the readers' faith in transnational feminist solidarities because, considering how enthusiastically they wanted (western) *Virgin* to be translated to other languages so that the cross-border networks of resistance it facilitated among variously located readers would continue expanding, I wondered if they would show the same enthusiasm for a geo-politically marked (eastern) *Virgin*.

Out of the seventeen readers who participated in the follow-up study, only three imagined that a traveling eastern *Virgin* would receive an absolutely unbiased reciprocity from western feminists:

Çise (follow-up interview): East or west wouldn't matter; I think west-ern feminists would embrace the book as well. Feminists wouldn't have any prejudices, but lay people could have ideas like, "wow the east is so barbaric," while in reality if they read their own histories, they would see very similar things.

Sezen (follow-up interview): I think western feminists would embrace the book. . . . Essentially it is the same problem, although its practical manifestations and historical progressions are different. Of course, there is prejudice everywhere, not just in the US. . . . But I don't think there would be a labeling, stigmatizing attitude among western feminists. I mean that is a legitimate doubt, but I can't generalize. I don't have much of that doubt for feminists.

Ayşegül (follow-up interview): I think a book produced here would have very similar stories in it. On the other hand, there is a lot of orientalist curiosity about what goes on in Turkey. . . . But by means of "sisterhood," I think feminists would not read the book with an orientalist curiosity. I mean, because I see feminism more in terms of sisterhood, I believe a feminist who lives in the US would read the book with a feminist agenda, not an orientalist agenda.

The trust that Çise, Sezen, and Ayşegül place in the anti-colonial western reception of the imaginary eastern text is extended only to feminist readers as they believe that non-feminist readers might still resort to colonial meaning-making mechanisms—i.e., using "barbaric" to describe nonwestern realities no matter how similar they are to those of the west. This doubt about the potential of orientalist western reception was raised by the rest of the participants (with varying degrees of intensity and confidence), who, however, unlike Çise, Sezen, and Ayşegül, also included western feminists among possible offenders. This interplay between doubt and trust in imagining "how the other sees you"—with loving perception or arrogant perception?—deserves closer analysis because, as much as "how you see the other" is a key part of imagined translational feminist communities, how you believe the other sees you matters just as much for the making of transnational feminist connectivities.

In articulating their concerns about interpretive hazards in eastern *Virgin*'s encounters with a western feminist audience, most of *Bekâret*'s readers discussed "orientalism" as the dominant paradigm of reception in the west, although this term was not used in any of the interview questionnaires. Given that the oppositional relationship between the west and the east (as well as the categories themselves) is a product of orientalism, it is not surprising that the readers brought up concerns of orientalist reception during a discussion of an eastern text traveling to the west. Yet, their accounts oscillating between trust and doubt, hope and disappointment, provide crucial geopolitical lessons on the affective making of transnational feminist solidarities, particularly for western feminists:

> Selma (follow-up interview): I would want such a book to be translated to English very much but I don't think books written in Turkish get to be translated to English that much. . . . I also wonder if such a book's travel would generate any orientalist reactions. I mean, would it further turn us into a victim? But their book was like that too! They didn't become victims in my eyes, but we could become victims in their eyes. After all, this is a matter of violence and violence is experienced everywhere. I mean, women actually don't differ much from each other on that front. That's why I believe it should be translated . . . But there is definitely a hegemonic relationship there. So, an orientalist perspective would certainly emerge, like, "oh my, look what kinds of horrible things happened there!" They would act as if that violence was far from them, like such things never happened to them. They would perceive the book as if they never went through that history themselves. But then again, if they could get passed that, the book could help establish commonalities. . . . Regardless, I would want that book to

be translated because such knowledge circulation is crucial. . . . I want to believe in the idea of sisterhood.

This comment designates the current global hierarchy of knowledge, rooted in the orientalist agenda of constructing the west as the place of epistemic, political, moral, and cultural superiority, as the central issue that transnational feminism must grapple with. In fact, the simultaneous appearance of the doubtful, "Would such an eastern *Virgin* even be allowed to travel to the west?"[6] and the hopeful, "Regardless of the risk of orientalist reception, it should be translated" points at the problem of a global hierarchy of knowledge, which elevates western texts to the status of "the truth" while positing eastern ones as irrelevant details ("non-knowledge") or relevant data to uphold *the* (western) truth ("case studies"). This "hegemonic relationship" was noted by other participants as well. For instance:

> Ece (follow-up interview): If the book traveled to the west, I think instead of explaining a theory like *Bekâret* did, it would turn into a case study. Like, "let's see what happens in Egypt about this issue, how do women in Iran deal with it?" I remember Saba Mahmood's work that explains to the west how Middle Eastern women perform agency and how they are not passive objects. This is in fact obvious, but we must illustrate, explain, and theorize it so that people in the west understand it as it is. I think this virginity book would have to do that as well. . . . Also, would that book go to the US? It would first have to prove its significance to the west.

Ece's comment, similarly unsure whether an eastern *Virgin* would make it to the west, calls attention to the disparities in the global traffic of feminist texts, which is a common critique in postcolonial feminist literatures.[7] This is a call to western feminists to question their protocols of translation and reception and engage in more ethical practices of world-traveling because "the possibilities of what the text can do for justice are in fact created in and through responsible receiving and interpretation" (Nagar, *Hungry Translations*, 153). So, it is not enough to translate more feminist texts into hegemonic languages; we also must create an ethical reception ethos to make sure those traveling texts do not end up reproducing the assimilative gestures of the "arrogant perception," which is "to perceive that others are for oneself and to proceed to arrogate their substance to oneself" (Lugones, *Pilgrimages*, 78).

Selma's comment above also illustrates another common element in the readers' responses: the expectation of "pity politics" (rescue mentality or savior complex) from western feminists in their encounters with nonwestern discourses on gender violence. When such a discourse originates in the east, violence against women becomes "oriental violence against oriental women."

In fact, the readers frequently used the phrase "looking down on" to describe that epistemic violence:

> Bilge Su (follow-up interview): They wouldn't read that book as we did. We read *Bekâret* in reference to anatomy. . . . But I think they would read it more in reference to the east. You know that "pitiful" condition of ours that they look down on, the claim that our society is the one where women are most subordinated, most exposed to sexism; they would read that. I don't think they would read the book only in reference to virginity. They'd read it as another layer of our "pitiful" condition. Here, we read "women" in the western context. But they wouldn't read "women." They wouldn't read the book in reference to women's common problems. They'd read "the oppressed woman of the eastern culture;" so, they'd read the east.

> Pembe (follow-up interview): Maybe the book would be considered a part of the orientalist repertoire. . . . In terms of embracing the book, they could have similar reading experiences, but perhaps they'd bring more orientalist readings in, like "this is something coming from a lesser culture." So, they could stigmatize it more. For them, solidarity would be more like being on the side of the oppressed, so they'd see that woman in more inferior terms. They perhaps wouldn't see her as their equal. The book's impact there would be more like looking down on.

> Dicle (follow-up interview): If the book was made here and translated to English, there could be a looking down on it—although they are quite behind on these issues as well, but they're not aware of it. When there is an issue about the Middle East or a Muslim country, they bring in a perspective as if they're at a very different point than the Middle Eastern "other." . . . But I think women's liberation is ultimately a universal struggle and we have a lot in common.

> Şeyma (follow-up interview): I feel like if they read that book in Europe and the US, they'd read it with a perspective like, "Oh poor things, how much they suffer!" They couldn't stay away from that orientalist perspective. When we read texts about the west, we try to critique it in equal terms. But when they look at us from that geography, there is always a looking-down-on. They'd say, "Look, they haven't overcome this problem and they can't anyway." Although, I must admit, what I'm doing right now is also a little like looking down on them. So, I'm not sure. This is hypothetical. . . . They might surprise us. We'd have to try and see.

I quote these comments at length because the geopolitical doubt they express about western feminists' colonial habits of "looking down on the other woman" is not only warranted by a long, persistent history of orientalist knowledge production and global activism, but also imbued with a hopeful invitation to change the current global economy of feminist reception. So, these critiques are not intended to reclaim the oppositional walls of orientalism and close off the chance of alliance-building across colonial borders; rather, they are to remind us of the possibility, and necessity, of transnational feminist solidarities. They are not just a testament to the presence of arrogant perception, but also an appeal to loving perception, because in Şeyma's words, "they might surprise us." Naeem Inayatullah calls this mode of post-oppositional, non-assimilative openness to the other (and the other's truth) the principle of "full generosity to the antagonist" (Inayatullah, "Pulling Threads," 336), which Richa Nagar explains as "understanding the simultaneous coexistence of inhumanity and humanity within each one of us" (*Hungry Translations*, 43). Inayatullah ("Pulling Threads," 341) further asks,

> Why do we work so hard to forget our overlap with others, so that what appears is our innocence and their guilt, and sometimes our guilt and their innocence, but never their overlap? Why do we strain to forget our simultaneous overlap but different embedding in violence, war, and even genocide? Why do we ignore our complicity?

Indeed, this mode of generosity to the antagonist appears in several readers' critiques of western feminism's complicity in orientalism—for instance, when Bilge Su turns the critical gaze to feminists in Turkey and says about the possibility of feminists yielding to "crude orientalist reflexes": "Just like what we do to women of Kurdistan." Or when Müjgan says, "Western feminists look to their east and see the east. Then, I turn and look to my east and see the east; then, that woman turns and looks to her east and sees the east, and this condescending cycle continues,"[8] pointing at the superficial (yet authoritative) presence of the categories "east" and "west." And finally, Yasemin says, "as people located in the west and in the east, we have so many prejudices against each other," highlighting orientalist estrangement as a two-way street (mutual but not equal). In other words, *Bekâret*'s readers recognize their own complicity in hegemonic power relations even as they criticize western feminists for their colonial attitudes. And as Nagar explains (*Hungry Translations*, 43, emphasis original),

> Such grappling with the simultaneous presence of the protagonist and antagonist in all of us is necessary for *just* translations—that is, for modes of retelling that agitate against the structures and epistemes invested in guarding the binary of "the emancipators" and "those in need of emancipation."

The hope, the desire, the dream encoded in the "surprise" that Şeyma expects from western feminists, as well as in the self-reflexive gestures of Bilge

Su, Müjgan, and Yasemin who attempt to see beyond the west/east binary while recognizing its divisive power are crucial because only through those complex, multilayered, post-oppositional modes of relationality that we can truly connect with one another. "Surprise" is the keyword here because embracing surprise—"playfulness" or "openness to uncertainty," in Lugones' words—is a key part of practicing loving perception (*Pilgrimages*, 26). So, when we encounter a translated other, we should remember that the text we are reading has traveled from another "world," which is not what we think it is, and can take us to that "world" if we are willing to go there playfully, not arrogantly; if we are willing to embrace "openness to being a fool, openness to self-construction or reconstruction and to construction and reconstruction of the 'worlds' we inhabit playfully" (96). This kind of world-traveling can be full of unknowns and surprises as a result of which subjectivities, including ours, get transformed and give birth to new forms of inter/subjectivity. So, the tentative border-space that translation forges between worlds is a space of uncertainty that we need to inhabit creatively, playfully, and bravely. Loss may be inevitable in this process of crossing but not all loss is impairing or depraving. Indeed, some loss is necessary in the process of learning to practice loving playfulness because that process involves unlearning our arrogant perceptions. The hope of solidarity that such loss entails is bigger than the hostile geohistories we have inherited; in fact, it is that very hope (and willingness to take the risk of translational surprises in a mode of generosity to the antagonist) that will bring us together in pursuit of global justice. That post-oppositional hope is exactly why *Bekâret*'s readers *always* ended up favoring translation, regardless of the intensity or legitimacy of their doubt about western feminists' interpretive parochialisms:

> Nil (follow-up interview): Of course, I'd want that book to go to the west. After all, virginity is not just a taboo in the Middle East; it is a taboo in the US as well, which *Bekâret* clearly shows. Based on those commonalities in our experiences, I think other political connectivities could be forged among feminists. But I am hoping that western feminists won't fall into orientalist traps that would jeopardize such bonds. But no matter what, it should be translated.

However, the intertwining appearance of doubt and hope about cross-border feminist connectivities requires that western feminists hear the disappointment, resentment, and frustration in these readers' (and other third world feminists') critiques that persistently emphasize the necessity of developing a more balanced global ethics of feminist perception that recognizes both commonalities and differences among women and their situated gender/sexuality realities (as opposed to the colonial habit of exaggerating the other's difference or the self's universality, or the "evolved" mode of indifference preached by cultural relativists). Indeed, there is another way to connect with one another, one that is not grounded in the missionary logic of orientalism, but we need to work hard for it:

> Ayşe (follow-up interview): If that book were translated to English—and I have this prejudice because I myself experienced it a lot—it'd be a text that went there from the *orient* [she uses the English word] and the stories would be more like the sins of the evil men of the east, while in reality the conceptualization of masculinity is quite a universal thing. I mean, our men are bad, okay, I accept that, but theirs are bad too. . . . But because that would be a book produced here and translated to there, and because there is unfortunately a hierarchical relationship between the east and the west, I don't think the text would be embraced over there. It wouldn't be like *Bekâret*. . . . But western feminists should question their feminisms because we need that kind of solidarity; we must mutually sustain each other. There is no situation where you can come and rescue me. If I rescue myself, you will rise from there. There is no other way.

Ayşe's comment reminds us that to achieve transnational solidarity, western feminists should not only let go of their (groundless) colonial rescue fantasies but also begin recognizing the plurality as well as the simultaneous "independence and interconnectedness" of patriarchies (and feminisms) in non-hierarchical frameworks (Gunning, "Arrogant Perception," 204). This re-relating to the other outside the objectifying fabric of orientalism—"not as parts, problems, or useful commodities, but from a connectionist view"— is not only an ethical imperative, but also a political necessity to achieve global justice (Anzaldúa, "Now Let Us Shift," 569). Our lives, movements, and stories are already so violently intertwined that to make the world a just place, we need to find nonviolent ways to connect with one another so that "my" self-defined journey to liberation enables "your" self-defined journey to liberation, and vice versa, until the boundaries that separate "my" and "your" blur into bigger and heterogeneous (contingent) grounds of "our." Thus, recognizing the dehumanizing effects of orientalism—not just intellectually, but also experientially—Ayşe offers western feminists a crucial political lesson in connecting across differences and borders; that is, lessons in world-traveling: "By traveling to other people's 'worlds,' we discover that there are 'worlds' in which those who are victims of arrogant perception are really subjects, lively beings, resisters, constructors of visions even though in the mainstream construction they are animated only by the arrogant perceiver and are pliable, foldable, file-awayable, classifiable" (Lugones, *Pilgrimages*, 97). This is not a new lesson but the fact that it is repeated so often by *Bekâret*'s readers points at the urgency of the task. So, I would like to end this section with the hopeful words of Gülümser and Müjgan, who, despite their serious reservations about orientalist possibilities, reject the political despair procured by that colonial history and reclaim transnational feminist solidarity, or "sisterhood" in Selma's words:

> Gülümser (follow-up interview): My wish and expectation are that, if that book reached them, feminists all around the world would read it with the same care and interest. I don't think they'd reject or sanctify it. I think they'd give the book its due and establish contact with it, remain in communication with it. Having more examples from different geographies reveals the big problem. We need this kind of collaboration. It's empowering. . . . Feminism has many different strands. Some feminists might disdain that book. Some might praise it too much. . . . I mean there is after all an orientalist doctrine. But I don't want to believe in such a world. And regardless, I say, the book should be translated and go there. Because I think experiences are unique and this is not an issue of Turkey, the US, India, etc.; every woman's, every human's, every living being's story is unique, and it is precious when all is heard and brought together.

> Müjgan (follow-up interview): That exclusionary, orientalist attitude is something I am familiar with. It is a question of "Where are you looking at me from? Why are you looking down on me like that?" But I want to be optimistic. We need people whose minds and hearts are open to understand the world. We need an open mind so they can responsibly transplant the book there. We need an open heart so they won't say, "Yes, I already know all this." Rather they will develop empathy.

These appeals to western feminists to treat nonwestern women as legitimate knowledge producers and capable political agents, to collaborate with them as equals, and to open their hearts and minds to their traveling stories reveal *Bekâret*'s readers' polyphonic dreams of solidarity inspired/facilitated by translational world-traveling. While they are keenly aware of the danger of cross-border travels reinforcing colonial tropes (which Bilge Su called "the orientalist tendency to find in the translated text things that confirm their preexisting suppositions"), they are more than willing to take the risk of translation because there is no other way of connecting across borders. It is indeed because of the possibility to translate and receive in translation differently (that is, ethically and politically responsibly) and the potential of translation to enable post-oppositional, cooperative connectivities between selves and others that *Bekâret*'s readers want the (imaginary) eastern *Virgin* to be translated to western languages, no matter what. While they are uneasy about the fact that this is "an ethics that remains a task" (Landes, "Weight of Others," 178), their yearnings for new becomings in solidarity and justice are bigger than their fears of betrayal because as Judith Butler beautifully puts it (*Precarious Life*, 44):

> When we ask for recognition for ourselves, we are not asking for an Other to see us as we are, as we already are, we have always been, as we were constituted prior to the encounter itself. Instead, in the asking, in the petition, we have already become something new, since we are constituted by virtue of the address, a need and desire for the Other that takes place in language in the broadest sense, one without which we could not be. To ask for recognition . . . is to solicit a becoming, to instigate a transformation, to petition the future always in relation to the Other.

In short, the geopolitical doubts raised by *Bekâret*'s readers indicate that the bridges they built while reading the book are not as sturdy or secure as they seemed earlier. In fact, the readers argued, those bridges can stand strong only if they are mutually sustained by feminists situated on the other side. That is, translational bridges bring us together (as tentative, yet promising collective becomings in/for solidarity)—"even as the bridge highlights the gap between us"—only if western feminists maintain and walk it with the same care, curiosity, commitment, and compassion required to engage with others (Bost, *Shared Selves*, 144). These bridges bond feminists across borders only in and through ethical practices of translation and reception, which, first and foremost, require western feminists to see feminism as a transnationally "polyversal" platform that does not belong to the west, and nonwestern women as feminist agents whose locally grown politics are not only legitimate but also globally relevant. As Zillah Eisenstein explains, calling for "a polyversal feminism—multiple and connected," "[Feminisms] have been wrongly homogenized as a unity, and then defined as of the West. This negates multiple forms of feminisms in the West *and* the multiple forms of feminisms outside the West. As such, feminisms lose their plurality of meanings which also express the similarities among women" (*Against Empire* 183, emphasis original). Considering the enduring legacies of colonial violence, engaging in ethical practices of translation and reception that appreciate and embrace (in non-assimilative, non-othering ways) feminist endeavors of the non-west is no easy task. However, as *Bekâret*'s readers emphasized (and showed), it is not impossible either. And it is urgent.

This is why feminists, particularly those of us who are products of the ideological currents of the west—call it colonial, orientalist, imperialist, neoliberal, even postcolonial—need to hone our skills of translating and reading in non-othering ways, practice loving perception and world-traveling in and through such textual encounters, and hear feminists in/of the global south as epistemic and political agents whose lessons of resistance are indispensable to transnational struggles for justice. Creating a decolonial feminist ethos of translation and reception is long overdue. We cannot get to that new world of justice and liberation that we dream of—"a new and more possible meeting," as Audre Lorde calls it below—without transnational solidarities and there can be no transnational solidarities without ethical translation and reception practices. While I continue exploring the urgency of this task in the concluding chapter, where I ask whether translation's connectionist potential is fully put to use for transnational feminist ends regardless of the geopolitical direction of textual flows, for now, I would like to leave you with a poetic lesson from Audre Lorde (*Sister Outsider*, 123):

> We have chosen each other
> and the edge of each other's battles
> the war is the same
> if we lose
> someday women's blood will congeal
> upon a dead planet
> if we win
> there is no telling
> we seek beyond history
> for a new and more possible meeting.

# Translation in Transnational/ Transnational in Translation

> Cultural translation is a process of yielding our most
> fundamental categories, that is, seeing how and why they
> break up, require resignification when they encounter the
> limits of an available episteme: what is unknown or not yet
> known. It is crucial to recognize that the human will only be
> built over time in and by the process of cultural translation,
> where it is not a translation between two languages that stay
> enclosed, distinct, unified. But rather, translation will compel
> each language to change in order to apprehend the other, and
> this apprehension, at the limit of what is familiar, parochial, and
> already known, will be the occasion for an ethical and social
> transformation. It will constitute a loss, a disorientation, but in
> which the human stands a chance of coming into being anew.
>
> —Butler, *Precarious Life*, 38

Virgin *Crossing Borders*, itself a traveling book, has told the story of *Virgin's* political journey from the US to Turkey—one of those "journeys enabled by trust with the ever-present possibility of distrust and epistemic violence; journeys of hope that must continuously recognize hopelessness and fears; journeys that insist on crossing borders even as each person on the journey learns of borders that they cannot cross" (Nagar, *Muddying the Waters*, 5). The reception studies I conducted with the feminist readers of the book, which was purposefully translated to disrupt Turkey's virginity regime, revealed that the traveling book did in fact intervene in the local virginity codes and reinforce the already existing feminist endeavors against biopolitical gender oppression. Moreover, the book accomplished such impact against all geopolitical odds, as the roads it traveled and the borders it crossed were paved with the oppositional, separatist forces of orientalism, imperialism, and nationalism. Despite all those reasons that situated the *western* book as irrelevant for, if not against, Turkey's cultural landscape, *Bekâret's* readers bridged across the "west vs. east" binary and engaged in constructive, egalitarian dialogues with the imported text. Such transcultural bridging has resulted in the growth of a local feminist repertoire of subversive virginity knowledges that stimulate crucial acts of resistance.

It seems that *Bekâret*'s subjectively and locally unsettling impact could take place across contentious borders partially because of the feminist translator's ethics of self-reflexivity and interconnectedness—particularly visible in my preface—and mostly because of the feminist readers' interpretive strategies of comparative accretion and differential universalization, all of which facilitated the formation of transnational feminist affinities and imagined translational feminist communities of solidarity against virginity oppression. So, in the course of its transplantation in Turkey, *Bekâret* became more than a book about western virginities; it grew epistemologically, experientially, and geopolitically as its translator and readers added to it from their subjective and local stocks of gender realities. And more importantly, the readers engaged in these connectionist reading practices despite the fact that they did not fully trust or always have confidence in western feminists' capacity for ethically receiving stories by and about eastern feminists. Indeed, while they themselves exercised post-oppositional readings—recognizing the ruling presence of and even borrowing from oppositional interpretive schemes but not letting themselves "become trapped within oppositional thought and action"—several of *Bekâret*'s readers expected oppositional readings from their "western sisters" (Keating, "Editor's Foreword," xi). Although that is not a barrier to *imagining* translational feminist communities, because the readers were still hopeful that western feminists could unlearn and escape deep-seated orientalist reflexes and prejudices in their encounters with the traveling stories of the other, this lack of mutual geopolitical trust is a barrier to the material formation of cross-border feminist alliances.

In first section of this chapter, I further elaborate on the implications of translational reading practices for the future of transnational feminist politics by hypothetically reversing the geopolitical direction of the traveling book, turning Edward Said's traveling theory on its head. Similar to what I asked *Bekâret*'s readers in the follow-up study, which I discuss in Chapter 6, I now ask you, dear reader, what if the book in question told a feminist history of "eastern virginities" and traveled to the US in English translation? How do you think US feminist readers would react to such a book? How would you react to that book? What kinds of interpretive strategies would you resort to in making sense of its alien stories, especially if they contradicted your preconfigured notions of the other or of virginity? What kinds of conclusions would you draw about your oriental other if the book's stories of gender violence overlapped with and confirmed sensationalist orientalist tropes that abundantly circulate in the west? In the end, would your reading strategies qualify as oppositional or post-oppositional? These are crucial questions since they help reveal the pitfalls of transnational feminism that we have yet to resolve. In the second section, I discuss two scenarios illustrating some of the disturbing reactions I received in response to the connectionist vision of Virgin *Crossing Borders* at various western academic settings. These oppositional responses are worth noting because they not only reveal the persistence of colonial encounters in translational epistemic border crossings, but also highlight the urgency of assuming geopolitical and ethical responsibility when it comes to hearing one another across differences and borders. In the third section, I discuss the figures of the feminist translator and the feminist reader as key actors of transnational feminist encounters, dialogues, and solidarities. I particularly underline the importance of not only disseminating feminist texts across borders—and across all geopolitical directionalities, not just from the global north to the global south as the colonial/imperial forces dictate—through politically conscious and ethically responsible translation practices, but also cultivating a new culture of "translation reception" that simultaneously celebrates the indeterminate alienness of the other, the fluidity and vulnerability of the self, and the fine possibility of transcultural hybridization. In the final section, I discuss the potential contributions of my research as well as its "blind" spots and omissions. It is my hope that with both its significance and limitations disclosed, the book will inspire a more intense cross-border traffic of transgressive discourses and greater knowledge production on the making of such translational travels.

## What If?

In *Strange Encounters*, Sara Ahmed writes, "Women in different nation spaces, within a globalised economy of difference, cannot not encounter each other, what is at stake is *how*, rather than *whether*, the encounter takes place" (167, emphasis original). Then, she asks, "How can women encounter each other differently, given that such encounters are already mediated by the divisions of labour and consumption that position women in different parts of the world in relationships of antagonism" (171)? *Virgin*'s Turkish translation and the reading narratives of its feminist readers provide us with an optimistic picture of transcultural encounters among women positioned hierarchically in the cultural economy of globalization. As the previous chapters have illustrated, the diverse meaning-making strategies utilized both by the feminist translator and the feminist readers in order to bridge the east/

west chasm seem to have facilitated the readers not only to experience a foreign book as a domestically relevant feminist project—without assimilating it into the local economy of sameness—but also to configure transcultural political commonalities among women and imagine translational communities of resistance against oppressive virginity (and broader biomedical gender) regimes.

Such cross-cultural operations of re/signification obviously posed a formidable challenge to *Bekâret*'s readers due to the hegemony of the globally and locally well-entrenched discourses of orientalism/occidentalism that only polarize and pit subjects and subjectivities marked as eastern and western against each other. Yet, instead of succumbing to the estranging and dividing force of such regulatory discourses and antagonistically rejecting the text for being on and of the west, the readers open-mindedly interacted with it. Such dismissal was not opted for even after noticing that, contrary to the universality its title claimed, the book exclusively told the history of the west and hardly mentioned cultures other than those deemed western. A few readers (e.g., Dicle, Ece, and Ayşe) even noted that the title could have been translated as "The 'Untouched' History of Virginity *in the West*" so that Turkish-speaking readers would know beforehand what to expect from the book in terms of its geohistorical scope. Interestingly, as the translator, I had considered that intervention, yet decided against it because I did not want to lose any readers to unwarranted prejudices fueled by nationalism or anti-westernism and deter readers from even turning the book's first page.[1] That is, I did not want the title to inflate the oppositional energies surrounding the book and burn bridges. Indeed, an example that well illustrates this geopolitical risk can be seen in the following excerpt from Milena:

> Milena (diary): Almost anyone who saw me holding and reading the book showed interest in it. They frequently asked me questions. These questions were generally on what the book was about and what they were most curious about was what it said about virginity. According to some [those who were conservative on gender issues], the reason why the book didn't embrace the "truths" about virginity they already had in their minds was because its author was from a foreign nation and didn't know our "values." That's why she had such [radical/different] ideas.

A marked "western" title could exacerbate such conformist and culturally purist (even xenophobic) perceptions and prevent potential readers from giving the book's "alien" voice a chance to unsettle their heteropatriarchal virginity truths.[2] However, as my study demonstrated, *Bekâret* could, and did, become more than a western history in Turkey. Its subversive theories and epistemologies held "universal" appeal as they could inform (and be informed by) the local virginity codes and realities excluded from the text. Eventually, the readers uncovered that potential because they were amenable to hearing such critical views—no matter what remote geography they traveled from or what "otherworldly" culture they were associated with. The delicate bridges the readers built with the book could have been undermined or foreclosed if the book were over-identified as "western" in its title.

In short, although they occasionally experienced geopolitical disjunctures, the readers did not quit reading *Bekâret* or close themselves off to its destabilizing epistemes. Instead of casting the book as "a product of an oppositional alien culture that has nothing to say to me" or as "the assimilative hegemonic voice of the imperialist west," they took it as a facilitator of cross-cultural dialogues and critical self-reflection. This attitude is key for building transnational feminist politics because as Charlotte Bunch explains, "We cannot depend on our perceptions alone as the basis for political analysis and action—much less for coalition. Feminists must stretch beyond, challenging the limits of our own personal experiences by learning from the diversity of women's lives" (*Passionate Politics*, 153).

As much as these findings provide us with a hopeful portrayal of transnational feminism (woven with "promises of radical vulnerability and love, reflexivity and risk, translation and coauthorship"), I would like to complicate (and perhaps deromanticize) them with an alternative argument, which posits that the travels of *Virgin* from the US to Turkey also hint at some cautionary possibilities about transnational feminist politics (Nagar, *Muddying the Waters*, 5). In the rest of this section, I present some speculative questions for you, the reader of this book, to highlight these potential pitfalls as well as to stimulate some "soul searching" to "unveil" and confront our geopolitically grounded assumptions (particularly those grounded in the discursive truth regimes of the global north) about feminist knowledge practices on and of other cultures.

So far, I have claimed that feminist translation, fostering a sense of political affinity or a vision of gender justice, paves the way for transnational activisms by making it easier for women to engage in cross-border conversations and collaborations. At the same time, I question whether this connective potential of feminist translation is fully put into practice no matter what the geopolitical direction of translational travels is. Can we indeed speak of cross-border feminist dialogics as an egalitarian conversation? Following this critical question, this section argues that the promising picture of *Bekâret* as a celebratory project of transnational feminism could emerge partly because of its particular geopolitical direction and trajectory. What if the textual travel being analyzed here were vice versa: from the east to the west? Could we then speak of a similarly hopeful case for transnational feminism?

Would a similar book on the history of "eastern virginities"—with its primary focus on critical historical analyses of Islam and its take on virginity in different geopolitical contexts typically deemed eastern in the global order—stand a chance if it migrated from the east to the west? Would it be allowed to speak to the western audience in a similarly "eye to eye" manner (Lorde, *Sister Outsider*, 145)? If yes, would this be an egalitarian epistemological exchange or an endorsement of the "rescue paradigm" that too often defines western perceptions of the other's gender realities (Tripp, "Challenges in Transnational," 302)? Also, if yes, with what political motivations would the book be released to the western markets? How would it be packaged and promoted? Would it simply replicate the trope of the "exotic veiled Third World woman" and present itself as a titillating case of "unveiling" the "mysterious" life of the "Oriental Woman"—perhaps with a picture of a veiled (supposedly) Muslim woman on its cover (Amireh and Majaj, "Introduction," 6)? Would the book be introduced to the local discursive fields of the west to unsettle its oppressive virginity codes? Would it be offered as a "feminist reference book" that would undergird the formation of resistance against virginity oppression? Or would it be used to advocate a corroborative "post-feminist" tale of the "liberated western woman" positioned once again against the "chronically oppressed eastern woman"? Would "the knowledge acquired by the Western reader as a result of this transcultural encounter" serve to "forge a bond between First and Third World women" or would it "merely emphasize the Western reader's superiority to these 'Other' women" (8)? More importantly, would the book's knowledge claims be elevated to the status of universal truths as in the case of *Bekâret*? Or would they remain as something exclusively "of the east"? Something that only affirmed the gulf between the east and the west? In other words, if this were a book traveling from the east to the west, would it be read in the same geopolitically expansive and connectionist manner and become more than a book about eastern virginities or would it simply recharge the oppositional energies of the west's orientalist meaning-making economy? In fact, would a book on eastern virginities even be permitted to travel to the west with a title that claimed universality, "The 'Untouched' *History* of Virginity"? Would the same gesture of geopolitical un-marking that is bestowed to *Virgin* be accorded to the eastern book? Could an eastern history book sit on a bookshelf anywhere in the world with a title as universal as "history"? Or is it only western books that can remain unmarked and be marketed as "history"?

All of these questions inquire whether the feminist theories and historical narratives of a book on eastern virginities would in the course of its travel to the west turn into "dislocated signs"—signs that "are plucked from their historical material context of exchange, and exist as free-floating signifiers that are then used for other purposes," such as to reproduce orientalist gender scripts (Ghosh, "Affair to Remember," 42). Thus, they need to be urgently addressed if we want to build truly egalitarian feminist relationalities, dialogues, and exchanges across all geopolitical directionalities around the globe. Although they are of speculative nature, since the reverse translation case being considered is hypothetical, they are predicated on the vast literatures on third world feminisms, transnational feminisms, and postcolonial feminisms, where the discursive and material operations of western hegemony in the global production, validation, and circulation of knowledges are widely recognized and critiqued (Nagar, *Muddying the Waters*). As Caren Kaplan nicely puts it ("Politics of Location," 139):

> Most important, feminists with socioeconomic power need to investigate the grounds of their strong desire for rapport and intimacy with the "other." Examining the politics of location in the production and reception of theory can turn the terms of inquiry from desiring, inviting, and granting space to others to becoming accountable for one's own investments in cultural metaphors and values. Such accountability can begin to shift the ground of feminist practice from magisterial relativism (as if diversified cultural production simply occurs in a cultural vacuum) to the complex interpretive practices that acknowledge the historical roles of mediation, betrayal, and alliance in the relationships between women in diverse locations.

This quotation reminds us once again that the world we live in is deeply divided and fragmented, yet the borders that delineate our different realities have the potential not just to separate us but also to connect us; that these borders *can* and *should* be crossed, if we want to remake the world a place of justice, equality, and peace for all peoples and communities. We need to learn to collaborate across borders, no matter how fanatically fenced, patrolled, and guarded they are, and share our words, stories, and worldviews with one another because it is only through that sharing that we can reach at common visions and worlds of solidarity and justice. And as Richa Nagar writes, "if feminist alliance work is to realize its transformative possibilities, collaborators must recognize each other as coauthors joined in relations of affect, trust, imagination, and critique, ever open to interrogation by their collaborators, and willing to forego the putative superiority of their protocols of understanding and sites of knowledge making" (*Muddying the Waters*, 174–75). That is, we need to think more self-reflexively about processes of mediating and cooperating across differences and the relationships we build, or fail to build, with the other standing across the border, whoever that is. We need to rethink borders as difficult and unfixed places of trial with imminent possibilities of much needed confrontation, reconciliation, collaboration, and revolution—acts that can take place only with sincere hospitality, radical vulnerability, and responsible commitment to connect with the other and co-exist with them no matter how challenging and frightening that is. In Inge Boer's words (*Uncertain Territories*, 13):

> Boundaries cannot be wished away but will serve their ordering purposes better—that is, without the lack of understanding and the ensuing hostilities that usually accompany them—if we accept their existence but take them as uncertain; not lines, but spaces, not rigid but open to negotiation. The resulting uncertain territories are the ground we stand on, together.

Then, no matter where we stand regarding the borders that divide us, if we want to accomplish global and local justice on intersecting grounds of oppression, we have to configure creative and responsible ways to travel more often to those uncertain spaces, where translating and reading are unavoidable, and necessary, practices of mediation and contact. In Sara Ahmed's words, "If we have been taught to turn away, we have to learn to turn toward" (*Feminist Life*, 32). We have to look each other in the eye and ask: "Why don't we meet each other's eyes? Do we expect betrayal in each other's gaze, or recognition?" (Lorde, *Sister Outsider*, 155). This question will force us to confront the fact that all those geopolitical boundaries that are made by structures and conditions of domination are also inside of us; that unless we transgress them from both within and without, our textual and discursive travels across those borders will be ridden with symbolic violence. *Bekâret's* feminist translation and readings have showed us what a promising project such transgressive traveling could be. Indeed, we must be better readers of translation precisely because "when we read, we travel into the worlds of others. Even if these journeys are always partial, always incomplete, they can still be transformational," particularly, I would add, if the journey takes you into the world of/in another language (Keating, "El Mundo Zurdo," 526). Therefore, despite all the geopolitical doubts and questions that I have presented above, and in Chapter 6, I would like to end this section with a hopeful note or an invitation by late Palestinian poet Samih al-Qasim's poem, "Travel Tickets," as translated by A.Z. Foreman:[3]

*The day I'm killed,*
*my killer, rifling through my pockets,*
*will find travel tickets:*
*One to peace,*
*one to the fields and the rain,*
*and one to the conscience of humankind.*
*Dear killer of mine, I beg you:*
*Do not stay and waste them.*
*Take them, use them.*
*I beg you to travel.*

## Not If

Backtracking slightly from the hopeful ending of the previous section, in this section, I discuss some disturbing responses that I received to the connectionist invitation that Virgin *Crossing Borders* extended to western audiences at various academic symposiums and conferences. These responses not only reveal the persistence of colonial encounters in translational border crossings, but also entail important cautionary lessons on transnational relationalities. The analysis also challenges (and augments) Edward Said's seemingly linear theoretical model to study textual flows by highlighting the possibility of "back travels" or the multidirectional messiness of traveling theories. Consider the following two scenarios:

### Scenario 1

I deliver a keynote address about my research on Virgin *Crossing Borders* at an international conference. I end my talk by asking the audience some of the questions I raised in the previous section regarding the hypothetical "eastern virginity book" and its possible translational travels to the Anglo/American west. During Q&A, a white British woman takes the microphone and asks,

> I just wonder, could we just not speculate that kind of an interventionist translation back the other way so it could be a history of Arab worlds, [their] history of the hymen and virginity but with an interventionist translation, a different cover,[4] and a preface so that western women can look at this and also then universalize it?

I start answering her by discussing the orientalist tendencies of western publishers in regard to text selection, translation, packaging, and promotion of books written by "brown women of the east" and by citing some of the immense amount of postcolonial literature that reveals those colonial trends in global knowledge production, dissemination, and reception. In fact, I do agree with her that such a hypothetical book on eastern virginities would have a better chance of facilitating ethical encounters if it were translated and presented to the western public with a locally interventionist and transnationally connectionist decolonial feminist agenda (a non-fetishizing cover page, non-othering promotional narratives about the traveling book, a detailed preface that emphasized the commonalities between different heteropatriarchal virginity regimes across the world and sought to prevent orientalist readings and build transcultural bridges among differently situated feminists, etc.). However, I disagree that the sole responsibility of ethical encounters falls on the shoulders of feminist translators, that an interventionist translation would eliminate the possibility of orientalist receptions. As I continue explaining my stance that ethically and geopolitically responsible translation is necessary but not adequate to eradicate or circumvent epistemic violences of the orientalist economy, the same audience member interrupts me and asks, "But could we imagine something different?" As if orientalism was a failure of my imagination. As if colonial meaning- and knowledge-making practices would disappear if I—along with numerous other feminist scholars and activists of color, including *Bekâret*'s readers—did not raise doubts about them. Something must have been wrong with my reasoning. I was perhaps too oversensitive, too resentful? After all, the geopolitical trajectory of the textual journey I was talking about—from the west to the rest—had not threatened the audience's multicultural illusion of one happy global village until I reversed that trajectory and asked, "what if?" Why did I have to do that?

Call it naïve or arrogant, when put like that, the question sounds more like a spin-off of color-blindness. Why couldn't I gratefully leave the stage without such a bitter, off-putting end to my talk? Why couldn't I be content with the promising stories of *Bekâret*'s readers being enlightened by western feminism's liberating, empowering touch? Why couldn't I leave the colonial fantasy of the happy native intact but "kill feminist joy" with my questions about the effects of orientalist legacies on feminist relationalities (Ahmed, *Promise of Happiness*, 67)? Seriously, why couldn't I imagine differently?

In fact, I did, I do imagine differently; otherwise, I would not write this book. And it is the very stories of *Bekâret*'s readers that sustain my hope in that "imagined otherwise" defined by cross-border togetherness in difference, justice, and peace—"a new and more possible meeting," in Audre Lorde's words (*Sister Outsider*, 123). The agitating questions I asked at the end of my talk (and here) about the epistemic vestiges of colonialism and how they manifest in global circulation of feminisms—and the "bad feelings" they stirred among subjects implicated by those questions—seek to help create, not hinder, the enabling conditions of possibility for that imagined otherwise:

> Bad feelings are seen as oriented toward the past, as a kind of stubbornness that "stops" the subject from embracing the future. Good feelings are associated with moving up, as creating the very promise of a future. This assumption that good feelings are open and bad feelings are closed allows historical forms of injustice to disappear. The demand that we be affirmative makes those histories disappear by reading them as a form of melancholia (as if you hold on to something that is already gone). . . . To let go would be to keep those histories present (Ahmed, *Promise of Happiness*, 217).

It is in order not to keep colonial histories present, which at times overlap with feminist histories, that I refuse to let go of those geopolitically loaded questions in my work, although I am tired of audience members reproaching me for voiding their picture-perfect visions of global sisterhood, even when my research is fundamentally dedicated to exploring questions of transnational feminist solidarity. I simply have had too many confrontational instances like the one I describe above (and below), or "feminist betrayals" as Aimee Carrillo Rowe calls them, to let go of my disturbing questions (*Power Lines*, 182). I am not claiming that those are the only kinds of reactions my work has received in academic settings. Luckily, the connectionist responses outnumber the oppositional ones. However, I have had enough of them to feel compelled to ask, "How do we forge feminisms of possibility out of the wreckage of our betrayals" (182)? This is an open invitation to question my/your place in history, so our encounters do not repeat the violence of that history. It is a question of hope—hope that you will hear me and the truths I re/tell—because "for me to assume that you will not hear me represents not only history, perhaps, but an old pattern of relating, sometimes protective and sometimes dysfunctional, which we, as women shaping our future, are in the process of shattering and passing beyond, I hope" (Lorde, *Sister Outsider*, 66–67). I hope.

## Scenario 2

I give a talk on Virgin *Crossing Borders* at another academic conference. During Q&A, a white US-American woman asks whether *Bekâret* has been censored or banned by the Turkish state for its "radical contents." I say no. She, then, asks if I or my publisher got into any trouble with the government because of the book. I say no. She does not seem satisfied by my responses.

She goes on to explain to me how repressive and violent Turkey's current government has been discharging "progressive" academics from their positions at universities; banning "progressive" books on political or moral grounds; prosecuting publishers and translators for disseminating "progressive" materials; imprisoning "progressive" academics, journalists, writers, activists, and politicians. All of that is true, I say. But it is not the single truth of Turkey. There are also truths of courage, dignity, resilience, solidarity, creativity, and resistance in Turkey. Just like my participant Ece, who is a doctoral student in the US, said in the follow-up interview: "Americans constantly expect me to talk about what an unlivable place Turkey has become with its problems of lack of freedom of expression, imprisoning of journalists and what has happened to Academics for Peace,[5] etc. But the Turkey that is in my reality is not just that." Besides, I add, suppression of "progress"—a language that reeks of the binary rhetoric of western enlightenment that once again positions the east as a place of backwardness and unfreedom—is not a uniquely Turkish problem. That we need to find a way to critique the Turkish state for its fascist policies and practices while also recognizing that this is part of a global rise in right-wing authoritarianism, neoliberalism, and conservatism and that dissent is alive and well in Turkey no matter how violent its forces of oppression are. Interestingly, this balancing act of "multiple mediations" is exactly what my talk had just attempted (Mani, ""Multiple Mediations"). Yet, in the end, all that was left with some audience members was stories of "Turkish oppression," a difference they wanted my work to confirm. Where I saw transcultural commonalities and potential solidarities, they saw insurmountable differences. I remember Trinh Minh-ha's words ("Difference," 14):

> Now, I am not only given the permission to open up and talk, I am also encouraged to express my difference. My audience expects and demands it; otherwise people would feel as if they have been cheated: We did not come to hear a Third World member speak about the First(?) World. We came to listen to that voice of difference likely to bring us what we can't have, and to divert us from the monotony of sameness.

How come a study exploring post-oppositional translationalities ended up affirming the (western) audience's sense of cultural superiority? Could it be something I said (or did not say) that caused such an arrogant perception fed by an affective economy of contempt and pity? Can I afford any gaps or ambiguities in the cross-border stories I tell? Or was it the power of "established [orientalist] cognitive structures in the reader" that constantly craved for juicy stories of Middle Eastern misery (Liddle and Rai, "Feminism, Imperialism," 496)? Can I be anything other than, or more than, different in the words I share? These questions about the geopolitics and ethics of feminist knowledge production, translation, dissemination, and reception are nothing but new. Indeed, transnational feminists have agonized over them so extensively and diligently that we might think we have exhausted them to the point of irrelevance.[6] We should have. Yet, my response to them still comes from decades ago:

> You are asking us to make ourselves more vulnerable to you than we already are before we have any reason to trust that you will not take advantage of this vulnerability. So you need to learn to become unintrusive, unimportant, patient to the point of tears, while at the same time open to learning any possible lessons. You will also have to come to terms with the sense of alienation, of not belonging, of having your world thoroughly disrupted, having it criticized and scrutinized from the point of view of those who have been harmed by it, having important concepts central to it dismissed, being viewed with mistrust, being seen as of no consequence except as an object of mistrust (Lugones and Spelman, "Have We Got," 580).

The two incidents I described above to illustrate certain kinds of feminist failures, betrayals, and disappointments in transnational/translational encounters reveal the urgency of assuming geopolitical and ethical responsibility when it comes to hearing one another across differences and borders. They are to remind us that, as feminist scholars, activists, teachers, storytellers, students, writers, readers, translators, editors, co-travelers, and collaborators, we need to do more to intervene into the violent structures of intimate and global knowledge-making, which requires the dialogic work of translation. It is in justice-driven practices of translation and reception (or "hungry translations" in Richa Nagar's terms), such as feminist translation, that, instead of indulging the colonial urge to rescue the other into (monolingual) sameness, hegemonic feminist subjects can learn to risk their selves for solidarity in difference. In the next section, I discuss this connectionist potential of translation in more detail.

## Only If

Of course, all the questions asked in the previous sections, the geopolitical criticisms they imply, and the promises and hopes they harbor are missing an important element: the political role and ethical agency of the feminist translator who is willing to navigate and mediate through differences and divisions among women to create non-othering contact zones and who strategically rewrites texts so that they can help build transcultural bridges. Although it would be naïve to claim that feminist translators hold all the decision-making power throughout the translation process and are not constrained by any institutional limitations in their textual choices or discursive interventions, their politically and ethically guided negotiations and mediations still do a substantial amount of subversive work both locally and transnationally. Acknowledging the feminist translator's political power does not disregard structural discrepancies in global textual flows nor the decisive role of the reader, which I emphasized in the previous section. However, my reception study with *Bekâret*'s readers has revealed the ways in which feminist translators can help generate transgressive effects against intersectional gender oppressions and facilitate connectionist reading practices against the alienating forces of geopolitics. Thus, it is my contention that if their trans/formative labor is recognized and their visibility as activists is increased, feminist translators' political impact will correspondingly grow.

One crucial task that feminist, or justice-oriented, translators can engage in is ethical and political disclosures, particularly in prefaces, footnotes, and promotional activities that can significantly increase the visibility of their politically creative labor. That is, feminist translators need to "sign" the texts they rework, which is an indispensable component of feminist translation ethics.[7] The feminist translator's textual signature is important because, as my research clearly shows, such disclosures (e.g., about the feminist agenda guiding the decisions regarding the text choice, linguistic strategies, paratextual additions, etc.) can help the reader of an imported text approach it with a more hospitable, vulnerable, and open-minded manner and thus increase the interventionist potential of the text. Ethical acts of disclosure about the discursive mediations and geo/political interventions that the text undergoes in the translation process can generate or solidify trust between the situated reader and the traveling text. In times of violent polarized borderings along racial, ethnic, national, and regional lines, which you might call the history of humanity, we particularly need such trust-building discursive spaces in translation. By specifying potential bridges (transcultural similarities and political commonalities) between the interchanging localities and the various feminist heritages and possible solidarities those thresholds harbor, ethically and geopolitically responsible translation practices can both facilitate the local embrace of the translated discourse (not in an appropriative mode, but rather in a connectionist manner) and foster the formation of imagined transnational feminist communities of resistance.

Another key task belongs to scholars, teachers, activists, publishers, and other makers of transnational feminism who need to acknowledge and endorse feminist translators' work because it is often thanks to these translators that feminist texts travel across borders and enter the discursive fields of different localities. Feminist movements grow with feminist translators' commitment to texts chosen for their subversive and disruptive potential in the face of hegemonic relations of power.[8] In order to appreciate and encourage such vital work done by feminist translators, we should engage in more conversations (for instance, in our classrooms) about feminist translation ethics, politics of translation, politics of reading and reception, and geopolitics of global textual flows. Beyond all that, we need to change our understanding of translation as a "second-hand copy" with no epistemic value and be willing to produce, read, and experience translation, first, as an enriching encounter with others, during which our subjectivity gets expanded and renewed with its boundaries stretched and blurred:

> The translation border is a space of transformation: a body, a tongue, a culture opens to elsewhere, and addresses itself to different directions, entering a contact zone, a transitional space of incessant gangways between cultures, between societary and individual histories, where words and worlds interact, and one's sense of identity transmutes and moves on (Zaccaria, "Translating Borders," 60).

As readers interpellated and implicated in global power relations, changing our intimate relationships with translation is more than necessary to engage in geopolitically accountable readings and encounters with the other that manage to "avoid reducing the work to an example of pleasurable exoticism" (Attridge, "Responsible Reading," 235). Then, in addition to seeing translation as a transformative act of self-reflection, we also need to reconfigure it as a necessary operation of transnational solidarity. This call to translational bridging and stretching across borders is central to transnational feminist politics. As Donna Kate Rushin says in her famous "The Bridge Poem," "Stretch or drown / Evolve or die" (267). *Bekâret*'s readers have provided us with ample examples of how to stretch when encountering the voice of the other and their stories told us that the feminist translator's undisguised mediating presence makes an enabling difference in the making of those stretching encounters.

To achieve such stretching and bridging, western feminists also need to unlearn their deep-seated ethnocentric reading habits that too often usurp and assimilate the intellectual voices and works of third world feminists in the service of western humanist universalism. Only by committing to such critical self-reflexivity and "feminist accountability," we can produce "knowledge tuned to resonance, not to dichotomy"—situated, partial knowledges that forge bonds, rather than deepen the chasms between feminists situated differently across localities (Haraway, "Situated Knowledges," 588). This is exactly why Donna Haraway calls for "accountability and responsibility for translations and solidarities linking the cacophonous visions and visionary voices that characterize the knowledges of the subjugated" (590). Exercising such interpretive retuning would both enable western feminists to learn local lessons from the experiences and theories of women situated in other parts of the world, and also devise commonalities and connectivities across borders and thus facilitate the formation of truly transnational solidarities and communities. As Aimee Carrillo Rowe explains in *Power Lines* (174),

> As long as competing notions of feminism emerge as a contested site of struggle, as long as alliances are defined and imagined in incompatible terms, the work of translation is necessary as we cultivate converging systems of meaning. Shared languages arise from shared experience, so the intimacies we generate in transracial alliances provide the context through which we cultivate such imagined communities [of radical women from diverse social locations, united by their investment in social justice].

At this point, one immediate act of critical self-reflection and feminist accountability you, dear reader, can engage in is to ask yourself, "how did I read the traveling stories of *Bekâret*'s translator and readers?" Yes, these stories were mediated through my analytical voice, translated into English only as fragments of (citations from) longer conversations held in another language, and repositioned as parts of an epistemological project with a specific agenda. Yet, you still had a glimpse at a different cultural gender reality with a distinctive virginity regime, a unique feminist heritage and presence, and differently situated interpretive communities that generate their own economy of meanings and reading habits. More importantly, while reading the book, you had some sort of discursive contact with a place that is typically defined as part of your oriental other. How did you imagine that place and women who inhabit it? What was your reading experience within that precarious threshold between the east and west? Whose response to the hypothetical translation resonated with you more—*Bekâret*'s readers or the two audience members'? How did you relate to *Bekâret*'s readers' stories that witnessed the transformation of a western book into a geopolitically hybrid one? Was your reading a case of arrogant perception through which you only heard stories that confirmed your preconceived notion of the "helpless oriental woman"? Or was it an egalitarian connection where you recognized both the differences and similarities between the stories being re/told and used them to build bridges paving the way for a transnational resistance against virginity oppression? In short, was this encounter an act of self-vulnerable solidarity with the other or an act of othering self-preservation? These questions, which we should ask ourselves every time we encounter a translation—including ones that seem not translated, like Virgin *Crossing Borders*—highlight not only the entanglement of the global with the intimate, but also the role of translation in framing the ethical and geo/political contours and effects of that cross-border entanglement. Therefore, if we want to co-exist in a world of polyphonic and polyversal togetherness, we have to learn to live in translation because, as George Steiner once said, "Without [translation] we would live in arrogant parishes bordered by silence" ("Introduction," 25).

Also, western feminists need to be willing to learn the languages and cultural realities of their so-called "sisters out there" since "learning languages might sharpen our own presuppositions about what it means to use the sign 'woman'" (Spivak, *Teaching Machine*, 215–16). Learning third-world languages should come with a political commitment to make feminist works produced in those languages available in hegemonic (as well as other non-hegemonic) languages through feminist translation ethics that aim to pull down the antagonistic—yet false/falsified—walls between the self and the other and pave the way for "strange encounters" with already encountered subjects (Ahmed, *Strange Encounters*). That is, western feminists need to take the responsibility to translate—in non-othering, non-assimilationist ways—their sisters' words and works to make flows of feminist discourses more egalitarian and the transnational space of feminist dialogics more polyphonic. This is a matter of building true solidarities and multidirectional bridges that connect us to each other for the purpose of changing the world. As Spivak asks in "The Politics of Translation," "How will women's solidarity be measured here? How will their common experience be reckoned if one cannot imagine the traffic in accessibility going both ways" (*Teaching Machine*, 214)? She responds (215):

> It is good to think that women have something in common, when one is approaching women with whom a relationship would not otherwise be possible. It is a great first step. But, if your interest is in learning if there is women's solidarity, how about . . . trying a second step? Rather than imagining that women automatically have something identifiable in common, why not say, humbly and practically, my first obligation in understanding solidarity is to learn her mother-tongue. You will see immediately what the differences are. You will also feel the solidarity every day as you make the attempt to learn the language in which the other woman learned to recognize reality at her mother's knees. This is preparation for the intimacy of cultural translation.

Developing a reception culture of heteroglossia and polyphony in the west is a crucial act of building transnational feminist solidarities. In Sara Ahmed's words, "The differences between us necessitate the dialogue, rather than disallow it—a dialogue must take place, precisely *because* we don't speak the same language" (emphasis original) (*Strange Encounters*, 180). And we neither need nor want to speak the same language. Dialogue across different languages and cultural codes is a fact of life and it often is a rewarding and exciting fact of life when experienced in egalitarian enunciative contexts. Translation is, therefore, a fact of life too and is quite an enriching one. It is up to us, translators and readers, to embrace that transformative and connectionist potential of translation and determine the particularities of its materialization. It is in such spirit of polyphonic solidarity that I say we have a lot to learn from the inspiring stories of *Bekâret*'s readers, who gave a potentially "threatening" western theory a chance to speak to them, listened to it, talked back to it, and eventually adopted it as locally empowering while also recognizing its potential universal standing. Their reading practices encapsulated "a necessary caution against generalizing the contingencies and contours of local circumstance, at the very moment at which a transnational, 'migrant' knowledge of the world is the most urgently needed" (Bhabha, *Location of Culture*, 306). This double gesture of recognizing the particular and making the transnational against the monopolist, essentialist urge of sameness that plagues contemporary globalization is the difficult task that awaits us. As Rosi Braidotti concurs, "The conclusion is clear: it is important to resist the uncritical reproduction of sameness on a planetary scale" (*Nomadic Subjects*, 6). In this context, we can think of the feminist translation and reading strategies of *Bekâret*'s translator and readers as both inspirational and navigational tools that can be used to create contact zones. And it is up to feminists situated in the west, and all around the world, to make sure that such a transformative meaning-making scheme is reciprocated in our encounters with critical texts traveling across geopolitically contentious routes (Anzaldúa, "Foreword," v):

> Mujeres, a no dejar que el peligro del viaje y la inmensidad del territorio nos asuste—a mirar hacia adelante y a abrir paso en el monte (*Women, let's not let the danger of the journey and the vastness of the territory scare us—let's look forward and open paths in these woods*). Caminante, no hay puentes, se hace puentes al andar (*Voyager, there are no bridges, one builds them as one walks*).

# Now What?

[Translation] has to do with linguistic translation, yes, but also with making a work available (with all the consequences this might have, all the "betrayals" and "erasures" it might include) to other audiences and letting it travel. It also has to do with opening scenarios of conversation and proposing new horizons for dialogue. It means opening your choices, your tastes, your affinities to others—which in politics can compromise (or strengthen) your principles.

—Prada, "Is Anzaldúa Translatable," 73

Virgin *Crossing Borders* put under the microscope translation configured not only as a cross-linguistic act of rewriting and a transcultural act of textual traveling, but also as a political intervention into local gender regimes (that of virginity, in this case) and into transnational feminist formations (in terms facilitating cross-border dialogues, self-reflections, and imagined communities of resistance). As Ana Rebeca Prada notes in the quotation above, translation has immense potential to build (or burn, for that matter) bridges across divides and differences—a potential whose yield depends most on the geohistorical contingencies of the text's translation and reception. That is, because translation is performed in a geopolitical and historical context defined by (material and symbolic) local and global asymmetries and borders, the political effects it creates are bound up with how the text is produced and signified in regard to the webs of power relations within which the text is re/made and received. If we want to increase the transgressive and connectionist potential of translation in the service of creating a just world, we need more research on the specificities of translation and reception so that we know what works and what does not when it comes to increasing the potential of translation to connect. The renovated analytical model of Said's traveling theory might prove helpful for other studies as well. Although every translation project is unique, studying the various facets of translational travels would provide us with key lessons both on local and subjective political trans/formations and global interconnectivities. Producing a rich transdisciplinary scholarship on translational borderings and border crossings, particularly in our age of cruel modes and manifestations of globalization, would enable us to develop ethical strategies of building stronger local and global resistances against hegemonic structures of power—by both enriching our repertoires of political action and fortifying our sense of affinity and togetherness in ways that embrace differences in the face of relentless social pressure to silence all but the homogenizing voice of convention. In Lawrence Venuti's words, studying translation would help us answer "whether and how it [translation] might constitute a cultural means of resistance that challenges multinational capitalism and the political institutions to which the global economy is allied. To what extent, then, might translation transform this political economy through its impact on contemporary cultural forms and practices" (*Translation Changes*, 141)?

Much of recent globalization literature and transnational feminist scholarship, in fact, acknowledge global flows of ideas and discourses as significant transcultural processes, but rarely studies the particularities of how normative and subversive texts travel across borders and become localized. By presenting an extensive case study tracing the cross-cultural trajectory of a specific text and focusing on the processes of its production, replantation, and reception, Virgin *Crossing Borders* aimed to expand the scarce literature on the global circulation of feminisms and the formation of transnational discursive regimes and counter-hegemonic mobilizations. It, moreover, provided an innovative analytical model to study translational border crossings of political discourses—a model that drew on Said's "traveling theory" but underpinned it with the critical theories of translation, transnational feminism, comparative literature, cultural studies, and reception studies, among others. The most innovative aspect of Virgin *Crossing Borders* is its use of reception theories to explore the political impact of translation in a specific geohistorical context through reading diaries, focus groups, and interviews. Adding reception analysis to "traveling theory" is particularly crucial for it illuminates whether the textual strategies deployed by the translator to reframe virginity in a subversive discourse achieved the intended effects. In the case of *Bekâret*, my study did reveal that the feminist translation strategies—particularly the addition of the translator's preface claiming a local and transnational feminist agenda for the book and the outright rejection of hetero/sexist language—did help the text intervene more decisively in Turkey's hegemonic virginity codes. This finding that feminist translation ethics did make a difference in the local signification and deployment of the text should give us, feminist translators, both self-affirmation in our often ignored (or worse, denigrated) translation work and motivation to engage in more interventionist projects of feminist, or justice-oriented, translation.

Yet, my study also has its limitations, the most important of which is the geopolitical directionality of the textual travel process under question. *Virgin* traveled from the west, mainly the United States, to Turkey, which is often designated as eastern (yet, with a self-admitted aspiration to become westernized). Therefore, the hegemonic economies of meaning prevailing throughout its cross-cultural trajectory are blatantly orientalist (and occidentalist) and my study focuses on the political implications of that specific truth regime in its interactions with *Bekâret* and the local truth regimes, such as Turkish nationalism and anti-Americanism, and the local feminist heritages. The Turkish translation of *Virgin*, then, reflects the contemporary global trend of the dissemination of western epistemologies to "the rest" of the world without a reciprocating attitude of western "hospitality" to textual importation from non-western localities. That is, the geopolitical directionality of *Virgin/ Bekâret* illustrates the dominant trajectory of the current global order. Due to that specific focus, my study cannot answer the following questions: How do feminist texts travel from the east to the west or from the global south to the global north and, more importantly, from the east to the east or the global south to the global south? What sorts of translation and reception issues would such a project bring to the table? What kinds of geopolitical lessons can we learn from studying those travel processes? Comparative translation studies examining texts traveling through those different geopolitical axes would reveal different global trends of textual dissemination and tell us more on what can be done to intervene in the existing power disparities that rule the course and outcome of transnational feminist dialogues and activisms.

Although my study cannot directly respond to the questions listed above, it can provide some strategies for geo/politically and ethically responsible translations. That is, comprehensive analyses of feminist translations (and translations charged with other justice-oriented agendas) would yield significant practical lessons for translators in terms of developing more effective translation strategies, producing more empowering texts for marginalized communities, disseminating more disruptive discourses across borders, and generating more actual and imagined communities of resistance. For instance, writing a preface where the translator discloses her political engagement with the text and highlights potential connections between the imported book and local feminist discourses may indeed result in more self-vulnerable and open-minded readings. If the text is traveling from the east to the west, or from the global south to the north, the feminist translator can also use this textual space to discuss the geopolitics of reception and help prevent global power asymmetries from undermining potential egalitarian reading practices and the formation of imagined transnational feminist communities. By doing that, the translator can disrupt orientalist readings before the reader begins engaging with the traveling text. Most importantly, however, we must keep translating, regardless of the geopolitical and ethical risks in translational encounters, because "the journey on which we have come thus far through trust, solidarity, and self-critique cannot stop at one or two critical experiments, one or two books, or one or two institutions. It is a dialogic process—a dialectical response—that can be sustained only through continuous movement and questioning" (Nagar, *Muddying the Waters*, 148).

It is a fact that translators do not have full autonomy when it comes to the selection, rewriting, promotion, and reception of the text. On the contrary, they are bounded by various apparatuses of knowledge production, validation, and distribution. Studies like Virgin *Crossing Borders* are important for that reason as they not only reveal politically effective translation procedures to exercise activist agendas, but also propose useful strategies to circumvent, perhaps even exploit, the institutional constraints with which dissident translators must contend. Therefore, we need more studies on the translations and receptions of different kinds of texts, in the largest sense of the term, traveling across multiple languages and geopolitical directionalities, and imbued with different political agendas. Hopefully, the research model presented in this book and its confirmation of the (locally and globally) subversive impact of feminist translation will inspire more politically conscious and ethically engaged translations—as well as research studies exploring those translations—that can help us recognize our planetary interconnectedness and achieve our dreams of social justice and peaceful co-existence across differences. Notwithstanding the risk of a romanticized vision of translation and textual travel, I would like to end this book with such an invitation to translators, scholars, activists, publishers, literary agencies, professional organizations, and readers to give a bigger chance to translation because translation has considerable power to transgress, to connect, and to bring us closer to each other and to our dreams. Audre Lorde once said, "As outsiders, we need each other for support and connection and all the other necessities of living on the borders. But in order to come together we must recognize each other" (*Sister Outsider*, 69–70). Translation can help us do exactly that, recognize each other.

# Notes

## Preface

1. Alevism is a belief system that is practiced among both Turks and Kurds in Turkey. It is a unique amalgamation of Shi'a Islam, Sufism, and shamanism, among others, and rejects some of the normative tenets of Islam. Alevis constitute the largest religious/cultural minority in Turkey and have been subjected to systematic discrimination and violence.

2. The "sister" reference is not meant as an essentializing gesture. Rather, it is a provoking rhetorical tool to remind the English-speaking reader of a particular subject position that is too readily available to them as feminists situated in and in relation to hegemonic western feminism—a subject position generated by the colonial discourse of "global sisterhood."

## Introduction

1. See Tambe's "Silences of #MeToo," Ajayi's "#MeToo, Africa," Onwuachi-Willig's "What About #UsToo," and Zarkov and Davis' "Ambiguities and Dilemmas." Also, see Farnush Ghadery ("#MeToo," 4), who argues that #MeToo could become a transnational phenomenon because it "allowed different groups of women in distinct places to take ownership of the individual manifestation of #MeToo in their specific context."

2. Another example is from Turkey, where, in 2015, two years before the latest surge of #MeToo, the murder of Özgecan Aslan, a twenty-year-old college student who was brutally killed after rape attempts galvanized the public in the streets and on the internet. Following the murder, a hashtag campaign flooded Twitter with users posting Aslan's name and #SenDeAnlat (Tell Your Story Too) inviting women to share their experiences with sexual violence. Although the case drew immense

worldwide attention, the campaign never turned into a transnational platform against violence against women.

3. Instagram post, July 28, 2020, https://www.instagram.com/p/CDL8teoBSbG/?utm_source=ig_embed.

4. Some responded to the critiques of "western whitewashing" of an online Turkish feminist campaign by disputing the Turkish origins of #ChallengeAccepted (e.g. *New York Times*' Taylor Lorenz) claiming that the Turkish and the US versions were parallel but unrelated events. These hasty denials appear problematic since rather than taking responsibility for the silencing (and appropriating) treatment that the "Turkish" campaign received in the US or simultaneously recognizing transnational heterogeneities and connectivities across borders, they simply claimed #Challenge-Accepted as "ours."

5. I should add that the murdered woman, Pınar Gültekin was also Kurdish, which got completely ignored in the feminist campaign that highlighted only the gender aspect of violence against women in Turkey. This erasure points to a larger problem in both feminist and mainstream discourses on femicide in Turkey, which is the failure to recognize "the entanglement of the Turkish state's assimilationist policies with gender-based killings" (Bakan and Saluk, "Challenge Accepted?"). Hence, before the local campaign went transnationally viral and got subjected to colonial erasures, it had already caused other colonial injuries by ignoring "the multi-layered violence that Kurdish women in Turkey experience as a result of the simultaneous exposure to heteropatriarchal structures and colonial state policies" (Bakan and Saluk). I am grateful to Ruken Işık for pointing out this colonial erasure in the local feminist responses to Gültekin's murder.

6. This does not mean that translation only has transgressive, connectionist potential regarding borders. Indeed, as Naoki Sakai ("Count a Language," 84) argues, "translation is not only a border crossing but also and preliminarily an act of drawing a border, of bordering." I do recognize this paradoxical work of translation, which Sakai explains in "Modern Regime": "translation can inscribe, erase, and distort borders; it may well give rise to a border where none was before; it may well multiply a border into many registers; it may erase some borders and institute new ones. . . . It shows most persuasively the unstable, transformative, and political nature of border" (106). Borders are seemingly fixed and fixated, but contested, in-between spaces where the conflicting dynamics of belonging and un/belonging not only foster antagonisms and violent, even deadly, operations of the nation, but also open transgressive spaces for subjugated peoples and communities to engage in unsettling dwellings and subversive crossings. Borders simultaneously deter and facilitate symbolic and material mobilities while continuously trying to contain and keep those im/mobilities under surveillance and control—with the itineraries and fates of those im/mobile bodies being deeply affected by the directionality of their cross-border travel. That is, borders both separate and connect across asymmetrically positioned localities; yet both of these mechanisms of power are relational and dialogic, no matter what political meaning or corporeal effect they generate. That relational and dialogic potential of

borders, in addition to the fact that they are "man-made," is exactly why translation can be a tool of trespassing, resistance, and solidarity. And it is that transgressive potential of translation that Virgin *Crossing Borders* explores. Also, see Baer's book on queering translation (*Queer Theory and Translation Studies*) and Mignolo and Schiwy's article on decolonial translation ("Beyond Dichotomies") for great discussions exploring the close connections between translation and borders.

7. The full Turkish title is "Bekâretin 'El Değmemiş' Tarihi," literally "Virginity's 'No Hands Touched' History."

8. Following Amrita Basu's ("Globalization," 76) suggestion that "global visions need to be further infused with local realities, while appreciating that the local is not merely local, but infused with global influences," I analyze both the local and the global aspects of *Virgin*'s translational travels between the US and Turkey. However, I do not conceive local/global as a binary, but rather as interdependent analytical categories that can be studied only in relation to specific socio-places and historical trajectories. So, I agree with Millie Thayer's (*Making Transnational*, 6) position that "the local matters . . . not simply as a passive and static counterpoint to the global, but as the primary site where globalization is constituted, as well as where its effects are played out." For more on the false local/global dichotomy, see Kaplan's "On Location," Katz's "Grounds of Globalization," and Mohanty's *Feminism Without Borders*.

9. According to Said, theories travel in four stages: (1) the point of "origin," "or what seems like one," where the theory comes into existence and enters local discursive fields, (2) the distance in time and location across which the theory travels and is meanwhile subjected to various pressures as a result of which its prominence is modified, (3) the set of conditions of acceptance and resistance that the transposed theory faces in its new environment, (4) the resultant fully or partially transplanted theory being "transformed by its new uses, its new position in a new time and place" (*The World*, 226–27).

10. Said's traveling theory has also been criticized by Friedman ("Locational Feminism," 16) for invoking the myth of originality, the modernist notion that dichotomously privileges only what is deemed original and relegates the rest (e.g., translation) to a secondary position. I do not completely agree that Said reasserts the myth of originality since in his book he acknowledges that originality not only is a contingent product of a specific historical context and is textually achieved, but also is always built on the pre-existing (*The World*, 126–39). That is, according to Said, every writing is in fact a rewriting, a creative recombination of citations. However, his use of phrases such as "a point of origin" and "the idea came to birth" seems to give way to such mis/understandings. I believe by these phrases Said refers to an illusionary point of origin, which, however, has been naturalized into our very conceptualizations of texts. In this book, when I refer to *Virgin* as the "original" (in cautionary quotation marks) it is only to refer to its given status as such. *Virgin* materially came into being in the US in 2007 with a distinctive ISBN number, but it is also derived from or built onto an existing repository of texts.

11. Said's traveling theory has also been criticized for its uncritical metaphorical

use of the term "travel," which carries problematical gender, class, and racial connotations regarding issues of accessibility (Clifford "Traveling Cultures" and *Routes*, 31–32, 39). However, like Clifford ("Traveling Cultures," 110), I prefer to use the term precisely for its "historical taintedness, its associations with gendered, racial bodies, class privilege, specific means of conveyance, beaten paths, agents, frontiers, documents, and the like" because very much like travels of embodied and historically situated individuals, travels of theories are also influenced by gender, class, racial, and geopolitical hierarchies of power. Just like individuals, theories also do not enjoy the same privileges or equal opportunities to travel and produce global and local knowledges.

12. Foundational works on feminist translation include Godard's "Speculum" and "Discourse/Translation," Flotow's *Translation and Gender*, Simon's *Gender in Translation*, de Lotbinière-Harwood's "Preface," and Chamberlain's "Gender and Metaphorics." For more recent works, see Alvarez et al.'s *Translocalities*, Baer and Kaindl's *Queering Translation*, Castro and Ergun's *Feminist Translation*, Flotow and Farahzad's *Translating Women*, Flotow and Kamal's *Routledge Handbook*, Robinson's *Transgender, Translation, Translingual Address*, and Spurlin's "Gender and Sexual Politics of Translation."

13. For an overview of the history of feminist translation, see Castro and Ergun's "Feminism and Translation."

14. "Transnational" here refers to cross-border relations, navigations, and negotiations anchored in and in-between nation-states and bound by local and global structures of power. I prefer the term to simultaneously highlight the local/national specificities of feminisms and global interconnectivities that are built among them in ways that transcend national borders.

15. Space, in this context, is not conceived as a permanently fixed location, but rather as a dynamic, relational sphere where borders are constantly made, solidified, contested, and redefined and where cross-border flows and encounters of ideas, goods, and people take place in connection to intersecting relations of power (Massey, "A Global Sense"). Geopolitics, then, is an analytical category of power that enables the study of the discursive and material constructions, implications, and experiential particularities of spaces. For strategies of geopolitical thinking and analysis see Friedman, *Mappings*, 131.

16. Moreover, discourses do not enjoy equal access to the apparatuses of global circulation since distribution networks and practices often reflect existing inequalities in the global capitalist economy. So, we usually do not see a reciprocal exchange of discourses between the global south and global north. For more on this inequality, see Costa's "Lost (and Found?)."

17. In my use of the bridge metaphor, I do not intend to claim that translation only connects across borders. As I noted before, as an act of bordering, translation both connects and separates, or in Sandro Mezzadra and Naoki Sakai's words, "produces both bridges and walls" ("Introduction," 9). My work focuses on the bridge-building work of translation.

18. For more on the paradox of the subversive use of orientalist cartography, see Yeğenoğlu's *Colonial Fantasies*, Bulbeck's *Re-Orienting Western Feminisms*, and Stam and Shohat's *Race in Translation*.

19. See Chapter 1 for more.

20. For an analysis of those cultural imaginaries and relationalities, see Gürel's *Limits of Westernization*.

21. Several studies (Freiwald's "Trans-Lation," Godard's "Speculum," Moorjani's "Translating Theory," Moses' "Made in America," Penrod's "Translating Cixous," Susam-Sarajeva's *Theories on the Move*; Varikas' "Traveling Concepts," Ward Jouve's "White Woman") argued that in the process of their selective and appropriative importations into the US context, Cixous, Irigaray, and Kristeva's diverse works were reconstructed as a coherent body of feminist theory under "French feminism," an umbrella term assumed to be representing France's complex (and contradictory) feminist politics.

22. Two exceptions, Costa's "Lost (and Found?)" and Thayer's *Making Transnational*, focus on travels of feminist discourses from the global north to the global south although neither attends to the textual specificities of translation.

23. By "experience," I am not talking about a modernist understanding of unmediated, "pure" perceptions of reality by autonomous subjects. I am rather referring to narratives constructed by situated individuals interacting with discourses, identity positions, and power relations circulating in the social setting in which they live. In Linda Alcoff's words ("Cultural Feminism," 416), "We are constructs—that is, our experience of our very subjectivity is a construct mediated by and/or grounded on a social discourse beyond (way beyond) individual control." For another critique of experience often authorized as the origin of explanation or foundation of knowledge, see Joan Scott's "Evidence of Experience."

24. In fact, Smith's (*Texts* and *Conceptual Practices*) theory appears quite fatalistic at times as her focus is on how "factual" texts activating objectified discourses ideologically guide readers to reproduce the relations of ruling. Although she emphasizes the reader as an active party in the production of meaning, readers' resistances or challenges to the text's ideological schemata are not included in Smith's textual analyses. Activeness seems to be used as limitedly referring to the reader's (often unconscious) collaboration with hegemonic power relations activated by the text. Therefore, Smith's theory is particularly useful for me in conceptualizing the active text, rather than the active reader.

25. Reception theory emerged in West Germany under the roof of Constance University in the late 1960s as a radical attempt to break away from New Criticism, a paradigm where the autonomy of the text and the fixity of meaning were proclaimed. Although the perspectives of reception schools and theorists differ significantly from each other, the main premise of the theory is that the text does not have a stable, intrinsic meaning to be discovered and absorbed by a passive reader; rather, it is the situated reader who actively engages with the text and makes it meaningful in that interpretive process.

26. Some studies that entirely or partly look at receptions of translated works include Brown's *Reception of Spanish* studying the reception of Latin American novels in West Germany, Caws and Luckhurst's edited collection on the receptions of Virginia Woolf's works across Europe (*Woolf in Europe*), Wirtén's analysis of the translations and editings of Harlequin novels in Sweden (*Global Infatuation*), Susam-Sarajeva's *Theories on the Move* on the reception of structuralism in Turkey and the construction of "French feminism" in the US, and Tahir-Gürçağlar's case study on the readers' letters published in *Varlık*, a prominent literature journal in Turkey (*Kapılar*). Although these works analyze the reception aspects of translated works, they mostly depend on written and/or published accounts of readers' responses, such as readers' letters, book reviews, and marketing and promotion materials, rather than oral studies or ethnographic studies like in-depth interviews.

27. Gonca Özmen, "Poetry Gives a Voice to the Voiceless," interview by Clare Roberts, *A New Divan*, June 22, 2020, https://newdivan.org.uk/blog/interview-with-gonca-ozmen/.

28. A few studies where the researcher analyzes their own translation include Díaz-Diocaretz (*Poetic Discourse*), Levine (*Subversive Scribe*), Maier ("Woman in Translation"), Reimóndez ("Curious Incident"), Simon (*Culture in Transit*), Venuti ("Translating Derrida").

29. The reading diaries were accompanied by a questionnaire I provided. The diary research provided data on the readers' "raw" and "intimate" reactions to the book and allowed me to see how those initial reading experiences were similarly or differently reconstructed later in the collective setting of the focus group and the individual interview. After reading and diary keeping processes were completed, the participants were divided into three semi-structured focus group sessions, which were all moderated by a professional, Esen Özdemir, from Amargi Women's Academy, a feminist organization that was based in Istanbul at the time. The focus groups were directed by a moderator, rather than me, since as the translator and researcher I was already too involved in every stage of the study and therefore, I believed, my presence could be a source of uneasiness in the collective discussions. I thought taking a step back in the middle of the study and giving the participants some space without my direct voice in it could help them raise their critiques of the book and my translation strategies more easily. While 17 of the 22 readers participated in all three steps of the study, 1 participant could take part only in the diary research and the focus group, and 4 participants participated only with their reading diaries.

30. This research study was supported by a Faculty Research Grant awarded by UNC Charlotte in 2017–2018.

## Chapter 1. Comparative Geohistories of Virginity

1. For instance, see the columns that appeared in *The Guardian* by Poppy Noor ("Check Your Hymen") and Jill Filipovic ("TI's Hymen Checks").

2. About a month later, when New York legislators proposed a bill to bar doctors

from performing "virginity tests," that also immediately hit the news in Turkey with similar elements of surprise.

3. For instance, according to Social Wit List, the show was the third most-followed new show on Instagram in December 2019: http://newsletters.worldscreen.com/newsflash/Social-Wit-List_2019–12.html (accessed on September 22, 2020).

4. Unless otherwise stated, all the translations in this book from Turkish into English are mine.

5. This actually points at the importance of feminist knowledge production on gender issues deemed "commonsensical," "natural," or "scientific" (read: factual)—institutionally authorized epithets that serve to prevent critical inquiries.

6. Turkey is the second largest TV drama exporter in the world behind the US and although the show started only in December 2019, "Sefirin Kızı" has already been sold to Uruguay, Paraguay, and Bolivia. Given that Turkish dramas have been exported to approximately 150 countries across Asia, Europe, South America, Middle East, and North Africa, "Sefirin Kızı," with the high ratings and immense social media attention it has received, will travel to many more countries.

7. See Chapter 5 to see the ways in which *Bekâret*'s feminist readers replaced that heteropatriarchal universality of virginity with a subversive one by deploying a reading strategy that I call "differential universalization."

8. Well aware of this urgency, UN Human Rights, UN Women, and the World Health Organization (WHO) released an interagency statement, "Eliminating Virginity Testing" in 2018 and called for a ban on virginity testing. The statement not only frames virginity testing as a harmful, discriminatory, and unscientific ("medically unnecessary and unreliable") practice that violates women's human rights, but also provides global strategies to eliminate it. Interestingly, the statement includes Turkey, but not the US, in its list of countries where the practice of medical virginity testing has been documented (see page 7). To see the full statement, visit: https://www.who.int/reproductivehealth/publications/eliminating-virginity-testing-interagency-statement/en/ (accessed on January 19, 2019.)

9. Hence, "the sick man of Europe" epithet used to describe the Ottoman Empire from the 1850s onward when the empire began losing vast amount of territory and population after disastrous wars and eventually fell under the control of European powers (Britain, France, Italy, and Greece). The epithet was employed both in the orientalist European rhetoric, and in the new Turkish state's official historiography to emphasize its self-disconnection from its Ottoman past (Ersanlı, *İktidar ve Tarih*, 132, 223).

10. Often defined as "Kemalist" referring to the role and impact of Atatürk's leadership in the ideological formation and implementation of these reforms.

11. The alleged granting of women's rights to vote and be elected for municipal and parliamentary office in 1930 and 1934 is also often cited among such "westernizing/modernizing" reforms.

12. Many of the legal codes passed into law in this period were translated and adopted from existing European codes. For instance, the Civil Code was translated

from the Swiss Code and the Penal Code was modeled after the Italian Code. Judicially, then, the new state itself was a "work of translation."

13. On the close connection between language, translation, and nation, see Sakai, who argues that "the modern regime of translation," with its claims of "the unities of national languages," played a key role in the formation of the modern nation-state ("Modern Regime," 106–7).

14. For more on the nation-building role of the Translation Bureau, see Tahir-Gürçağlar's *The Politics and Poetics of Translation*.

15. Anderson (*Imagined Communities*, 45–46) sees this imposition of "compulsory romanization" as a bilateral attempt "to heighten Turkish-Turkey's national consciousness at the expense of any wider Islamic identification" and "to align Turkish nationalism with the modern, Romanized civilization of Western Europe."

16. The new dress codes emulated European codes and imposed the western style of hats and clothing instead of fezzes, turbans, and baggy trousers for men. Although there were no such official dress codes for women, they were encouraged to adopt western feminine garments and remove their veils.

17. The aftermath of the 1980 coup is often regarded as the most repressive period in Turkey's history. The new constitution, passed in 1982, was designed to build a centralized and authoritative state (backed up by the military now endowed with extensive powers to guard the nation's secularism and assumed unity) and create an extremely depoliticized society by imposing severe restrictions on political and civil rights within an atmosphere of fear and intimidation.

18. Often described as a pro-Islamist party advocating a neoliberal market economy, Evren Savcı calls AKP's political, economic, and social model (with a complex politics of morality) "neoliberal Islam" (*Queer in Translation*, 16–24).

19. The waves metaphor, which is the dominant periodization tool in conceptualizing US feminisms, is also occasionally used to describe the genealogy of Turkey's feminist movements. However, the metaphor has been rightly criticized by US feminists for privileging the political experiences of white upper-class women, reinscribing hierarchies and omissions in women's history, obscuring plurality among feminist activists and activisms, failing to capture the historical complexities of feminist politics, misrepresenting feminisms as a singular homogeneous movement, and fostering generational divisions among feminists. For an overview of the debate see Laughlin et al.'s "Jump Ship," Nicholson's "Feminism," and Thompson's "Multiracial Feminism." Also see Rowley's "Idea of Ancestry" on the problematics of using the waves metaphor transatlantically to describe other feminist genealogies.

20. Another genealogy that is more closely modeled after the US wave scheme classifies the feminist movements in Turkey under three waves on the basis of political agenda: the first wave of the early republican era with its focus on civic and political rights; the second wave of the 1980s with its focus on violence against women; and the ongoing third wave of the 1990s with its focus on diversity, intersectionality, and identity politics (a change mainly resulting from critiques by Kurdish and Islamist feminists toward the *Turkish* feminist movement). See Diner and Toktaş ("Waves of Feminism") for details.

21. Also, see Tekeli's "80'lerde Türkiye'de."

22. So much so that one of the most popular documentaries about feminism in Turkey, *İsyan-ı Nisvan*, is fully dedicated to the "origin" story of the Women's Circle. See Ergun's "Translational Beginnings" for an analysis of the documentary.

23. I am thankful to Carole McCann for this historical insight.

24. These contestations around importing foreign concepts, particularly from western languages, also reflected some geopolitical anxieties. For instance, Stella Ovadia ("Feminist Hareketin," 63), one of the founding figures of the feminist movement, notes how their "feminist page" in the periodical *Somut*, which was the project that brought together several members of the Women's Circle and paved the way for the translation group, was criticized by famous woman fiction writer, Tomris Uyar. Uyar's apparently leftist-oriented, anti-imperialist critique that the language of the feminist writings published in *Somut* "reeks of west" was wittily countered by Ovadia as "some languages reek of west, others reek of male." These critiques of Turkish feminism being borrowed from the imperial/bourgeois west continued.

25. For a retelling of the feminist movement's "origin story" that recognizes its history in translation, see Ergun's "Translational Beginnings."

26. See Çakır's *Osmanlı Kadın*; Demirdirek's *Osmanlı Kadınlarının*; Durakbaşa's *Halide Edib*; Ekmekçioğlu and Bilal's *Bir Adalet Feryadı*; Sirman's "Feminism in Turkey;" and Zihnioğlu's *Kadınsız İnkılap*.

27. To challenge that erasure, the Women's Library and Information Centre, founded in 1990, has undertaken a project called "Ottoman Women's Memories Publication Series" to transliterate Ottoman women's periodicals to Turkish script.

28. For a discussion on the problematics of the term "state feminism" in Turkey, see Arat's "Turkish Women."

29. Sinha 2004, 255. See also Delaney (1995) for an illuminating discussion on the ways in which gender played a central role in the nationalist conceptualization of Turkey as the "motherland" (*anavatan*) to be protected by the "father state" (*devlet baba*) drawing on the heteropatriarchal narratives of the nuclear family and procreation.

30. See Durakbaşa's "Cumhuriyet;" Sancar's "Otoriter;" Sirman's "Feminism in Turkey." The New Turkish Woman was also a product of the new state's Turkification policies, which had started in the late Ottoman history. These policies actively sought to assimilate a wide range of ethnic and religious groups into the category "Turk" and erase all ethnic and religious diversity passed on by the Ottoman Empire.

31. Modern Girl Around the World Research Group reveals that the "Modern Girl" is itself/herself a case of translation.

32. For more on Dersim Genocide caused by those military operations in 1837–38, see Deniz's "Re-assessing the Genocide."

33. Despite the women's organizations' objections, the Justice Commission refused to use the term "virginity examination" in the code by claiming that it was covered under "genital examination," and so, they failed to criminalize the practice.

34. A telling case took place in January 2013 in the northwestern city of Edirne, where forensic doctor Prof. Gürcan Altun refused to force three girls (between the

ages of ten and thirteen), who were allegedly sexually abused, to undergo virginity tests and therefore was sued by the attorney general's office for professional negligence ("Profesöre Bekâret"). Altun was later acquitted ("Bekaret Kontrolü" and "Yargının Derdi"). He was sued for a similar case in 2016 and was acquitted again. Another similar case also happened in Edirne in 2010 when forensic doctor Prof. Ahmet Yılmaz was sued after he refused to examine a fifteen-year-old girl against her will. He was acquitted as well (Keskinkılıç, "Bekaret Davası"). These cases dispute the TPC and may play a crucial role in the medical treatment and legal handling of similar cases in the future.

35. The article proposes an imprisonment sentence (from three months to one year) for perpetrators forcing or performing a genital examination on a woman without a legal order but not a single case of prosecution has taken place since 2004.

36. For more on the hymen, see Mishori et al., "Little Tissue," and McKeon Olson and García-Moreno, "Virginity Testing."

37. However, this should not be understood in absolute terms in a domination/oppression dichotomy, since the Ottomans did resist and intervene in orientalist discourses. See Lewis' *Rethinking Orientalism* for an account of Ottoman women writers negotiating orientalist gender discourses in their writings targeting primarily western audiences.

38. Occidentalism refers to the binary conceptualization and representation of the "superior" west (Occident) as opposed to the "inferior" east. An extension of the self-naming global regime of Europe, occidentalism is internalized orientalism. Turkey's eagerness to shake off the "Oriental Ottoman" tag and embrace the "western" title, captured by the phrase "admiration for the west" (*batı hayranlığı*), is an example of occidentalism. Gürel calls this "method of social engineering" "selective westernization" (*Limits of Westernization*, 4).

39. Also see Göknar, whose analysis of novelist Tanpınar's writings reveals this "crisis of mind" rooted in the "pervasive duality extant in Ottoman/Turkish culture," which according to Tanpınar, "first began in public life, then it split our society in two in terms of mentality, and in the end, deepening and changing its progress, it settled within us as individuals" ("Ottoman Past," 658–59).

40. I claim that *Virgin* only *partially* dismantles the "liberated Western Woman" notion because the book's narratives at times reinforce this notion by emphasizing that women living in the contemporary west do not have to choose to remain virgins until marriage. As Blank notes, "this option has only quite recently—within the last thirty years or so—become widely acceptable" (15). More importantly, sporadic references to non-western cultures and their virginity practices (such as "honor killings") could also be read through the ideology of the "progressive" west (with its "liberated women") versus the "backwards" non-west (with its "women in need of rescue"), and, thus, could reproduce orientalist readings.

41. It seems that this claim is strategically made to convince US readers that virginity is *still* a relevant issue for them despite its defeat after the so-called sexual revolution of the 1960s. In this sense, dismantling the myth of the expired western virginity could be seen as a major motive of the book in the political context of the United States.

42. Accessed on May 12, 2013 at *Milliyet*'s website (March 15, 2011): http://saglik .milliyet.com.tr/yeni-trend-bekaret-/cinselsaglik/haberdetay/15.03.2011/1364486/ default.htm.

43. Accessed on May 12, 2013 at *Haber 365*'s website (March 15, 2011): http://www .haber365.com/Haber/ABDde_Yeni_Kadin_Modasi_Bekaret/.

44. Accessed on February 9, 2020 at newspaper Hürriyet's website (November 7, 2019): https://www.hurriyet.com.tr/galeri-kizini-her-yil-bekaret-kontrolune-goturuyor -41368666/4.

45. For more on the politics and/or history of virginities in the US, see Allan, Santos, and Spahr's *Virgin Envy*, Bernau's *Virgins*, Bouris' *The First Time*, Carpenter's *Virginity Lost*, Kelly's *Performing Virginity*, and Valenti's *The Purity Myth*.

46. A story that appeared in *Marie Claire* in 2019, based on an interview study conducted in partnership with the Fuller Project revealed the prevalence of virginity tests in the US: "[We] have found that not only is virginity testing being requested in the United States with frequency by both religious and secular communities and occurring here, but the practice remains wholly unregulated" (Jones). While the article importantly defies virginity's medical testability, it also makes some orientalist statements, such as: "[People] think it only happens in the Middle East with child brides. But it happened to me."

47. I am using "honor" in scare quotes because of the term's colonial and orientalist load. For a critique of "honor" as "an overdetermined term" that sticks exclusively to Muslim bodies and communities, see Grewal, "Feminist Encounters," 15. For a discussion of the "modern infrastructures of honor crimes" as well as how to engage in complex non-colonial analyses of the so-called honor crimes, see Abu-Lughod, who writes, "The seductive power of the honor crime, with its unique mix of sexual titillation and moral horror and its polymorphous interpretive capacity, has allowed it to emerge in the last couple of decades as a robust category that does significant political and cultural work" ("Orientalism," 50). Finally, I should note that there has been a concerted orientalist effort within Turkey to attribute "honor killings" exclu- sively to the Kurdish population. In fact, the mainstream media have consistently called them "murders of tradition" (*töre cinayeti*) to insinuate that it is the "tribal and feudal" culture of the Kurdish people that cause such gender violence. This problematic naming practice, which has been deeply challenged by both Kurdish and Turkish feminists in the country, is a colonial attempt to frame "honor" as an innocent, benevolent norm in contrast to "*töre*," conceived in the hegemonic Turkish imaginary as a deadly extension of "Kurdish backwardness." See Çağlayan's *Women in the Kurdish Movement*, Kışanak's *Kürt Siyasetinin Mor Rengi*, and Kogacioglu's "Tradition Effect" for more on the colonial framing of honor killings in Turkey.

48. A striking example that illustrates the role of medicine in the construction of virginity as a control mechanism over women comes from Nobel laureate Orhan Pamuk's novel, *The Museum of Innocence*. In the novel, where virginity appears as a recurring theme along with tensions of westernization, the main character Kemal engages in a conversation with Doctor Barbut in his engagement party. After Kemal humorously informs the doctor about his fiancé's refusal to get her tonsils taken out,

the doctor offers the following response, which is disturbingly realistic as it seems to allude to hymen tests: "Well, these days modern medicine has more modern ways of scaring beautiful girls into submission" (106).

## Chapter 2. Re-visioning Virginity in the Rewriting of *Virgin*

Part of this chapter was published in *Trans/Scripts* with the title, "Reconfiguring Translation as Intellectual Activism: The Turkish Feminist Remaking of *Virgin: The Untouched History*" [vol. 3, 2013, 264–89].

1. For a discussion of Rich's concept of "re-vision" framed as translation, her poetic use of translation as a powerful metaphor, and her emphasis on translation as an indispensable practice of feminist activism, see Bermann's "Re-vision."

2. According to my personal communication with Blank, the publisher wanted to make the book shorter mainly for commercial reasons. Their reasoning behind the deleted sections was that long books would not sell as well as short ones. The publisher also deleted many references to virginity-related cultural practices performed outside the geopolitical terrain of the west to ensure coherence and consistency in the book, which claimed an exclusively "western" history of virginity. So, in the publication process, *Virgin* became more "western" than Blank had originally intended it to be. *Virgin*'s Turkish translation did not include any of these deleted parts as the copyright agreement was based on the final published text.

3. *Virgin* was reviewed in *Washington Post* (Warner), *New York Times* (Kuczynski), *New York Observer* (Grossman), *San Francisco Chronicle* (Blaisdell), *San Diego Union Tribune* (Mayhew), and the *Bitch* magazine (Blasi) among many others.

4. In Gordon's words, *Virgin* provides on virginity "an alternative diagnostics . . . to link the politics of accounting, in all its intricate political-economic, institutional, and affective dimensions, to a potent imagination of what has been done and what is to be done otherwise" (*Ghostly Matters*, 18).

5. *Virgin* does not use an academic citation style. A "selected bibliography" is given for each chapter at the end of the book, where sources are not alphabetically ordered, or explicitly cited, but rather presented in brief annotations.

6. And *Bekâret* is even more intertextual because, as a work of translation, it is simultaneously constituted by both "foreign" and "domestic" codes and echoes.

7. For example, the sacred vestal virgins held enormous power in Ancient Rome until the institution was abolished in 394 (Blank, *Virgin*, 128–31).

8. The question of genre is also a factor in turning the textual traces of the feminist translator more or less visible. For instance, feminist translations of experimental writings, where language is recycled through linguistic strategies such as neologisms, puns, unconventional spellings, and subversions of grammatical and semantic gender systems, yield more visible examples of feminist translation. However, in translations of other genres, such as non-fictional or scholarly texts, the feminist translator's political strategies may not be as manifest to readers as they are in experimental texts.

9. As Blank notes, what all virginity tests have in common is that they "do not look for virginity, but for signs of virginity;" "virginity tests cannot tell us whether an individual woman is a virgin; they can only tell us whether or not she conforms to what people of her time and place believe to be true of virgins;" "women may not speak for themselves" (*Virgin*, 77).

10. I got acquainted with Aksu Bora in 2006 while working on a translation of hers for a research study. For the study, I interviewed her, during which we established a lasting feminist affinity. Aksu Bora's partner, Tanıl Bora, was also one of the main editors of İletişim Publications and played a major facilitating role in the initiation process of the translation project. İletişim Press was established in Turkey in the restrictive aftermath of the 1980 military coup by a collective of leftist activists and intellectuals to address the country's arising political concerns with (heavily curtailed) democratization.

11. This emphasis is well expressed on their website: "We aimed to encourage liberation incentives, skills of autonomous action and intellectual thinking in every domain of society and we aimed to achieve this without being 'didactic;' with an attitude that, rather than talking to people, would make them talk." (İletişim Publications, "Hakkımızda" (About Us), accessed on December 15, 2011 at http://www.iletisim.com.tr/iletisim/hakkimizda.aspx)

12. Just as I was thinking that things were going too smoothly, when İletişim contacted the book's copyright agent, they were informed that another publisher, İnkılâp Press had already taken an interest in the book, so we had to wait for their decision. I reluctantly emailed İnkılâp and let them know that if they decided to publish the book, I would like to be its translator—reluctantly because İnkılâp does not take as critical and subversive a stance as İletişim does in its publishing practices. Moreover, while İletişim encourages feminist knowledge production, İnkılâp pays no such systemic attention to feminist scholarship. Although İnkılâp seemed genuinely pleased with my interest in translating the book, they decided not to publish *Virgin* because of its exclusive geographic focus on the western and Christian history.

13. The most notorious example of such patriarchal translation is the first English translation of Simone de Beauvoir's *The Second Sex*. For more on this, see Simons' "The Silencing" and Moi's "While We Wait."

14. In addition to textual cooperations, after *Bekâret* was published, Bora interviewed me for *Amargi*, the renowned Turkish feminist quarterly of the time ("Bekâretin"). In that interview Bora did not focus exclusively on *Bekâret* but also highlighted feminist translation as a form of activism. At the end of the interview, she also asked me to write an introductory essay on feminist translation for the same magazine, which was published a year later (Ergun, "Feminist Çeviri").

15. Bayraktar's "Bekaretin," Gülen and Eren's "Bekâret Kavramı," Kızılarslan's "Utanç," Kurnaz's "Bedenden Öte," and Öğüt's "Yamuk Bakış."

16. I discuss how *Bekâret*'s readers responded to this potential of the book to facilitate the formation of imaginary feminist collectivities in Chapter 6.

17. I should note that translation necessarily involves some degree of familiariza-

tion; otherwise, the text risks being utterly unintelligible. By "familiarization" here I am referring more to recreating an imported text that target readers can more easily enter and connect with, rather than to the assimilation of all foreign elements or differences within the text.

18. This note about my use of simplistic language is not a claim of achievement. Some readers actually found *Bekâret*'s language dense and said that readers who were not used to academic texts could struggle with understanding the book.

19. "A mayden faire of ye greene sicknesse late
Pitty to see, perplexed was full sore
Resolvinge how t'amend her bad estate,
In this distresse Apollo doth implore
Cure for her ill; ye oracle assignes,
Keepe ye first letter of these severall lines" (*Virgin*, 69).

20. "Bir güzel genç kız, yakalanmış yeşil hastalığa
İçi parçalanır görenin, kızsa bilemez derdi ne
Rahatsızlığı nedendir nasıl iyileşir acaba
Çabucak kıza cevap verir Apollon şöyle
Üzülme, çaresi vardır hastalığının, der kahin
Kurtuluşun ilk harflerde bak da gör kendin" (*Bekâret*, 130).

21. The term "prick" is also used later in the book in a quotation from *My Secret Life*, "a four-thousand page sexual diary" (*Virgin*, 195): "The street boys' dirty pricks went up their little cunts first." I translated this "prick" as "*çük*" as well, but since the pricks in this case already belonged to "boys," my translation did not come out as interventionist as before.

22. This is the reason why I sometimes refer to *Virgin/Bekâret*'s imagined reader or subject as "she," not with essentialist intentions, but to draw attention to the gendered configuration of virginity and virginity's constitutive role in the making of "womanhood" as an embodied "fact of nature." So, very much like gender, virginity is also a regulatory fiction anchored in the body through scientific complicity. And the fact that "the body is an historical idea but a set of possibilities" is precisely why virginity can be modified, rejected, and eradicated with feminist action (Butler, "Performative Acts," 521).

23. Also, the use of a colon in book titles is not as common in Turkish. Thus, keeping the title's "foreign" punctuation could underline the importedness of the book excessively, which could result in the local audience's rejection of the book. I believed making the title more fluent, meaningful, and memorable in Turkish alleviated such a risk of immediate dismissal.

24. Another politically invested familiarization decision made in the title was the translation of "untouched" as "*el değmemiş*," which literally translates as "no hands touched." Both terms in both languages connote "virgin." Yet, while the English word implies a wide range of abstract and concrete forms of touching, the Turkish phrase underlines the embodied action by explicitly naming the body part performing the touching. In doing so, the Turkish title invites the reader to engage with the book

not only intellectually, but also bodily. The reader is intimately positioned in the reading process as a corporeal being who is expected to experience the book both as an epistemological project and as an embodied process of resignification. With such an emphasis on physical contact, the Turkish title provokes the reader to touch and retouch the text of their own body, whether written by them or others, as they touch the book (and the history of virginity told in it).

25. It would perhaps be a fair critique to say that the book, in English or in Turkish, does not openly point out the cisgender nature of virginity, but rather treats cisgender in unmarked and universal terms. In this regard, *Virgin* might be criticized for potentially perpetuating an essentialist and cisgenderist perception of "womanhood," while de-essentializing virginity.

26. Discussing *Our Bodies, Ourselves'* Bulgarian translation, Davis notes, "the problem facing the translators was what to do about the ubiquitous 'we' in the U.S. text." The question of how to translate the US "we" "in a form that sounds natural and inviting enough for a Bulgarian woman reader to identify with" resonates with my case (*How Feminism Travels*, 190).

27. How did *Bekâret*'s readers respond to being textually included in this western history, while being geopolitically excluded? How did they handle this push-pull relation with the text? I address these questions in the upcoming chapters.

28. Accessed on November 6, 2012 at http://ayrimcisozluk.blogspot.com/2012/02/turkce-ayrmc-deyis-deyim-ve-atasozleri.html. According to an interview with Ahmet Özcan, the compiler of the dictionary, Bilgi UP, Istanbul, is planning to publish the online dictionary as a book. (Accessed on December 4, 2012 at http://www.haberturk.com/medya/haber/762662-bu-da-ayrimci-sozluk.)

29. For instance, "A girl is asked for by a thousand, taken by one" (*Bir kızı bin kişi ister, bir kişi alır.*)

30. Ironically, the protest was against the killing of a leftist retired teacher who had died of a heart attack triggered by the police's use of tear gas during a demonstration.

31. Accessed on September 12, 2012 at the news channel CNN-Turk's official website: http://www.cnnturk.com/2011/yazarlar/06/04/basbakan.o.kadin.kiz.midir.kadin.midir/618955.0/.

32. Indeed, the *kız* discourse is so conspicuously packed with misogyny that Erdoğan's words sparked off major feminist protests in Istanbul and Ankara, where feminists responded with slogans such as "Tayyip, get your hands off my body!"

33. The hymen, which has been deployed in heteropatriarchal societies to create perhaps the most rigid binary regarding virginity, is strategically used by Derrida to illustrate his deconstructive notion of "undecidable." According to Derrida, the hymen, by simultaneously referring to virginity and consummation of marriage (desire and fulfillment), implies both communion and impediment of that communion and lies between these assumed poles at once being neither inside nor outside. As he notes, "the one—the veil of virginity where nothing has yet taken place—remains in the other—consummation, release, and penetration of the antre" (*Dissemination*, 215). However, Derrida's deconstruction of the hymen does not bring about a

feminist problematization of the concept. On the contrary, while problematizing the dichotomy, he reiterates the hetero/sexism of virginity discourses by participating in the same male gaze that objectifies, appropriates, and sexualizes women's bodies for masculine ends. Although Derrida rightly describes the hymen as "a tissue on which so many bodily metaphors are written," his rereading of these metaphors falls short of disclosing the violent body politics behind the conceptualization of the hymen (213). I am thankful to Luise von Flotow for alerting me to this discussion.

34. Since *himen* is imported from English, it could also be read as populated with imperialist intentions. Depending on the reader's political stance, this could be perceived as a more or less risky move in the Turkish translation of a western book.

35. Accessed on December 2, 2012 at the Turkish Medical Association's official website: http://www.ttb.org.tr/index.php/Etik-Kurul/etik-1347.html.

36. Accessed on December 2, 2012 at the Turkish Medical Association's official website: http://www.ttb.org.tr/kutuphane/etik_bldgeler2010.pdf.

37. This example also illustrates that the translator's agency is always partial because as Spivak notes, the translator is at the same time "written by her language" (*Teaching Machine*, 201).

38. For instance, Bozkurt's "Kadın Mı," Kurnaz's "Bedenden Öte," and Tekin's "Namus."

39. For instance, Elbek's "Himen Vesayeti," Işık's "Mona Eltahawy'den," Özgökçe's "Geleneksel," Saraç's "Erkeklik Zarı," and Tahaoğlu's "Himen Tazminat." Several examples of such expansion of *himen* can be seen on the online news site *Bianet*, particularly in op-eds written by medical doctors. For instance, in a 2009 op-ed reporting on a case of two teenagers who went on a vacation without informing their families and were then forced to undergo virginity tests to "prove" that they had not "fooled around," Osman Elbek, a medical school faculty member, responds to the widely (and hegemonically) televised event. In his op-ed titled, "Himen Vesayeti" [The Hymen Guardianship], he critiques Turkey's virginity politics, including its thorny virginity lexicon. *Kızlık zarı* is not used in his article at all and *himen* is simply defined in a footnote as "vaginal membrane." In another recent *Bianet* op-ed titled "Erkeklik Zarı" [The Membrane of Manhood], gynecologist Irmak Saraç draws on *Bekâret* (including the translator's preface) to dismantle virginity myths. Under a subheading that would translate as "*Himen*, Not *Kızlık Zarı*," she rejects *kızlık zarı* as a hetero/sexist term. Also see Chapter 1.

40. Another striking example is an instructional video series presented by gynecologist Müjdegül Karaca, who consistently uses *himen* in her several videos on virginity and the hymen. In fact, under the one on "Virginity," she openly mentions and recommends *Bekâret*: https://www.youtube.com/watch?v=EpDTRGKICe0 (accessed on September 20, 2020).

41. My use of these national and regional markers does not mean that the virginity regimes associated with those two geopolitical territories are completely detached from each other. They are not because virginity is a translationally constituted, ever-

ramifying discourse that is both local and global, universal and particular at the same time. In other words, just because they are different and distinct enough does not mean they do not have any similarities or commonalities.

42. I included the "joke" in the preface to criticize the intersectional configuration of virginity, honor, and violence against women in Turkey: "A man, two days after getting married, kills his wife and is taken to the court. The judge asks him, 'Why did you kill your wife, son?' The man answers, 'She wasn't a virgin, your honor.' When the judge asks him, 'Then, why didn't you kill her on the first day?' he replies, 'Your honor, she was a virgin on the first day'" (Ergun, "Önsöz," 12).

43. An exception is Marco Sonzogni's book (*Re-covered Rose*), which analyzes the translations of the cover designs of Umberto Eco's internationally renowned book, *Il nome della rosa* [*The Name of the Rose*].

44. The 414-page long *Bekâret* was first published in paperback in October 2008 with 1,000 copies printed. 1,000 might seem to be a ludicrously low number to a US-American audience but it is a common practice for publishers in Turkey to print first editions (particularly of academic books) in 1,000 copies unless the book is expected to be a bestseller. İletişim printed *Bekâret*'s second edition in 2012, third edition in 2013, fourth edition in 2014, fifth edition in 2017, sixth edition in 2019, and seventh edition in 2021, which points at a steady sales record and the ongoing relevance of the book in Turkey.

45. Personal email correspondence, November 14, 2011.

46. For a discussion on the readers' reactions to the cover, see Chapter 4.

## Chapter 3. Remaking Feminist Subjectivity in Feminist Translation

A shorter version of this chapter was published in *Women & Language* with the title, "'Reading Is an Act of Survival': Remaking Feminist Subjectivity in Translation" [vol. 43, no. 1, 2020, 203–37].

1. For more on theorizing the intricate relation between experience, discourse, and knowledge, see Joan Scott's "Evidence of Experience" and Section I Introduction in McCann, Seung-kyung, and Ergun's *Feminist Theory Reader* (17–19).

2. For a brilliant discussion of reading a translated text as a case of "strange encounter" with the other, see Ahmed's *Strange Encounters*, particularly the boxed sections in Chapter 7, "Ethical Encounters," where she narrates her reading of Mahasweta Devi's short story, "Douloti the Beautiful," translated by Gayatri Chakravorty Spivak (147–48, 152–54, 158–60).

3. The diaries were partly guided by a questionnaire I provided. It was composed of three groups of questions: "before you start reading the book," "while you are reading the book," and "when you finish reading the book." While almost all the readers used the questionnaire to organize their diary entries, their responses diverged in terms of length, complexity, writing style, and degree of intimate disclosure. The diaries

greatly exceeded my expectations as I did not anticipate that the readers would commit such intense concentration and meticulous treatment to writing down their reading experiences.

4. The research participants are referred to by the pseudonyms of their choice.

5. The backside of Turkish national ID cards includes detailed information about family registry, and after marriage, a woman's records are transferred from her father's registry into her husband's.

6. This concern has been most vocally raised by Third World and postcolonial feminists. For more, see Amireh and Majaj's *Going Global* and Spivak's *Teaching Machine*.

7. In this chapter, I refer to the reader as "she" when I discuss a particular body that has been called and configured in the binary gender regime as a "woman" and thus been recruited into the hegemonic hymen-centered virginity discourse. This does not mean that *Virgin/Bekâret* exclusively speaks of and to bodies called and configured as "women."

8. The consecrated vestal virgins were "guardians of the sacred flame that symbolized the hearth of Rome's patron goddess, Vesta" and held enormous political, religious, and social power in Ancient Rome until 394 (*Virgin*, 129).

9. Leylak, who was a school counselor and had worked on several child abuse cases in her school, did not report any memories or signs of experiencing a sexual trauma during childhood. So, her self-questioning was exclusively caused by the lack of vaginal bleeding during her first (hetero)sexual intercourse.

10. Vaginismus can simply be described as a condition of the vagina not allowing penetration due to "involuntary" contractions of pelvic muscles. For an in-depth discussion of vaginismus, see Chapter 5.

## Chapter 4. Local Politics of Feminist Translation

1. Indeed, we observe a steady increase in the feminist virginity scholarship (in English) since the 2000s. For instance, see Allan, Santos, and Spahr's *Virgin Envy*, Bernau's *Virgins*, Bouris's *The First Time*, Carpenter's *Virginity Lost*, Kelly's *Performing Virginity*, and Valenti's *The Purity Myth*.

2. A quick google search reveals that *Bekâret* has indeed been incorporated into almost every reading list and/or course syllabus in Women's Studies programs and other political institutions, such as the (leftist) teachers' union, EğitimSen.

3. Interestingly, in our post-focus-group interview, Dicle told me that after the group discussion, she took another look at the book and changed her perception of its language being too dense, although she still categorized it as academic.

4. One example is the verb, "to experience," which is used frequently in both theoretical and everyday language in English. When translated into Turkish, this quite accessible verb becomes "*deneyimlemek*," which, at the time of the study, was a newly coined word with a somewhat limited sociolinguistic area of usage.

5. This term comes up earlier in the discussion when the participants debate why

women participate in and perpetuate the hegemonic virginity regime. Bilge Su jokingly calls women, including herself, who unknowingly support heteropatriarchal ideologies like virginity "accomplices" because "they have internalized and taken as natural the fiction/ality of virginity."

6. Accessed on May 10, 2010 at the web-based collective dictionary: http://www.eksisozluk.com/show.asp?t=virgin%20the%20untouched%20history.

7. For instance, Frank et al.'s "Virginity Examinations."

8. Another participant, Leylak, who worked as a guidance counselor at a school, regretfully told me about an incest case involving a female student in her school. She said that the child was taken to a virginity test as part of the forensic medical investigation with her approval. She further noted that if she had read the book and known about the unreliability of the test at the time of the incident, she would have convinced the prosecutor and not allowed the child to undergo the test.

9. See Chapter 5 for more on how Bekâret's feminist readers used the reading strategy of "differential universalization" to subvert the heteropatriarchal universality of virginity while making a new subversive universal claim of virginity instead.

10. Several readers actually noted that the intersectional discussions could be more in-depth in the book. Dicle, for instance, criticized, in the group discussion, Blank's (Virgin, 11–12) narration of the case of the eighteen-year-old college student Rosie Reid, who sold her virginity in an online auction in 2004 to help pay for her education. While Blank focused on the heteronormative configuration of virginity in the public perception of Reid's virginal status despite her being in a long-term sexual relationship with a woman, Dicle articulated her disappointment with Blank, who failed to intersectionally analyze the commodification of women's bodies in relation to the corporatization of education in the case.

11. I cannot provide bibliographic information for this blog quotation to ensure confidentiality.

12. This is a paraphrased version of the last sentence on page 20 in Virgin.

13. In 2020 alone, 410 women were murdered in Turkey, mostly by their partners and relatives. For more, see We Will Stop Femicide Platform's website, http://www.kadincinayetlerinidurduracagiz.net/for-english and their "Monument Counter" at http://anitsayac.com/?year=2020 for the exact numbers of femicide victims in Turkey recorded since 2008.

14. Gülümser is repeating a sentence from the translator's preface, which, she noted, gave her hope (Blank, Bekâret, 33).

15. A great example of such an impact of the book on doctors is gynecologist Irmak Saraç's 2019 newspaper article, "Erkeklik Zarı" [The Membrane of Manhood], which clearly draws on Blank's Bekâret. See Chapter 2.

16. Inspired by Eve Ensler's The Vagina Monologues and its subsequent Turkish translations, İşte Böyle Güzelim (Adak et al.) was compiled by four feminist academics and printed twice in the same year. It is composed of narratives of a diverse group of women's sexuality experiences, which were collected orally through workshops held across Turkey. Gülümser was a volunteer in the project and her real name is

not mentioned in the book; so, her identity is not disclosed by this mention. *İşte Böyle Güzelim* has been a success in Turkey being performed at numerous venues by more than 150 people. It was then translated into German in 2009, followed by several multilingual public readings in Germany. One of the co-editors of the Turkish book, Ayşe Gül Altınay adds on the political significance of this border-crossing saying, "these readings inspired debates among German feminists regarding their stereotypical (often orientalist) perceptions of Turkish and Kurdish women" (Nagar et al., "Cross-Disciplinary Roundtable," 126).

17. Kırmızı's comment on the problematics of using the word "virgin/ity," which was also raised by other participants like Dîlan, points to the paradox of deconstruction that emerges when one makes use of a metaphysical concept and at the same time puts it into question and under erasure but does not erase it. In fact, when read after Derrida's (*Of Grammatology*, 24) words, it becomes clear that Kırmızı's confusion is an inherent aspect of deconstruction: "Operating necessarily from inside, borrowing all the strategic and economic resources of subversion from the old structure, . . . the enterprise of deconstruction always in a certain way falls prey to its own work." We always inhabit the discursive field that we attempt to deconstruct, because as Derrida puts it, "There is nothing outside of the text" (158). Yet, the political potentiality, albeit unknowable in advance, of the deconstructive act for revealing, contesting, and reworking remains.

## Chapter 5. Feminist Translation as a Praxis of Cross-Border Interconnectivity

1. Given that *Virgin* was first rejected by İnkılâp Publishing in Turkey (before it was adopted by İletişim Publishing) because it was considered to be exclusively about the west proves that debilitating risk of "cultural irrelevance."

2. Other participants also shared similar observations. For instance, Dicle wrote in her diary: "We probably invariably see the 'bright/enlightened' face of the west in movies and in books."

3. For more on the problematics of this term, see Abu-Lughod's "Orientalism" and Grewal's "Feminist Encounters."

4. There is a lot of controversy about whether *Quran* makes such a promise or not.

5. The disease of virgins, also called "greensickness," had a collection of symptoms (e.g. "lack of menstruation, paleness, lack of appetite, and pica") and was "not only a common diagnosis but had a substantial medical literature as well" in the pre-20th century western medicine (Blank, *Virgin*, 65–66). "Marriage and particularly childbearing were believed to be a sovereign cure" (66).

6. For more, see Turan Yunusoğlu's recent book, *Yatak Odasındaki Kalabalık* [The Crowd in the Bedroom], which reveals the vaginismus narratives of women in Turkey from a feminist and anti-medicalizing perspective.

7. It is debatable how successful Blank is in this counteraction, since although she is

careful with not reasserting such orientalist beliefs, her discourse may at times activate problematic readings due to her implied hierarchical juxtaposition of "the west and the rest," particularly in the conclusion chapter, and also due to the pervasiveness of orientalist myths in *Virgin*'s reception context. In fact, in her review, Warner ("Virgin Territory") criticizes *Virgin* for containing some "misleading sweeping comments." The example she discusses to illustrate this is that of "female genital mutilation," which is briefly mentioned in the epilogue along with "honor crimes" as happenings of "the Islamic world" (*Virgin*, 255). Although *Virgin* is almost exclusively about the western history (at least on the surface), the epilogue brings up the issue of "other cultures" and "their cultural problems" in a way that presents "female genital mutilation" and honor-based violence against women as problems of an assumed monolithic "Islamic world" without giving any reference to the global interconnectedness of violent gender practices or local feminist activisms carried out against them. As a result, women living in societies with those issues appear as helpless victims of barbaric local traditions. Moreover, the brief section provides neither a local/global contextualization nor a complex geohistorical background for the practices and presents them in a hegemonic western paradigm, where, by implication, the west appears as the locus of "progress" and the non-west rest as "not there yet." In this respect, *Virgin* seems to reproduce the symbolic violence of the "western feminism as cultural imperialism" discourse. Given the care with which Blank presents her findings in the rest of the book to prevent colonial readings, this rhetoric appears not only problematic, but also inconsistent with the book's overall discourse.

8. This is also a good moment for you, the reader of this book, to stop and check whether you are interpreting this statement—"Turkey's virginity regime generates more systematic and extreme forms of violence against women"—as a confirmation of colonial tropes about "brutally oppressed oriental women waiting to be rescued," or whether you are reading it in a connectionist manner to expand your understanding of virginity as a diversely violent heteropatriarchal ideology that cuts across borders and manifests itself in various cultural codes and practices, some more deadly than others.

9. This is why a few participants noted that the book could emphasize the diversity of the west more. For instance, Bilge Su said in the interview, "It could be more comparative within the west." Ayşe similarly wrote, "I wish the historical account continued geographically as well although that doesn't look very possible. The thing that we call 'west' in fact contains such a vast geography and after a while what we read inevitably turns into an exclusive narrative of the US."

10. For instance, Şeyma's diary comments written right after reading the translator's preface, which presented such a "gruesome" portrayal of Turkey's virginity realities, illustrate that risk: "The preface has already shaken me quite a bit; I've started wondering if the preface is like this, how the book itself will be like, for how many nights it will give me nightmares."

11. In fact, the six participants of the third focus group session engage in a long discussion about this danger. The discussion begins when Kırmızı asks whether the

book's disregard for non-western virginity realities while making universal claims on virginity is an orientalist reflex. Eventually, they conclude that Blank's universality claims are valid, unlike "pseudo universals, where western criteria are proclaimed and imposed on all cultures" (Bilge Su), and her disregard for the non-western realities seems to be a research necessity or induced by the limitations of her cultural situatedness, rather than reflecting an imperialist gesture. In Bilge Su's words, Blank has an "exclusive, but not exclusionary" geopolitical approach to virginity: "I mean, deliberately rejecting something is different from making it invisible. Of course, she must have some limitations or blind spots caused by her coming from the west. But if we asked her that, I feel like she would respond with 'oh yes, is that so?' and confront that; she wouldn't say, 'no, it's not like that.'" These comments illustrate a sense of geopolitical trust for the author, which is admitted by most of the readers and seems to be enhanced both by the author's candid remarks about her geopolitical limitations and the feminist translator's ideological backing-up of the book.

12. While Mohanty (*Feminism Without Borders*, 19) calls these supposedly universal assumptions "ethnocentric universality," Keating (*Transformation Now*, 136) calls them "pseudo-universals."

13. An anecdotal study conducted in England by Paterson-Brown, M.D., which revealed that "63 percent of her respondents—and possibly more, since some of the women she asked could not remember—had not experienced any bleeding when they lost their virginity" (Blank, *Virgin*, 89).

14. Although I have not conducted a reception study with *Virgin*'s English-speaking readers, I can tell from my teaching experiences in Introduction to Women's and Gender Studies classes in the US, where I have my students read excerpts from *Virgin*, including the part on the Gitano, that they do at times read the Gitano's virginity code as an affirmation of their orientalist conceptions of non-western cultures and their gender practices. Of course, this is a partial observation. Yet, the consistency with which such initial problematic interpretations have ensued over the years is quite disconcerting.

15. The word "Gitano" was not mentioned anywhere in the research questionnaires used in the reception study.

16. *Virgin*, 77.


## Chapter 6. Imagined Translational Feminist Communities

1. "'Imagined' not because it is not 'real' but because it suggests potential alliances across divisive boundaries" (Mohanty, *Feminism Without Borders*, 46). Benedict Anderson (*Imagined Communities*, 6–7) uses "imagined communities" to refer to nations as imaginary collectivities of people whose common identification and "horizontal comradeship" is the product of an invention process. An interesting sidenote about Anderson's book is that he added into the revised edition a long afterward titled, "Travel and Traffic: On the Geo-biography of *Imagined Communities*," where he talks

about the translations and travels of the book into 29 languages and 37 countries (as of 2007). After discussing the transformations that the book has gone through during translation, he humbly ends the chapter saying, "*IC* is not my book anymore" (229). See Walkowitz ("Comparison Literature") for an analysis of Anderson's theoretical take on translations and crosscultural travels of books. Finally, see Mackie's "Language of Globalization" for an overview of "imagined transnational feminist communities."

2. For productive discussions and applications of Lugones' theory of world-traveling, in addition to Lugones' *Pilgrimages*, also see Ortega's *In-Between* (especially Chapter 4), Pitts' "World-traveling," Alcoff's "Lugones's World-Making," Gunning's "Arrogant Perception," Runyan's "World-Traveling," and Bardwell-Jones' "Home Making."

3. In fact, as a discursive regime of truth, orientalism itself is an ongoing work of translation.

4. For detailed explorations of the links between the intimate and the global, see Nagar's *Hungry Translations* and Pratt and Rosner's *The Global and the Intimate*.

5. I cannot provide any bibliographic information on the documentary to ensure confidentiality.

6. Or as Yasemin said, "You asked me if it were translated, but would it actually be translated?"

7. For a great discussion of this issue, see de Lima Costa's "Lost (and Found?)."

8. This statement reminds me of Chilla Bulbeck, who, referring to Robert Young, writes, "'Move a yard to your right' and you become an easterner" or, then, move a yard to your left and you become a westerner (*Re-Orienting Western feminisms*, 6).

## Conclusion

1. It seems that the publisher had a similar concern since *Bekâret*'s blurb—the book's most widely used promotion material—did not mention anything about the geohistorical scope of the book either.

2. In fact, this geopolitical risk was so real that a reader who wrote a review of *Bekâret* in her blog titled noted, "The book draws on the literature of the west as its primary source. Yet, do not immediately interpret unfavorably the fact that it works its way through the western history because Blank sweetly explains that she has started from the place she knows best and that she draws on the west only to narrow down her scientific focus" (Günyüzü, "Ve Tanrı").

3. I quote A.Z. Foreman's translation, which is not published in print but circulated widely on the internet. For a different translation of the poem and its Arabic "original," see al-Qasim (*Sadder Than Water*, 52–53).

4. Referring to the fact that my PowerPoint presentation showed a fake cover image for that hypothetical book on eastern virginities—a close-up black and white half-headshot of a woman wearing a hijab that covers her face except for her eye.

5. Founded in 2012 to support Kurdish prisoners' demands for peace in Turkey, Academics for Peace became well-known for our petition, "We will not be a party to

this crime!" publicized in 2016. Since then, the signatories have been under massive attack by the Turkish state. For more on Academics for Peace, visit https://barisicin akademisyenler.net

6. For a discussion on the dilemmas of Middle Eastern feminist scholars, also see Abu-Lughod's "Orientalism."

7. For a discussion of decolonial feminist translation ethics, see Ergun's "Feminist Translation Ethics."

8. For more on the role of translation in the growth of feminist movements, see Alvarez et al.'s *Translocalities*, Castro and Ergun's *Feminist Translation*; Flotow and Kamal's *Routledge Handbook*; and Flotow and Farahzad's *Translating Women*.

# Bibliography

Abdo, Diya. "Textual Migration: Self-Translation and Translation of the Self in Leila Abouzeid's *Return to Childhood* and *Ruju' 'Ila Al-Tufulah*." *Frontiers* 30, no. 2 (2009): 1–42.

Abu-Lughod, Lila. "'Orientalism' and Middle East Feminist Studies." *Feminist Studies* 27, no. 1 (2001): 101–13.

———. "Seductions of the 'Honor Crime.'" *differences* 22, no. 1 (2011): 17–63.

Adak, Hülya, Alyşe Gül Altınay, Esin Düzel, and Nilgün Bayraktar, editors. *İşte Böyle Güzelim . . .* [That's How It Goes My Sweetie . . .]. Sel, 2008.

Ahıska, Meltem. "Occidentalism: The Historical Fantasy of the Modern." *The South Atlantic Quarterly* 102, nos. 2/3 (2003): 351–79.

Ahmed, Sara. *Living a Feminist Life*. Duke UP, 2017.

———. *Strange Encounters: Embodied Others in the Post-Coloniality*. Routledge, 2000.

———. *The Promise of Happiness*. Duke UP, 2010.

Aiken, Susan Hardy, Ann Brigham, Sallie Marston, and Penny Waterstone, editors. *Making Worlds: Gender, Metaphor, Materiality*. U of Arizona P, 1998.

Ajayi, Titilope. "#MeToo, Africa and the Politics of Transnational Activism." 2018, https://africasacountry.com/2018/07/metoo-africa-and-the-politics-of-transnational -activism. Accessed 30 November 2019.

Alcoff, Linda Martín. "Cultural Feminism Versus Post-structuralism: The Identity Crisis in Feminist Theory." *Signs* 13, no. 3 (1988): 405–36.

———. "Lugones's World-Making." *Critical Philosophy of Race* 8, nos. 1–2 (2020): 199–211.

Alexander, Jacqui. "Remembering *This Bridge*, Remembering Ourselves: Yearning, Memory, and Desire." *This Bridge We Call Home*, edited by Gloria Anzaldúa and AnaLouise Keating, 81–103. Routledge, 2002.

Alexandra, Rae. "'Empowerment' Selfies Are Burying a Turkish Women's Rights Campaign." 2020, https://www.kqed.org/arts/13883979/empowerment-selfies -are-burying-a-turkish-womens-rights-campaign. Accessed 4 September 2020.

Allan, Jonathan, Cristina Santos, and Adriana Spahr, editors. *Virgin Envy: The Cultural (In)Significance of the Hymen.* U of Regina P, 2016.

Allen, Amy. "Solidarity After Identity Politics: Hannah Arendt and the Power of Feminist Theory." *Philosophy and Social Criticism* 25, no. 1 (1999): 97–118.

Alpar, Asli, editor. *Jinekolog Muhabbetleri* [Conversations of/on Gynecologists]. Kaos GL, 2020.

al-Qasim, Samih. *Sadder Than Water.* Translated by Nazih Kassis, Ibis, 2006.

Altınay, Ayşe Gül. "Bedenimiz ve Biz: Bekâret ve Cinselliğin Siyaseti" [Our Bodies and Us: Virginity and the Politics of Sexuality]. *90'larda Türkiye'de Feminizm* [Feminism in Turkey in the 90s], edited by Aksu Bora and Asena Günel, 323–43. İletişim, 2009.

———. "Giriş: Milliyetçilik, Toplumsal Cinsiyet ve Feminizm" [Introduction: Nationalism, Gender and Feminism]. *Vatan, Millet, Kadınlar* [Homeland, Nation, Women], edited by Ayşe Gül Altınay, 15–32. İletişim, 2009.

———. "Ordu-Millet-Kadınlar: Dünyanın İlk Kadın Savaş Pilotu Sabiha Gökçen" [Military-Nation-Women: The First Woman Combat Pilot in the World Sabiha Gökçen]. *Vatan, Millet, Kadınlar*, edited by Ayşe Gül Altınay, 261–94. İletişim, 2009.

Alvarez, Sonia, Claudia de Lima Costa, Verónica Feliu, Rebecca Hester, Norma Klahn, and Millie Thayer, editors. *Translocalities/Translocalidades: Feminist Politics of Translation in the Latin/a Américas.* Duke UP, 2014.

Amireh, Amal, and Lisa Suhair Majaj, editors. *Going Global: The Transnational Reception of Third World Women Writers.* Garland, 2000.

———. 2000. "Introduction." *Going Global: The Transnational Reception of Third World Women Writers*, edited by Amal Amireh and Lisa Suhair Majaj, Garland, 1–25.

Anderson, Benedict. *Imagined Communities: Reflections on the Origin and Spread of Nationalism*, revised edition, Verso, 2006.

Anzaldúa, Gloria. "Foreword to the Second Edition." *This Bridge Called My Back: Writings By Radical Women of Color*, 2nd edition, edited by Cherríe Moraga and Gloria Anzaldúa, iv–v. Kitchen Table: Women of Color Press, 1983.

———. *Interviews/Entrevistas.* Edited by AnaLouise Keating, Routledge, 2000.

———. "Now Let Us Shift . . . The Path of Conocimiento . . . Inner Work, Public Acts." *This Bridge We Call Home*, edited by Gloria Anzaldúa and AnaLouise Keating, 540–78. Routledge, 2002.

———. "Preface: (Un)natural Bridges, (Un)safe Spaces." *This Bridge We Call Home*, edited by Gloria Anzaldúa and AnaLouise Keating, 1–5. Routledge, 2002.

Apter, Emily. *The Translation Zone: A New Comparative Literature.* Princeton UP, 2006.

Arat, Zehra. "Turkish Women and the Republican Reconstruction of Tradition." *Reconstruction Gender in the Middle East*, edited by Fatma Müge Göçek and Shiva Balaghi, 57–78. Columbia UP, 1994.

Attridge, Derek. "Responsible Reading and Cultural Distance." *Postcolonial Audi-*

ences: *Readers, Viewers and Reception*, edited by Bethan Benwell, James Procter, and Gemma Robinson, 234–44. Routledge, 2012.

Baca Zinn, Maxine, and Bonnie Thornton Dill. "Theorizing Difference from Multiracial Feminism." *Feminist Studies* 22, no. 2 (1996): 321–31.

Baer, Brian James, and Klaus Kaindl, editors. *Queering Translation, Translating the Queer*. Routledge, 2018.

Bakan, Ronay, and Seda Saluk. "Challenge Accepted? Systemic Erasures in Femicide Narratives from Turkey." *Jadaliyya*, 14 August 2020. https://www.jadaliyya.com/Details/41561. Accessed 12 October 2020.

Bakhtin, Mikhail. *The Dialogic Imagination*. Translated by Caryl Emerson and Michael Holquist, U of Texas P, 2011.

Bardwell-Jones, Celia. "'Home Making; and 'World-Traveling': Decolonizing the Space-Between in Transnational Feminist Thought." *Decolonizing Feminism: Transnational Feminism and Globalization*, edited by Margaret Maclaren, 151–76. Rowman & Littlefield, 2017.

Barthes, Roland. *Image/Music/Text*. Translated by Stephen Heath, Hill and Wang, 1977.

Basu, Amrita. "Globalization of the Local/Localization of the Global." *Feminist Theory Reader*, 3rd edition, edited by Carole McCann and Seung-kyung Kim, 68–76. Routledge, 2013.

"Batı'da Bekarete Dönüş" [The Return to Virginity in the West]. *Haberdesin: Kadın*, 25 May 2012, http://haberdesin.com/haber/kadin/batida-bekarete-donus. Accessed 12 May 2013.

Bayraktar, Işıl. "Bekaretin El Değmemiş Tarihine Yolculuk [Journey to the Untouched History of Virginity]. *Taraf Kitap*, no. 4, 4 Nov. 2008, 2.

"Bekaret Kontrolü Yapmayı Reddeden Doktora Beraat" [Acquittal for the Doctor Who Refused to Perform a Virginity Test]. *Radikal*, 23 May 2013, http://www.radikal.com.tr/turkiye/bekaret_kontrolu_yapmayi_reddeden_doktora_beraat-1134719. Accessed 28 May 2013.

Benjamin, Walter. *Illuminations*. Edited by Hannah Arendt, translated by Harry Zohn, Schocken, 1968.

———. "The Task of the Translator: An Introduction to the Translation of Baudelaire's *Tableaux Parisiens*," translated by Harry Zohn. *The Translation Studies Reader*, 2nd edition, edited by Lawrence Venuti, 75–85. Routledge, 2004.

Berktay, Fatmagül. *Tarihin Cinsiyeti* [Gender of History]. Metis, 2003.

Berman, Antoine. *The Experience of the Foreign: Culture and Translation in Romantic Germany*. Translated by Stefaan Heyvaert, SUNY Press, 1992.

Berman, Jessica. *Modernist Commitments: Ethics, Politics, and Transnational Modernism*. Columbia UP, 2011.

Bermann, Sandra. "Re-vision and/as Translation: The Poetry of Adrienne Rich." *Translating Women*, edited by Luise von Flotow, 97–117. U of Ottawa P, 2011.

Bernau, Anke. *Virgins: A Cultural History*. Granta, 2007.

Bhabha, Homi. *The Location of Culture*. Routledge, 1994.

Blaisdell, Bob. "Behind Men's Obsession with Virginity. Review of *Virgin: The Untouched History*, by Hanne Blank." *San Francisco Chronicle*, no. 11, March 2007, M-1.

Blank, Hanne. *Bekâretin "El Değmemiş" Tarihi*. Translated by Emek Ergun, İletişim, 2008.

Blank, Hanne. *Virgin: The Untouched History*. Bloomsbury, 2007.

Blasi, Iris. "Virgin Territory. Review of *Virgin: The Untouched History*, by Hanne Blank." *Bitch* 7, no. 37 (2007): 70–75.

Boer, Inge. "Remastering the Master Narrative or Feminism as a Travelling Theory." *Changing Stories: Postmodernism and the Arab-Islamic World*, edited by Inge Boer, Annelies Moors, and Toine van Teeffelen, 107–20. Rodopi, 1995.

———. *Uncertain Territories: Boundaries in Cultural Analysis*. Edited by Mieke Bal, Bregje van Eekelen, and Patricia Spyer, Rodopi, 2006.

Bora, Aksu. "Emek Ergun ile Söyleşi: 'Bekâretin El Değmemiş Tarihi' [A Conversation with Emek Ergun: The Untouched History of Virginity]. *Amargi* 12, Spring 2009, 82–84.

Bost, Suzanne. *Shared Selves: Latinx Memoir & Ethical Alternatives to Humanism*. U of Illinois P, 2019.

Bouris, Karen. *The First Time: Women Speak out about "Losing Their Virginity."* Conari Press, 1993.

Bozkurt, Deniz. "'Kadın Mı Kız Mı Belli Değil'in Dildeki Yeri ve Kökeni Üzerine" [The Linguistic Position and Root of 'Not Sure Whether a Girl or a Woman']. *Birgün*, 24 Aug. 2014, http://www.birgungazetesi.net/news/view/kadin-mi-kiz-mi -belli-degilin-dildeki-yeri-ve-kokeni-uzerine/4357. Accessed 12 Sep. 2014.

Brah, Avtar. *Cartographies of Diaspora: Contesting Identities*. Routledge, 1996.

Braidotti, Rosi. *Nomadic Subjects: Embodiment and Sexual Difference in Contemporary Feminist Theory*. Columbia UP, 2011.

———. *Transpositions: On Nomadic Ethics*. Polity Press, 2006.

Brown, Meg. *The Reception of Spanish American Fiction in West Germany 1981–1991*. Niemeyer, 1994.

Bulbeck, Chilla. *Re-Orienting Western Feminisms: Women's Diversity in a Postcolonial World*. Cambridge UP, 1998.

Bunch, Charlotte. *Passionate Politics: Feminist Theory in Action*. St. Martin's Press, 1987.

Burwell, Catherine. "Reading Lolita in Times of War: Women's Book Clubs and the Politics of Reception." *Intercultural Education* 18, no. 4 (2007): 281–96.

Butler, Judith. "Performative Acts and Gender Constitution: An Essay in Phenomenology and Feminist Theory." *Theater Journal* 40, no. 4 (1988): 519–31.

———. *Precarious Life: The Powers of Mourning and Violence*. Verso, 2004.

Carpenter, Laura. *Virginity Lost: An Intimate Portrait of First Sexual Experiences*. NYU P, 2005.

Carrillo Rowe, Aimee. *Power Lines: On the Subject of Feminist Alliances*. Duke UP, 2008.

Castro, Olga, and Emek Ergun. "Feminism and Translation." *The Routledge Handbook of Translation and Politics*, edited by Fruela Fernández and Jonathan Evans, 125–43. Routledge, 2018.

———., editors. *Feminist Translation Studies*. Routledge, 2017.

Caws, Mary Ann, and Nicola Luckhurst, editors. *Reception of Virginia Woolf in Europe*. Continuum, 2008.

Chamberlain, Lori. "Gender and the Metaphorics of Translation." *Signs* 13, no. 3 (1988): 454–72.

Clifford, James. "Notes on Travel and Theory." *Inscriptions* 5, (1989): 177–88.

———. *Routes: Travel and Translation in the Late Twentieth Century*. Harvard UP, 1997.

———. "Traveling Cultures." *Cultural Studies*, edited by Lawrence Grossberg, Cary Nelson, and Paula Treichler, 96–116. Routledge, 1992.

Comay, Rebecca. "Geopolitics of Translation: Deconstruction in America." *Stanford French Review* 15, nos. 1/2 (1991): 47–79.

Çağlayan, Handan. *Women in the Kurdish Movement: Mothers, Comrades, Goddesses*. Translated by Simten Coşar. Palgrave, 2019.

Çakır, Serpil. "Feminism and Feminist History-Writing in Turkey: The Discovery of Ottoman Feminism." *Aspasia* 1, (2007): 61–83.

———. *Osmanlı Kadın Hareketi* [Ottoman Women's Movement]. Metis, 1996.

Davis, Kathy. *The Making of Our Bodies, Ourselves: How Feminism Travels across Borders*. Duke UP, 2007.

Delaney, Carol. "Father State, Motherland, and the Birth of Modern Turkey." *Naturalizing Power*, edited by Sylvia Yanagisako and Carol Delaney, 177–99. Routledge, 1995.

de Lauretis, Teresa. *Alice Doesn't: Feminism, Semiotics, Cinema*. Indiana UP, 1984.

de Lima Costa, Claudia. "Lost (and Found?) in Translation: Feminisms in Hemispheric Dialogue." *Latino Studies* 4, (2006): 62–78.

de Lima Costa, Claudia, and Sonia Alvarez. "Dislocating the Sign: Toward a Translocal Feminist Politics of Translation." *Signs* 39, no. 3 (2014): 557–63.

de Lotbinière-Harwood, Susanne. "Preface: About the *Her* in the Other." *Letters from an Other*, Lise Gauvin, translated by Susanne de Lotbinière-Harwood. Women's Press, 1989.

———. *Re-belle et infidèle: La traduction comme pratique de réécriture au féminin/ The Body Bilingual: Translation as a Re-writing in the Feminine*. Women's Press, 1991.

Demirdirek, Aynur. *Osmanlı Kadınlarının Hayat Hakkı Arayışının Bir Hikayesi* [A Story of Ottoman Women's Search for the Right to Live]. İmge, 1993.

Deniz, Dilşa. "Re-assessing the Genocide of Kurdish Alevis in Dersim, 1937–38." *Genocide Studies and Prevention* 14, no. 2 (2020): 20–43.

Dennis, Anna. "The #MeToo Movement: A Global, Social Media Sensation." *The Advocate: Newsletter of WomenSafe* 24, no. 1 (2018): 1, 5.

Derrida, Jacques. *Dissemination*. Translated by Barbara Johnson, U of Chicago P, 1981.

———. "Living On," translated by James Hulbert. *Deconstruction and Criticism*, 62–142. Continuum, 2004.

———. *Of Grammatology*. Translated by Gayatri Chakravorty Spivak, Johns Hopkins UP, 1976.

Devi, Mahasweta. *Imaginary Maps: Three Stories by Mahasweta Devi*. Translated by Gayatri Chakravorty Spivak. Routledge, 1995.

Díaz-Diocaretz, Myriam. *Translating Poetic Discourse: Questions on Feminist Strategies in Adrienne Rich*. John Benjamins, 1985.

Diner, Cagla, and Şule Toktaş. "Waves of Feminism in Turkey: Kemalist, Islamist and Kurdish Women's Movements in an Era of Globalization." *Journal of Balkan and Near Eastern Studies* 12, no. 1 (2010): 41–57.

Dogan, Sultan. "Vaginismus and Accompanying Sexual Dysfunctions in a Turkish Clinical Sample." *Journal of Sexual Medicine* 6, no. 1 (2009): 184–92.

Durakbaşa, Ayşe. "Cumhuriyet Döneminde Kemalist Kadın Kimliğinin Oluşumu" [The Formation of the Kemalist Woman Identity in the Republican Era]. *Tarih ve Toplum* 9, no. 51 (1993): 39–43.

———. *Halide Edib: Türk Modernleşmesi ve Feminizm* [Halide Edib: Turkish Modernization and Feminism]. İletişim, 2000.

Eisenstein, Zillah. *Against Empire: Feminisms, Racisms, and the West*. Zed Books, 2004.

Eker, Arzu. "Building Translations in the Social Sciences Since the 1980s: An Alternative View of Culture Planning in Turkey." MA Thesis, Boğaziçi University, 2001.

Ekmekçioğlu, Lerna, and Melissa Bilal, editors. *Bir Adalet Feryadı: Osmanlı'dan Türkiye'ye Beş Ermeni Feminist Yazar, 1862–1933* [A Cry for Justice: Five Armenian Feminist Writers from the Ottoman Empire to Turkey, 1862–1933]. Aras, 2006.

Elbek, Osman. "Kadın Hakları: Himen Vesayeti" [Women's Rights: The Hymen Guardianship]. *Bianet*, 8 Aug. 2009, http://www.bianet.org/biamag/saglik/116362-himen-vesayeti. Accessed 6 Oct. 2012.

Ergun, Emek. "Feminist Çeviri, Feminist Çevirmen, Feminist Hareket" [Feminist Translation, Feminist Translator, Feminist Movement]. *Amargi* 17, Summer 2010, 11–13.

———. "Feminist Translation Ethics." *The Routledge Handbook of Translation and Ethics*, edited by Kaisa Koksinen and Nike K. Pokorn, 114–30. Routledge, 2020.

———. "Önsöz: Türkiye'de Bekâretin 'El Değmemiş' Tarihi" [Preface: The "Untouched" History of Virginity in Turkey]. *Bekâretin "El Değmemiş" Tarihi*, Hanne Blank, translated by Emek Ergun, 11–34. İletişim, 2008.

———. "Translational Beginnings and Origin/izing Stories: Writing the History of the Contemporary Feminist Movement in Turkey." *Translating Women: Different Voices and New Horizons*, edited by Luise von Flotow and Farzanah Farahzad, 41–55. Routledge, 2017.

Ergun, Emek, and Necla Akgökçe. "Neyle Ölçerseniz Ölçün, Bekâret Yoktur" [Whatever You Measure it with, Virginity Does Not Exist]. *Psikeart* 2, nos. March-April 2009, 60–7.

Ergun, Zeynep. *Erkeğin Yittiği Yerde: 21. Yüzyıl Romanında Toplumsal ve Siyasal Arayışlar* [When Man Disappears: Social and Political Quests in the 21st Century Novel]. Everest, 2009.

Ersanlı, Büşra. *İktidar ve Tarih: Türkiye'de "Resmî Tarih" Tezinin Oluşumu (1929–1937)* [Political Power and History: The Formation of the "Official History" Thesis in Turkey (1929–1937)]. İletişim, 2003.

Felski, Rita. "The Doxa of Difference." *Signs* 23, no. 1 (1997): 1–21.

Felski, Rita, and Susan Stanford Friedman. "Introduction." *Comparison: Theories, Approaches, Uses*, edited by Rita Felski and Susan Stanford Friedman, 1–12. Johns Hopkins UP, 2013.

Ferguson, Kathy. *The Man Question: Visions of Subjectivity in Feminist Theory*. U of California P, 1993.

Filipovic, Jill. "TI's Hymen Checks Are Horrific. So Is the Entire Concept of Virginity." *The Guardian*, 8 Nov. 2019, https://www.theguardian.com/commentisfree/2019/nov/08/ti-hymen-virginity-daughter?CMP=Share_iOSApp_Other. Accessed 10 Dec. 2019.

Fish, Stanley. *Is There a Text in This Class?* Harvard UP, 1980.

Flotow, Luise von. *Translation and Gender: Translating in the "Era of Feminism."* St. Jerome, 1997.

Flotow, Luise von, and Farzanah Farahzad, editors. *Translating Women: Different Voices and New Horizons*. Routledge, 2017.

Flotow, Luise von, and Hala Kamal, editors. *The Routledge Handbook on Translation, Feminism and Gender*. Routledge, 2020.

Flynn, Elizabeth. "Gender and Reading." *Gender and Reading: Essays on Readers, Texts, and Contexts*, edited by Elizabeth Flynn and Patrocinio Schweickart, 267–88. Johns Hopkins UP, 1986.

Foucault, Michel. *The Archaeology of Knowledge and the Discourse on Language*. Translated by A.M. Sheridan Smith, Vintage Books, 1972.

Frank, Martina, Heidi Bauer, Nadir Arican, Sebnem Korur Fincanci, and Vincent Iacopino. "Virginity Examinations in Turkey: Role of Forensic Physicians in Controlling Female Sexuality." *JAMA* 282, no. 5 (1999): 485–90.

Freiwald, Bina. "The Problem of Trans-Lation: Reading French Feminisms." *TTR* 4, no. 2 (1991): 55–68.

Friedman, Susan Stanford. "Locational Feminism: Gender, Cultural Geographies, and Geopolitical Literacy." *Feminist Locations*, edited by Marianne DeKoven, 13–36. Rutgers UP, 2001.

———. *Mappings: Feminism and the Cultural Geographies of Encounter*. Princeton UP, 1998.

———. "Why Not Compare?" *Comparison: Theories, Approaches, Uses*, edited by Rita Felski and Susan Stanford Friedman, 34–45. Johns Hopkins UP, 2013.

Genette, Gerard. *Paratexts: Thresholds of Interpretation*. Translated by Jane Lewin, Cambridge UP, 1997.

Ghadery, Farnush. "#MeToo—Has the "Sisterhood" Finally Become Global or Just

Another Product of Neoliberal Feminism?" *Transnational Legal Theory* 10, no. 2 (2019): 252–74.

Ghosh, Bishnupriya. "An Affair to Remember: Scripted Performances in the 'Nasreen Affair.'" *Going Global*, edited by Amal Amireh and Lisa Suhair Majaj, 39–83. Garland, 2000.

Godard, Barbara. "Theorizing Feminist Discourse/Translation." *Translation, History and Culture*, edited by Susan Bassnett and André Lefevere, 87–96. Cassell, 1990.

———. "Translating (with) the Speculum." *TTR* 4, no. 2 (1991): 85–121.

Gordon, Avery. *Ghostly Matters: Haunting and the Sociological Imagination*. U of Minnesota P, 2008.

Göknar, Erdağ. "Ottoman Past and Turkish Future: Ambivalence in A. H. Tanpınar's *Those Outside the Scene*." *The South Atlantic Quarterly* 102, nos. 2/3 (2003): 647–61.

Greslé-Favier, Claire. "Sexual Abstinence Education and the Reassertion of the 'Biblical' Patriarchal Family Unit in the Contemporary United States." *Pieties and Gender*, edited by Lene Sjørup and Hilda Rømer Christensen, 65–81. Brill, 2009.

Grewal, Inderpal. "Feminist Encounters, Transnational Mediations, and the Crime of 'Honor Killings.'" *International Feminist Journal of Politics* 15, no. 1 (2013): 1–19.

Grewal, Inderpal, and Caren Kaplan, editors. *Scattered Hegemonies: Postmodernity and Transnational Feminist Practices*. U of Minnesota P, 1994.

Grossman, Anna Jane. "The 2000-Year-Old Virgin: Purity, Chastity, Mystery. Review of *Virgin: The Untouched History*, by Hanne Blank." *New York Observer* 21, no. 12, 26 March 2007, C14.

Gunning, Isabelle. "Arrogant Perception, World Travelling and Multicultural Feminism: The Case of Female Genital Surgeries." *Columbia Human Rights Law Review* 23, 1991/1992, 189–248,

Gülen, Hande, and Dilan Eren. "Bekâret Kavramı Yeniden Sorgulanıyor" [The Virginity Concept Is Being Revisited"]. *Birgün*, 29 July 2009, http://www.birgun.net/life_index.php?news_code=1248860206&year=2009&month=07&day=29. Accessed 5 Aug. 2010.

Günyüzü, Oza. "Ve Tanrı Himeni Yarattı! Yoksa Yaratmadı Mı?" [And God Created the Hymen! Or Did They Not?]. 24 July 2010, http://bilgilidunya.net/1821/ve-tanri-himeni-yaratti-yoksa-yaratmadi-mi/. Accessed 23 Sep. 2010.

Gürel, Perin. *The Limits of Westernization: A Cultural History of America in Turkey*. Columbia UP, 2017.

Haraway, Donna. "A Manifesto for Cyborgs: Science, Technology, and Socialist Feminism in the 1980s." *Feminism/Postmodernism*, edited by Linda Nicholson, 190–233. Routledge, 1990.

———. "Situated Knowledges: The Science Question in Feminism and the Privilege of Partial Perspective." *Feminist Studies* 14, no. 3 (1988): 575–99.

Hemmings, Clare. *Why Stories Matter*. Duke UP, 2011.

Hill Collins, Patricia. *Black Feminist Thought: Knowledge, Consciousness, and the Politics of Empowerment*, 2nd edition. Routledge, 2000.

———. "Preface: On Translation and Intellectual Activism." *Feminist Translation Studies*, edited by Olga Castro and Emek Ergun, xi–xvi. Routledge, 2017.

hooks, bell. "Feminism: A Transformational Politic." *Race, Class, and Gender in the United States*, 8th edition, edited by Paula Rothenberg, 670–7. Worth Publishers, 2010.

Inayatullah, Naeem. "Pulling Threads: Intimate Systematicity in *The Politics of Exile*." *Security Dialogue* 44, no. 4 (2013): 331–45.

Iser, Wolfgang. *The Implied Reader*. Johns Hopkins UP, 1974.

Işık, Ruken, translator. "Mona Eltahawy'den: Bizden Neden Nefret Ediyorlar?" [From Mona Eltahawy: Why Do They Hate Us?] *Bianet*, 26 May 2012, http://hwww.bianet.org/biamag/dunya/138636-bizden-neden-nefret-ediyorlar. Accessed 7 Feb. 2013.

*İsyan-ı Nisvan* [Women's Rebellion]. DVD. Directed by Melek Özman. Filmmor Kadın Kooperatifi (Filmmor Women's Cooperative), 2008.

Jauss, Hans. *Toward an Aesthetic of Reception*. U of Minnesota P, 1982.

Jones, Sophia. "A Test with No Answers." *Marie Clare*, 30 Oct. 2019. https://www.marieclaire.com/health-fitness/a29488743/virginity-testing-america-doctors/. Accessed 3 Sep. 2020.

Kabakçı, Elif, and Senar Batur. "Who Benefits from Cognitive Behavioral Therapy for Vaginismus?" *Journal of Sex & Marital Therapy* 29, no. 4 (2003): 277–88.

Kandiyoti, Deniz. "Emancipated but Unliberated? Reflections on the Turkish Case." *Feminist Studies* 13, no. 2 (1987): 317–38.

Kaplan, Caren. "On Location." *Making Worlds: Gender, Metaphor, Materiality*, edited by Susan Hardy Aiken, Ann Brigham, Sallie Marston, and Penny Waterstone, 60–65. U of Arizona P, 1998.

———. *Questions of Travel: Postmodern Discourses of Displacement*. Duke UP, 1996.

———. "The Politics of Location as Transnational Feminist Critical Practice." *Scattered Hegemonies*, edited by Inderpal Grewal and Caren Kaplan, 137–52. U of Minnesota P, 1994.

Kardam, Nüket, and Yakın Ertürk. "Expanding Gender Accountability: Women's Organizations and the State in Turkey." *International Journal of Organization Theory and Behavior* 2, nos. 1–2 (1999): 167–97.

Katz, Cindi. "On the Grounds of Globalization: A Topography for Feminist Political Engagement." *Signs* 26, no. 4 (2001): 1213–34.

Kaufman, Rona. "'That, My Dear, Is Called Reading': Oprah's Book Club and the Construction of a Readership." *Reading Sites: Social Differences and Reader Response*, edited by Patrocinio Schweickart and Elizabeth Flynn, 221–55. MLA of America, 2004.

Keating, AnaLouise. "Forging El Mundo Zurdo: Changing Ourselves, Changing the World." *This Bridge We Call Home*, edited by Gloria Anzaldúa and AnaLouise Keating, 519–30. Routledge, 2002.

———. "'I'm a Citizen of the Universe': Gloria Anzaldúa's Spiritual Activism as Catalyst for Social Change." *Feminist Studies* 34, nos. 1/2 (2008): 53–69.

———. "Series Editor's Foreword." *Hungry Translations*, Richa Nagar, xi-xii. U of Illinois P, 2019.

———. *Transformation Now! Toward a Post-Oppositional Politics of Change*. U of Illinois P, 2013.

Kelly, Kathleen Coyne. *Performing Virginity and Testing Chastity in the Middle Ages*. Routledge, 2000.

Keskinkılıç, Fırat. "Bekaret Davası İlk Celsede Düştü" [Virginity Lawsuit Is Dismissed at the First Session]. *Radikal*, 8 Dec. 2010, http://www.radikal.com.tr/turkiye/bekaret _davasi_ilk_celsede_dustu-1031823. Accessed 28 May 2013.

Kışanak, Gültan, editor. *Kürt Siyasetinin Mor Rengi* [The Purple Color of Kurdish Politics]. Dipnot, 2018.

Kızılarslan, Yeliz. "Utanç, Saflık, Erdem Simgesi Bekaret Zaten Hiç Yok Muydu?" [So Virginity—the Symbol of Shame, Purity, Virtue—Never Existed Anyway?] *Bianet*, 7 Feb. 2009, http://bianet.org/bianet/kadin/112388-utanc-saflik-erdem-simgesi -bekaret-zaten-hic-yok-muydu. Accessed 11 March 2009.

Kogacioglu, Dicle. "The Tradition Effect: Framing Honor Crimes in Turkey." *differences* 15, no. 2 (2004): 119–51.

Kuczynski, Alex. "Sweet Chastity. Review of *Virgin: The Untouched History*, by Hanne Blank." *New York Times Book Review*, 25 March 2007, 6.

Kum, Berivan, Fatma Gülçiçek, Pınar Selek, and Yeşim Başaran, editors. *Özgürlüğü Ararken: Kadın Hareketinde Mücadele Deneyimleri* [In Search of Liberation: Experiences of Struggle in the Women's Movement]. Amargi Kadın, 2005.

Kurnaz, Işıl. "Bedenden Öte Mit: Kadınca Bilinmeyişler ve Bekâret" [Myth Beyond the Body: Womanly Unknowns and Virginity]. *Bianet*, 13 Feb. 2013, http://bianet .org/biamag/bianet/144301-bedenden-ote-mit-kadinca-bilinmeyisler-ve-bekaret. Accessed 24 March 2013.

Landes, Donald. "The Weight of Others: Social Encounters and Ethics of Reading." *Body/Self/Other: The Phenomenology of Social Encounters*, edited by Luna Dolezal and Danielle Petherbridge, 161–84. SUNY Press, 2017.

Laughlin, Kathleen, Julie Gallagher, Dorothy Sue Cobble, Eileen Boris, Premilla Nadasen, Stephanie Gilmore, and Leandra Zarnow. "Is It Time to Jump Ship? Historians Rethink the Waves Metaphor." *Feminist Formations* 22, no. 1 (2010): 76–135.

Lazreg, Marnia. "The Triumphant Discourse of Global Feminism: Should Other Women Be Known?" *Going Global: The Transnational Reception of Third World Women Writers*, edited by Amal Amireh and Lisa Suhair Majaj, 29–38. Garland, 2000.

Levine, Suzanne Jill. *The Subversive Scribe: Translating Latin American Fiction*. Graywolf, 1991.

Lewis, Reina. *Rethinking Orientalism: Women, Travel and the Ottoman Harem*. Rutgers UP, 2004.

Liddle, Joanna, and Shirin Rai. "Feminism, Imperialism and Orientalism: The Challenge of the 'Indian Woman.'" *Women's History Review* 7, no. 4 (1998): 495–520.

Liu, Lydia. *Translingual Practice: Literature, National Culture, and Translated Modernity—China 1900–1937*. Stanford UP, 1995.

Lorde, Audre. *Sister Outsider*. Freedom, The Crossing Press, 1984.

Lugones, María. *Pilgrimages/Peregrinajes: Theorizing Coalition Against Multiple Oppressions*. Rowman & Littlefield, 2003.

———. "Toward a Decolonial Feminism." *Hypatia* 25, no. 4 (2010): 742–59.

Lugones, María, and Elizabeth Spelman. "Have We Got a Theory for You!" *Women's Studies International Forum* 6, no. 6 (1983): 573–81.

Lukic, Jasmina, Sibelan Forrester, and Borbála Faragó, editors. *Times of Mobility*. Central European UP, 2020.

MacKie, Vera. "The Language of Globalization, Transnationality and Feminism." *International Feminist Journal of Politics* 3, no. 2 (2001): 180–206.

Maier, Carol. "A Woman in Translation, Reflecting." *Translation Review* 17 (1985): 4–8.

Mani, Lata. "Multiple Mediations: Feminist Scholarship in the age of Multinational Reception." *Feminist Review* 35 (1990): 24–41.

Mansbridge, Jane. "Complicating Oppositional Consciousness." *Oppositional Consciousness: The Subjective Roots of Social Protest*, edited by Jane Mansbridge and Aldon Morris, 238–64. U of Chicago P, 2001.

———. "The Making of Oppositional Consciousness." *Oppositional Consciousness: The Subjective Roots of Social Protest*, edited by Jane Mansbridge and Aldon Morris, 1–19. U of Chicago P, 2001.

Mansbridge, Jane, and Katherine Flaster. "*Male Chauvinist, Feminist, Sexist*, and *Sexual Harassment*: Different Trajectories in Feminist Linguistic Innovation." *American Speech*, 80, no. 3 (2005): 256–79.

Massey, Doreen. "A Global Sense of Place." *Space, Place, and Gender*. U of Minnesota P, 1994, 146–56.

Mayhew, Kelly. "Pure and Not Simple. Review of *Virgin: The Untouched History*, by Hanne Blank." *The San Diego Union-Tribune*, 18 March 2007.

McCann, Carole, Seung-kyung Kim, and Emek Ergun, editors. *Feminist Theory Reader*, 5th edition. Routledge, 2021.

McKeon Olson, Rose, and Claudia García-Moreno. "Virginity Testing: A Systematic Review." *Reproductive Health* 14, no. 1 (2017): 61.

Merrill, Christi. *Riddles of Belonging: India in Translation and Other Tales of Possession*. Fordham UP, 2008.

Mezzadra, Sandro, and Naoki Sakai. "Introduction." *Translation* 4, Spring 2014, 9–29.

Mignolo, Walter, and Freya Schiwy. "Beyond Dichotomies: Translation/Transculturation and the Colonial Difference." *Beyond Dichotomies: Histories, Identities, Cultures, and the Challenge of Globalization*, edited by Elisabeth Mudimbe-Boyi, 251–86. SUNY Press, 2002.

Minh-ha, Trinh. "Difference: 'A Special Third World Women Issue.'" *Discourse* 8, Fall/Winter 1987, 11–38.

Mishori, Ranit, Hope Ferdowsian, Karen Naimer, Muriel Volpellier, Thomas McHale.

"The Little Tissue That Couldn't—Dispelling Myths about the Hymen's Role in Determining Sexual History and Assault." *Reproductive Health* 16, no. 1 (2019): 74.

Modern Girl Around the World Research Group, editors. *The Modern Girl Around the World: Consumption, Modernity, and Globalization.* Duke UP, 2008.

Mohanty, Chandra Talpade. *Feminism Without Borders: Decolonizing Theory, Practicing Solidarity.* Duke UP, 2003.

Moi, Toril. "While We Wait: The English Translation of 'The Second Sex.'" *Signs* 27, no. 4 (2002): 1005–35.

Moorjani, Angela. "Translating Theory and Feminism(s) from the French." *Contemporary Literature* 37, no. 4 (1996): 671–92.

Morley, David. "Texts, Readers, Subjects." *Culture, Media, Language: Working Papers in Cultural Studies, 1972–79,* edited by Stuart Hall, Dorothy Hobson, Andrew Lowe, and Paul Willis, 163–73. Routledge, 2006.

Moses, Claire Goldberg. "Made in America: 'French Feminism' in Academia." *Feminist Studies,* 24, no. 2 (1998): 241–74.

Nagar, Richa. *Hungry Translations: Relearning the World through Radical Vulnerability.* U of Illinois P, 2019.

———. *Muddying the Waters: Coauthoring Feminisms across Scholarship and Activism.* U of Illinois P, 2014.

Nagar, Richa, Kathy Davis, Judith Butler, AnaLouise Keating, Claudia de Lima Costa, Sonia Alvarez, and Ayşe Gül Altınay. "A Cross-Disciplinary Roundtable on the Feminist Politics of Translation." *Feminist Translation Studies,* edited by Olga Castro and Emek Ergun, 111–35. Routledge, 2017.

Nicholson, Linda. "Feminism in 'Waves': Useful Metaphor or Not?" *New Politics* 12, no. 4 (2010): 34–39.

Noel, Ann, and David Oppenheimer, editors. *The Global #MeToo Movement: How Social Media Propelled a Historic Movement and the Law Responded.* Full Court Press, 2020.

Noor, Poppy. "'Now I Have to Check Your Hymen': The Shocking Persistence of Virginity Tests." *The Guardian,* 9 Dec. 2019, https://www.theguardian.com/life andstyle/2019/dec/09/hymen-virginity-tests-us-ti?CMP=Share_iOSApp_Other. Accessed on 10 Dec. 2019.

Onwuachi-Willig, Angela. "What About #UsToo?: The Invisibility of Race in the #MeToo Movement." *The Yale Law Journal* 128, (2018): 105–20.

Ortega, Mariana. *In-Between: Latina Feminist Phenomenology, Multiplicity, and the Self.* SUNY Press, 2016.

Ovadia, Stella. "Feminist Hareketin İlk Günleri: Örgütlenme Zorlukları, Özgün Örgütlenme Deneyimleri" [First Days of the Feminist Movement: Organization Difficulties, Individual Organization Experiences]. *Özgürlüğü Ararken: Kadın Hareketinde Mücadele Deneyimleri* [In Search of Liberation: Experiences of Struggle in the Women's Movement], edited by Berivan Kum, Fatma Gülçiçek, Pınar Selek, and Yeşim Başaran, 59–80. Amargi Kadın, 2005.

Öğüt, Hande. "Bekârete Yamuk Bakış" [A Skewed Look at Virginity]. *Radikal Kitap*, 31 Oct. 2008, http://www.radikal.com.tr/Radikal.aspx?aType=RadikalEklerDetay V3&ArticleID=905979&Date=22.10.2011&CategoryID=40. Accessed 5 Nov. 2008.

Özgökçe, Zozan. "Kadının 'Geleneksel' Olarak Aşağılanması" ["Traditional" Humiliation of Women]. *Demokrat Haber*, August 2011, http://www.demokrathaber.net/kadinin-%E2%80%98geleneksel-olarak-asagilanmasi-makale,1886.html. Accessed 2 March 2012.

Paker, Saliha. "Unmuffled Voices in the Shade and Beyond: Women's Writing in Turkish." *Textual Liberation: European Feminist Writing Century*, edited by Helena Forsas Scott, 270–300. Routledge, 1991.

Pamuk, Orhan. *The Museum of Innocence*. Translated by Maureen Freely, Alfred A. Knopf, 2009.

Park-Fuller, Linda. "Voices: Bakhtin's Heteroglossia and Polyphony, and the Performance of Narrative Literature." *Literature in Performance* 7, (1986): 1–12.

Parla, Ayse. "The 'Honor' of the State: Virginity Examinations in Turkey." *Feminist Studies*, 27, no. 1 (2001): 65–88.

Patil, Vrushali. "From Patriarchy to Intersectionality: A Transnational Feminist Assessment of How Far We've Really Come." *Signs* 38, no. 4 (2013): 847–67.

Penrod, Lynn. "Translating Hélène Cixous: French Feminism(s) and Anglo-American Feminist Theory." *TTR* 6, no. 2 (1993): 39–54.

Pitts, Andrea. "World-traveling." *50 Concepts for a Critical Phenomenology*, edited by Gail Weiss, Ann Murphy, and Gayle Salamon, 343–50. Northwestern UP, 2019.

Prada, Ana Rebeca. "Is Anzaldúa Translatable in Bolivia?" *Translocalities/Translocalidades*, edited by Alvarez et al., 57–77. Duke UP, 2014.

Pratt, Geraldine, and Victoria Rosner, editors. *The Global and the Intimate: Feminism in Our Time*. Columbia UP, 2012.

"Profesöre 'Bekaret Kontrolü' Davası" ["Virginity Test" Lawsuit Against Professor]. *Radikal*, 10 May 2013, http://www.radikal.com.tr/turkiye/profesore_bekaret_kontrolu_davasi-1132862. Accessed 28 May 2013.

Qureshi, Sadiah. "A Manifesto for Survival." *To Exist Is to Resist: Black Feminism in Europe*, edited by Akwugo Emejulu and Francesca Sobande, 205–18. Pluto Press, 2019.

Radhakrishnan, R. "Why Compare?" *Comparison: Theories, Approaches, Uses*, edited by Rita Felski and Susan Stanford Friedman, 15–33. Johns Hopkins UP, 2013.

Reimóndez, María. "The Curious Incident of Feminist Translation in Galicia: Courtcases, Lies and Gendern@ations." *Galicia* 21 A, (2009): 68–89.

Rich, Adrienne. *On Lies, Secrets, and Silence: Selected Prose 1966–1978*. W. W. Norton, 1979.

Robinson, Douglas. *Transgender, Translation, Translingual Address*. Bloomsbury Academic, 2019.

Rowley, Michelle. "The Idea of Ancestry: Of Feminist Genealogies and Many Other Things." *Feminist Theory Reader*, 3rd edition, edited by Carole McCann and Seungkyung Kim, 77–82. Routledge, 2013.

Runyan, Anne Sisson. "World-Traveling Feminisms in an Era of Global Restructuring." *Partial Truths and the Politics of Community*, edited by Mary Ann Tétreault and Robin Teske, 67–85. U of South Carolina P, 2003.

Rushin, Donna Kate. "The Bridge Poem." *Feminist Theory Reader*, 3rd edition, eds. Carole McCann and Seung-kyung Kim, 266–67. Routledge, 2013.

Said, Edward. *Orientalism*. Vintage Books edition. Random House, 1979.

———. *The World, the Text, and the Critic*. Harvard UP, 1983.

———. "Traveling Theory Reconsidered." *Critical Reconstructions: The Relation of Fiction and Life*, edited by Robert Polhemus and Roger Henkle, 251–65. Stanford UP, 1994.

Sakai, Naoki. "How Do We Count a Language? Translation and Discontinuity." *Translation Studies* 2, no. 1 (2009): 71–88.

———. "The Modern Regime of Translation and the Emergence of the Nation." *The Eighteenth Century* 58, no. 1 (2017): 105–8.

Sancar, Serpil. "Otoriter Türk Modernleşmesinin Cinsiyet Rejimi" [The Gender Regime of Authoritarian Turkish Modernization]. *Doğu Batı* 29, (2004): 197–211.

Santaemilia, José. "Feminists Translating: On Women, Theory, and Practice." *Translating Gender*, edited by Eleonora Federici, 55–77, Peter Lang, 2011.

Santos, Boaventura de Sousa, João Arriscado Nunes, and Maria Paula Meneses. "Introduction: Opening up the Canon of Knowledge and Recognition of Difference." *Another Knowledge Is Possible: Beyond Northern Epistemologies*, volume 3, edited by Boaventura de Sousa Santos, xix-lxii. Verso, 2008.

Saraç, Irmak. "Erkeklik Zarı" [The Membrane of Manhood]. *BirGün*, 21 Dec. 2019, https://www.birgun.net/haber/erkeklik-zari-280991. Accessed 1 Sep. 2020.

Savcı, Evren. *Queer in Translation: Sexual Politics under Neoliberal Islam*. Duke UP, 2021.

Scott, Joan. "The Evidence of Experience." *Critical Inquiry* 17, no. 4 (1991): 773–97.

Sen, Purna, editor. *#MeToo: Headlines from a Global Movement*. UN Women Headquarters: United Nations Entity for Gender Equality and the Empowerment of Women, 2020, https://www.unwomen.org/en/digital-library/publications/2020/08/brief-metoo-headlines-from-a-global-movement. Accessed 23 Oct. 2020.

Shohat, Ella, and Robert Stam. *Unthinking Eurocentrism: Multiculturalism and the Media*. Routledge, 1994.

Shread, Carolyn. "Metamorphosis or Metramorphosis? Towards a Feminist Ethics of Difference in Translation." *TTR* 20, no. 2 (2007): 213–42.

———. "On Becoming in Translation: Articulating Feminisms in the Translation of Marie Vieux-Chauvet's *Les Rapaces*." *Translating Women*, edited by Luise von Flotow, 283–303. U of Ottawa P, 2011.

Shrestha, Nanda, and Dennis Conway. "Globalization's Cultural Challenges: Homogenization, Hybridization and Heightened Identity." *Globalization's Contradictions: Geographies of Discipline, Destruction and Transformation*, edited by Dennis Conway and Nik Heynen, 196–211. Routledge, 2006.

Simon, Sherry, editor. *Culture in Transit: Translating the Literature of Quebec.* Véhicle, 1995.

———. *Gender in Translation.* Routledge, 1996.

Simons, Margaret. "The Silencing of Simone de Beauvoir: Guess What's Missing from *The Second Sex.*" *Women's Studies International Forum* 6, no. 5 (1983): 559–64.

Sinha, Mrinalini. "Gender and Nation." *Women's History in Global Perspective*, volume 1, edited by Bonnie G. Smith, 229–74. U of Illinois P, 2004.

Sirman, Nükhet. "Feminism in Turkey: A Short History." *New Perspectives on Turkey* 3, no. 1 (1989): 1–34.

Smith, Dorothy. *Texts, Facts, and Femininity: Exploring the Relations of Ruling.* Routledge, 1990.

———. *The Conceptual Practices of Power: A Feminist Sociology of Knowledge.* Northeastern UP, 1990.

Sonzogni, Marco. *Re-covered Rose: A Case Study in Book Cover Design as Intersemiotic Translation.* John Benjamins, 2011.

Spivak, Gayatri Chakravorty. *Outside in the Teaching Machine.* Routledge, 2009.

Spurlin, William, editor. "The Gender and Sexual Politics of Translation: Literary, Historical, and Cultural Approaches." Special issue of *Comparative Literature Studies* 51, no. 2, 2014.

Stam, Robert, and Ella Shohat. *Race in Translation: Culture Wars Around the Postcolonial Atlantic.* NYU Press, 2012.

———. "Transnationalizing Comparison: The Uses and Abuses of Cross-Cultural Analogy." *New Literary History* 40, no. 3 (2009): 473–99.

Steiner, George. "Introduction." *The Penguin Book of Modern Verse Translation*, edited by George Steiner, Penguin, 1966.

Stone-Mediatore, Shari. *Reading Across Borders: Storytelling and Knowledges of Resistance.* Palgrave Macmillan, 2003.

Susam-Sarajeva, Şebnem. *Theories on the Move: Translation's Role in the Travels of Literary Theories.* Rodopi, 2006.

Tahaoğlu, Çiçek. "Himen Tazminat Davası: 'Karar Bekâret Olgusunu Meşru Kılmamalı'" [Claim for Damages for the Hymen: "The Verdict Should Not Legitimize the Virginity Notion"]. *Bianet*, 3 Oct. 2011, http://hwww.bianet.org/bianet/kadin/133134-karar-bekaret-olgusunu-mesru-kilmamali. Accessed 5 Feb. 2013.

Tahir-Gürçağlar, Şehnaz. *Kapılar: Çeviri Tarihine Yaklaşımlar* [Doors: Approaches to the History of Translation]. Scala, 2005.

———. *The Politics and Poetics of Translation in Turkey, 1923–1960.* Rodopi, 2008.

Tambe, Ashwini. "Reckoning with the Silences of #MeToo." *Feminist Studies* 44, no. 1 (2018): 197–203.

Tekeli, Şirin. "Birinci ve İkinci Dalga Feminist Hareketlerin Karşılaştırmalı İncelemesi Üzerine Bir Deneme" [An Essay on the Comparative Analysis of the First and Second Wave Feminist Movements]. *75 Yılda Kadınlar ve Erkekler* [Women and Men in 75 Years], edited by Ayşe Berktay Hacımirzaoğlu, 337–46. İş Bankası ve Tarih Vakfı Yayınları, 1998.

————. "80'lerde Türkiye'de Kadınların Kurtuluşu Hareketinin Gelişmesi" [The Development of the Women's Liberation Movement in Turkey in the 80s]. *Birikim* 3, July 1989, 34–41.

Tekin, Nilüfer. "Namus Bekaret Değildir" [Honor Is Not Virginity]. *Tanrı Boşluklardadır* (blog), 10 Jan. 2010, http://nilufertekin.blogspot.com/2010/01/namus-bekaret-degildir.html. Accessed 13 March 2011.

Thayer, Millie. *Making Transnational Feminism: Rural Women, NGO Activists, and Northern Donors in Brazil.* Routledge, 2010.

Thompson, Becky. "Multiracial Feminism: Recasting the Chronology of Second Wave Feminism." *Feminist Studies* 28, no. 2 (2002): 337–60.

Timisi, Nilüfer, and Meltem Ağduk Gevrek. "1980'ler Türkiye'sinde Feminist Hareket" [Feminist Movement in the 1980s' Turkey]. *90'larda Türkiye'de Feminizm* [Feminism in Turkey in the 90s], edited by Aksu Bora and Asena Günel, 13–39. İletişim, 2009.

Tosun, Funda. "Bekâretin Kanla Yazılan Tarihinden 'El Değmemiş' Bilgiler" ["Untouched" Knowledges on the Blood-Written History of Virginity]. *Agos*, 23 Jan. 2009, 13.

Treichler, Paula. "Escaping the Sentence: Diagnosis and Discourse in 'The Yellow Wallpaper.'" *Tulsa Studies in Women's Literature* 3, nos. 1/2 (1984): 61–77.

Tripp, Aili Mari. "Challenges in Transnational Feminist Mobilization." *Global Feminism: Transnational Women's Activism, Organizing, and Human Rights*, edited by Myra Marx Ferree and Aili Mari Tripp, 296–312. NYU Press, 2006.

Tsing, Anna Lowenhaupt. *Friction: An Ethnography of Global Connection.* Princeton UP, 2005.

————. "Transitions and Translations." *Transitions, Environments, Translations: Feminisms in International Politics*, edited by Joan Scott, Cora Kaplan, and Debra Keates, 253–72. Routledge, 1997.

Turan Yunusoğlu, Yeliz. *Yatak Odasındaki Kalabalık: Türkiye'de Kadınların Vajinusmus Deneyimleri* [The Crowd in the Bedroom: Vaginismus Experiences of Women in Turkey]. Metis, 2021.

Valenti, Jessica. *The Purity Myth: How America's Obsession with Virginity Is Hurting Young Women.* Seal Press, 2009.

Varikas, Eleni. "Traveling Concepts: Feminist Theory in Cross-cultural Perspective." *Trends and Issues in the Theoretical Psychology*, edited by Ian Lubek, Rene van Hezewijk, Gail Pheterson, Charles Tolman, 60–65. Springer, 1995.

Venuti, Lawrence. *Translation Changes Everything.* Routledge, 2013.

————. "Translating Derrida on Translation." *The Yale Journal of Criticism* 16, no. 2 (2003): 237–62.

Walkowitz, Rebecca. "Comparison Literature." *New Literary History* 40, (2009): 567–82.

Ward Jouve, Nicole. *White Woman Speaks with Forked Tongue: Criticism as Autobiography.* Routledge, 1991.

Warner, Marina. "Virgin Territory. Review of *Virgin: The Untouched History*, by Hanne Blank." *The Washington Post*, 15 Apr. 2007, Arts & Living, Books.

White, Jenny. "State Feminism, Modernization, and the Turkish Republican Woman." *NWSA Journal* 15, no. 3 (2003): 145–59.

Wirtén, Eva Hemmungs. *Global Infatuation: Explorations in Transnational Publishing and Texts: The Case of Harlequin Enterprises and Sweden.* Uppsala UP, 1998.

"Yargının Derdi Fiziksel Bulgu" [The Judicial Concern is Physical Evidence]. *Radikal*, 11 May 2013, http://www.radikal.com.tr/turkiye/yarginin_derdi_fiziksel_bulgu-1132995. Accessed 28 May 2013.

Yeğenoğlu, Meyda. *Colonial Fantasies: Towards a Feminist Reading of Orientalism.* Cambridge UP, 1998.

Zaccaria, Paola. "Translating Borders, Performing Transnationalism." *Human Architecture: Journal of the Sociology of Self-Knowledge* 4, no. 3 (2006): 57–70.

Zarkov, Dubravka, and Kathy Davis. "Ambiguities and Dilemmas around #MeToo: #ForHow Long and #WhereTo?" *European Journal of Women's Studies* 25, no. 1 (2018): 3–9.

Zihnioğlu, Yaprak. *Kadınsız İnkılap* [Reform Without Women]. Metis, 2003.

# Index

directionality, 5, 10, 15–16, 152, 194–96, 198
disjunctures, 14, 70, 72, 100–102, 124, 179
dissemination, 4–5, 42, 125, 129, 177, 184–87, 195
domestication, 7, 49, 61. *See also* familiarization
doubt, xix, 68, 79, 83, 129, 165–66, 168, 170

eastern text, 165, 166, 180
eastern virginities, 125–26, 176, 180–81, 183, 184, 219n4
Eisenstein, Zillah, 13, 145, 173
Ekmekçioğlu, Lerna, 205n26
embodied encounter, 20, 74–85
embodied subjectivity, 39–40, 67, 74, 81–82, 84, 121
embodiment, 29, 32, 51, 75, 77, 79–80, 83–84, 116, 162
English language, 17, 27, 49, 50–51, 53–54, 99, 197n2, 210n24, 212n34, 214n4
epistemic violence, 168, 175, 184
Erdoğan, Recep Tayyip, 25, 53–54, 211n32
Ergun, Emek, 37, 47, 50, 89, 94, 111, 136
Ergun, Zeynep, 31
essentialism, 12, 25, 72, 155, 157, 192, 197n2, 210n22, 211n25
ethical encounters, xx, 66, 73–74, 154, 160, 184, 213n2
ethical reading/reception, 74, 152, 167, 173–74
ethical translation, xviii, 40, 45, 46, 60, 74, 84, 156, 173–74, 188
Europe, 4, 25, 34, 147, 168, 203n9, 203n12, 204nn15–16, 206n38
exoticism, 180, 189
experience, 65, 201n23, 213n1, 214n4

familiarization, 49–53, 61, 64, 209–10n17, 210–11n24
family, 30, 32, 35–37, 53, 76, 92, 94, 113, 118, 133, 134, 135, 151, 205n29, 214n5
Felski, Rita, 128, 162
"female genital mutilation," 217
femicide, 2, 109, 121, 136, 137, 198n5, 215n13
"feminism as cultural imperialism," 5, 217n7
*Feminism Without Borders*, 123, 147, 150, 155, 199n8, 218n12, 218n1
feminist: accountability, 189–90; activists, 4, 26, 48, 60, 81, 184, 187, 204n19; betrayals, 185–87; connectivities, 12, 18–19, 21, 38, 123, 163, 166, 170; discourse, 2, 3, 6, 8,
9, 13, 26, 44, 49, 57, 73, 80–81, 88–89, 98, 101, 107, 121–22, 144, 191; fidelity, 45; historiography, 27–28, 30; intertext, 44, 60; "killjoy," 119, 184; knowledge production, xvii, 6, 96, 187, 203n5, 209n12; language, 26–28, 121; literature, 10, 27, 95–96; movements in Turkey, xvi, 4, 26–28, 32–33, 80, 112, 119, 164, 204n20, 205n24; "objectivity," 45; reader, xvii, 5, 19, 21, 44, 65, 67, 74, 84, 98, 101, 121–22, 124, 126, 166, 175–78, 203n7, 215n9; resistance, 3, 16, 19, 101, 104, 106; solidarity, xi, 4, 11, 16, 18, 47–48, 112, 124, 154–56, 165–66, 169, 172, 185, 192; subjectivity, 65–66
feminist translation: as activism, 4, 19, 46, 58, 88–89, 160–64, 179, 188, 209n14; as a call for action, 104–120; ethics, 40, 176, 188–91, 194, 220n7; as knowledge production, 89–104; literature, 47, 51; praxis, 8, 45–46, 123; strategies, 20, 74, 125, 192, 194; studies, 8–9, 13, 40, 47, 51, 200n12; *Virgin*, 15, 28, 125, 182
feminist translator, 17–18, 40, 45–48, 74, 113, 121, 137, 177, 184, 187–89, 194–95, 208n8
Ferguson, Kathy, 160
fidelity (in translation), 8, 45, 49
"first wave," 26, 29, 204n20
Fish, Stanley, 15
Flotow, Luise von, 200n12, 212n33, 220n8
Flynn, Elizabeth, 69
focus group, 67, 112, 145, 194, 202n29
footnotes, 43, 54, 57, 188, 212
foreignness, xv, 5, 20, 27, 49, 58, 60, 65, 69, 71, 74, 88, 127, 157, 178, 205n24, 208n6, 210n17, 210n23
Foucault, Michel, 49, 83–84
freedom of expression, 186
"French feminism," 13, 201n21, 202n26
*Friction*, 9, 11, 96, 123, 146, 147, 151
frictions, 9, 10, 96, 123
Friedman, Susan Stanford, 9–10, 127, 128, 199n10, 200n15

gender: binary, 51, 214n7; discourse, 15, 154; justice, 3, 121, 179; pronouns, 17, 51–52
genealogy, 151, 204n19, 204n20
generosity, xix–xx, 16, 69, 84, 164, 169–70
genre, 41–43, 99, 208n8
geopolitics, 5, 8, 9–10, 21, 51, 187–89, 195, 200n15; of translation, 8–10

politics of location, 181
politics of reception, xix, 8, 13, 84, 189
polyphony, xviii, xx, 48, 58, 68, 172, 191, 192
"polyversal feminism," 2, 173
postcolonialism, 5, 7, 9, 12, 13, 51, 151, 167,
174, 181, 184, 214n6
post-feminism, 129, 159, 180
post-oppositionality, ix–xi, 10–11, 15–16,
20–21, 127, 153, 156, 160, 164, 169–72, 177
power of books, xiv, xv
Prada, Ana Rebeca, 193
progress, 28–29, 112, 186, 206n40, 216–17n7

Quebec, 8
queering translation, 199n6
*Quran*, 216n4

race, xix, 31, 107, 123, 188, 200n11
"radical vulnerability," 11, 69, 84, 157, 164,
179, 182
Rai, Shirin, 149, 186
reader, 13–15, 43, 49–51, 56–57, 66–84,
186–88, 201n24, 210–11n24, 214n7
reader's subjectivity, 20, 64, 65–68, 82–84
reading diaries, 18, 67, 69, 105, 194, 202n29,
213n3
reading translation, 15, 65–69, 141
reception theory, 13–15, 194, 201n25
reciprocity, 2–3, 21, 154, 162, 165, 200n16
regulatory discourse, 76, 104, 178
relationality, 11, 140, 156, 157, 170
"relations of ruling," 12–13, 49, 56, 201n24
religion, 25, 42, 95, 104, 130–31, 138, 146,
207n46, 214n8
rescue fantasies, xix, 167, 171, 180, 187, 206,
217n8
re-vision, 15, 39–41, 44, 48, 65, 75, 208n1
Rich, Adrienne, 39, 65, 208n1
Rushin, Donna Kate, 189

Said, Edward, 6–15, 176, 183, 193, 194,
199–200nn9–11
Sakai, Naoki, 157, 198, 200n17, 204n13
sameness, x–xi, 11, 85, 143–44, 150, 160, 178,
186–87, 192
Santaemilia, José, 45
Savcı, Evren, 204n18
savior complex, 167. *See also* rescue fantasies
*Scattered Hegemonies*, 144, 145
science, 17, 23, 33, 42, 44, 56, 75–77, 92,
94–95, 203n5, 210n22, 219n2

scientific discourse, 17, 95, 99
Scott, Joan, 201n23, 213n1
"second wave," 8, 26, 204n20
secularism, xiv, 25, 26, 29, 130, 204n17,
207n46
self/other, x, xx, 11, 21, 66–69, 88, 132,
139–41, 156, 170–71, 177, 191
sex education, 36–38
sexual: abuse, 1, 80, 214n9; freedom, 36, 82,
95, 139; harassment, 1, 27; intercourse,
33, 79, 82, 83, 133, 214n9; liberation,
81–82, 119; revolution, 23, 35–36, 206;
violence, 1, 197n2
sexually active, 76–78, 82, 118
Shohat, Ella, 5, 12, 130, 144, 201n18
Shread, Carolyn, 46, 68
silence, xix, 1, 8, 32, 58, 69, 73, 88, 125, 154,
191, 193, 198n4
Simon, Sherry, 45, 202n28
Sinha, Mrinalini, 30, 205n29
Sirman, Nükhet, 31, 205n26, 205n30
sisterhood, 2, 124, 154, 164–67, 172, 185,
197n2
"sisterhood is global," 124
*Sister Outsider*, xvi, xix, 1, 153, 174, 180, 182,
184, 185, 196
situated knowledges, 89, 189–90
Smith, Dorothy, 13–14, 49, 88, 201n24
social change, 11, 67, 105, 109–13, 120–21, 159
Sonzogni, Marco, 213n43
Spelman, Elizabeth, 187
Spivak, Gayatri Chakravorty, 7, 191,
212n37, 213n2, 214n6
Stam, Robert, 5, 12, 130, 144, 201n18
"state feminism," 26, 28, 205n28
Steiner, George, 191
Stone-Mediatore, Shari, 65
*Strange Encounters*, 66, 69, 144, 160, 177,
191, 192, 213n2
"strange encounters," 66, 191, 213n2
"strategic universalisms," 147
subversive discourse, 16, 48, 50, 74, 87, 92,
162, 194
surprise, 35, 69, 90, 148, 149, 156, 168–70,
202–3n2
survival, xxi, 39, 65, 81, 107, 138, 156
Susam-Sarajeva, Şebnem, 201n21, 202n26
symbolic violence, 182, 216–17n7

Tahir-Gürçağlar, Şehnaz, 15, 202n26, 204n14
teen pregnancy, 36
Tekeli, Şirin, 26, 28, 205n21

television/TV, 23–24, 43, 54, 92, 133, 147, 161, 203n6
text choice, 17, 19, 46–48, 183, 188, 196
textual analysis, 13, 16, 40, 46–64
Thayer, Millie, 199n8, 201n22
"third wave," 204n20
Third World, 42, 147, 150, 186, 191; feminisms, 155, 170, 181, 189, 214n6; women, 5, 13, 147, 180
Thornton, Dill Bonnie, 153
threshold/thresholder, 156, 162, 188, 190
togetherness, 162–64, 184, 191, 193
*Transformation Now!*, 11, 128, 135, 140, 141, 144, 151, 156, 160, 218n12
translation: connectionist potential of, 11, 66, 152, 161, 163, 174, 187, 192–93, 198n6, 200n17; geopolitics of, 8, 9–10, 187–89; studies, x, 8, 13, 15, 17, 60, 194, 195; as paradoxical, 156–57, 198n6; process of, x, 40, 60, 188; political power of, xv, xvii, 3–4, 7, 15–16, 84, 87, 105, 151, 159, 172, 194, 199n6; as "telling in turn," xviii. *See also* feminist translation
translational border crossings, 10, 24, 183, 193–94
translational feminist communities, 20, 153–56, 158, 166, 176
translator's: agency, 8, 17, 40, 58, 187, 212n37; preface, 19, 24, 54, 57–60, 73–77, 99, 101–4, 111–12, 120–22, 132, 135, 161–63, 194, 217n10; signature, 52, 74, 188; visibility, 8, 17, 40, 58, 189
*Translocalities/Translocalidades*, 200n12, 220n8
transnational feminism, xiii, 3–4, 6, 8–10, 14, 20, 74, 124–25, 150, 154, 167, 177, 179–80, 188, 194
traveling theory, 6–15, 176, 193–94, 199n10, 199n11
Treichler, Paula, 77
Tripp, Aili Mari, 180
trust, xix, 21, 47–48, 72–73, 101, 121–22, 154, 164–66, 175–76, 181, 187–88, 195, 218n11
truth claim, 5, 44, 49–50, 58, 70–72, 90, 94, 102
truth regime, 19, 43, 58, 90, 94–95, 104, 179, 195
Tsing, Anna Lowenhaupt, 9, 11, 96, 123, 146–47, 151
Turkish: feminism, 204n20, 205n24, 207n47; imaginary, 35, 38, 125, 207; language, 17, 25, 27–28, 50–57, 120, 210n23, 210–11n24, 214n4; nationalism, 25, 30–31, 35–38, 195, 204n15; Penal Code, 33, 102, 203–4n12; state, 26–28, 33, 185–86, 198n5, 203n9, 220n5

universalism, 11, 143, 146–47, 152, 189
universality claim, 25, 144–46, 215n9, 218n11
"us versus them," x, 68, 151

vagina, 37, 52, 55, 133–35, 147, 214n10
vaginal bleeding, 24–25, 79, 94–95, 135, 148–49, 214n9, 218n13
*Vagina Monologues,* 115, 215n16
vaginismus, 80, 132–35, 214n10, 216n6
veil, 30, 180, 204n16, 219n4
Venuti, Lawrence, 17, 161, 194, 202n28
Vesalius, Andreas, 33, 106
violence against women, 2, 24, 37–38, 42–44, 81, 105, 119, 128, 137, 167, 198n5
*Virgin: The Untouched History*, xiii, xvii, 3–4, 12; contents of, 35–37, 41–45, 49–52, 58, 75–78, 91, 95–96, 106, 110–11, 147–49, 206n40; cover page of, 61–62; reception context of, 36–37; reviews of, 43, 99, 208n3, 217n7
virginity: as a control mechanism, 30–36, 44, 75–77, 90, 110, 120, 160, 207n48; discourse, 37, 41, 45, 54, 57, 60, 76–77, 79, 81, 92, 111, 119–20, 124, 212n33, 214n7; "does not exist," 42–43, 49, 70–72, 82–83, 106, 136, 150; as embodied, 32, 44, 46, 75–77, 80, 82, 120, 210n22; as "fake," 37, 147, 150; as fiction, 72, 79, 106, 146, 159, 210n22, 215n5; knowledges, 3, 25, 54, 58, 75–76, 93, 103–4, 127, 148, 176; literature, 91, 96; "loss," 52, 61, 78–79, 80–83, 117, 134–37, 149, 161, 218n13; myths, xvii, 19, 23–24, 72, 134–35, 212n39; norm, 24, 36, 57, 80, 108, 118, 133, 137, 164; politics, 19, 36–38, 88–91, 109–12, 121, 131, 136, 141–42, 157; premarital, 31–32, 34, 36, 133; reconstruction, 56, 59; regime, 4, 32–48, 78, 124–39, 151, 159, 165, 175, 184, 217n8; scholarship, 96–97, 214n1; taboo, 32, 51, 64, 83, 88, 92, 104–5, 114–18, 121–25, 130, 133–34, 142, 170; tests, 23, 32–37, 41, 46, 55, 77, 93 102–3, 150, 203n2, 205n33, 206n34, 207n46, 209n9, 212n39; violence, xvi, 25, 41–43, 59–60, 95, 109–11, 128, 162–64; as white, 42, 51

EMEK ERGUN is an associate professor of women's and gender studies and global studies at the University of North Carolina at Charlotte. She is the coeditor of *Feminist Translation Studies: Local and Transnational Perspectives* and *Feminist Theory Reader: Local and Global Perspectives*, fifth edition.

Transformations: Womanist, Feminist,
and Indigenous Studies

The University of Illinois Press
is a founding member of the
Association of University Presses.

———————————————————

University of Illinois Press
1325 South Oak Street
Champaign, IL 61820-6903
www.press.uillinois.edu